NEW PATTERNS OF ADULT LEARNING: A SIX-COUNTRY COMPARATIVE STUDY

Titles of Related Interest

BÉLANGER & VALDIVIELSO

The Emergence of Learning Societies: Who Participates in Adult Learning?

TUIJNMAN

International Encyclopedia of Adult Education and Training Second Edition

Volume 1 **R. H. DAVE**
Foundations of Lifelong Education

Volume 2 **R. SKAGER & R. H. DAVE**
Curriculum Evaluation for Lifelong Education

Volume 3 **A. J. CROPLEY**
Lifelong Education: A Psychological Analysis

Volume 4 **R. SKAGER**
Lifelong Education & Evaluation Practice

Volume 5 **A. J. CROPLEY & R. H. DAVE**
Lifelong Education & the Training of Teachers

Volume 6 **J. B. INGRAM**
Curriculum Integration & Lifelong Education

Volume 7 **A. J. CROPLEY**
Towards a System of Lifelong Education: Some Practical
Considerations

Volume 8 **L. H. GOAD**
Preparing Teachers for Lifelong Education

Volume 9 **R. SKAGER**
Organizing Schools to Encourage Self-direction in Learners

New Patterns of Adult Learning: A Six-Country Comparative Study

Edited by

Paul Bélanger, UNESCO
and
Albert Tuijnman, OECD

PERGAMON
and

UNESCO INSTITUTE FOR EDUCATION

U.K.   Elsevier Science Ltd, The Boulevard, Langford Lane, Kidlington, Oxford OX5 1GB, U.K.

U.S.A.   Elsevier Science Inc., 655 Avenue of the Americas, New York 10010, U.S.A.

JAPAN   Elsevier Science Japan, Higashi Azabu 1-chome Building 4F, 1-9-15, Higashi Azabu, Minato-ku, Tokyo 106, Japan

First edition 1997

Library of Congress Cataloging in Publication Data
A catalog record for this book is available from the Library of Congress

British Library Cataloguing in Publication Data
A catalogue record for this book is available from the British Library

ISBN 0-08-0430694

Printed and bound in Great Britain by Biddles Ltd.

Contents

New Patterns of Adult Learning:
A Six-Country Comparative Study

Blurb

With the transition toward the post-industrial society increasingly complete, the challenge to make learning a common, continuous and even universal experience and to reduce the exclusive tendencies in adult education and training is becoming more urgent than ever. In such societies some workers will have stable, good jobs in knowledge- and learning-intensive workplaces, while many others will be underemployed or locked into a series of precarious, low-skill jobs at the periphery of the economy. The design of successful intervention strategies will depend crucially on the knowledge base of adult education, especially improved insights into the factors and contexts of learning that are associated with participation and non-participation. It is by improving this knowledge base that this volume, which reports on a six-country comparative investigation of the patterns of adult education participation, seeks to make a contribution to policy and research.

This publication presents, for the first time, a systematic, empirical and comparative analysis of the multiple factors that explain a substantial part of the variance in the patterns of adult education participation. The same data set is analyzed in all chapters. Collected in 1994 as part of the International Adult Literacy Survey, it involves records collected from over 20,000 individual respondents in samples representative of the adult population aged 16-65 in six countries: Canada, the Netherlands, Poland, Sweden, Switzerland, and the United States.

Foreword

This book presents, for the first time, a systematic, empirical and comparative analysis of the multiple factors that explain a substantial part of the variance in the patterns of adult education participation. The same data set is analyzed in all chapters. Collected in 1994 as part of the International Adult Literacy Survey, it involves records collected from over 20,000 individual respondents in samples representative of the adult population aged 16-65 in six countries: Canada, the Netherlands, Poland, Sweden, Switzerland, and the United States.

While the criterion of adult education participation and non-participation is constant across the ten chapters, the authors focus on different contextual, explanatory, and mediating variables. The authors' choice of these variables is influenced by the findings of previous research studies on adult education participation as well as by their use of different sociological, economic, social-psychological and anthropological conceptual frameworks, theories, and research methodologies.

Collectively, the chapters in this volume seek to contribute to cross-disciplinary theory building in the field of adult learning, to offer an international perspective on the phenomenon, scope and patterns of adult education participation in the countries studied, and to identify the factors that explain this phenomenon and the observed cross-national similarities and differences.

The book is significant not only because it marks the first time an international data set is being used for the comparative investigation of the patterns and determinants of adult learning. Its findings make an important contribution to the knowledge base of adult education, which itself is increasingly moving to the center stage of educational policy and research as all industrialized countries more intently pursue strategies for making lifelong learning a reality for all. Clearly, improved knowledge about the demand and provision of adult learning is needed for the design of strategies that will be equitable, inclusive and efficient.

Knowledge is needed not only about the type and number of institutions providing learning opportunities, or the number and characteristics of the learners they reach, but also about the multiple factors that influence the expression of demand, the participation process, and the individual and social outcomes. Obviously, the knowledge base of adult education should also have an international dimension, because it is within comparative frameworks that questions about the appropriateness of often implicit system goals and the adequacy of provisions and outcomes are best addressed, by using information drawn from various countries and contexts as a point of reference that is external to the functioning of any one adult education system.

This volume does not include information about the survey designs employed, instruments, the procedures used for the data collection, and the achieved coverage and response rates. Readers who wish to obtain this information are referred to the sources mentioned in the footnote.[1] No project of this size could have been accomplished without considerable effort and dedication from a large number of people. Among those who have rendered invaluable services in the collection of the data, special thanks are due, firstly, to T. Scott Murray, the international survey director, and secondly, to the national study managers in the concerned countries: Ireneusz Bialecki (Poland); Marilyn Binkley (United States); Willem Houtkoop (Netherlands); Mats Myrberg (Sweden); Jean Pignal (Canada); and François Stoll and Philipp Notter (Switzerland). A special debt of gratitude is due to Stephen Arrowsmith, Nancy Darkovitch and Richard Porzukzecm, all of Statistics Canada, who have made important contributions to the data analyses presented in this volume. Finally, we are grateful to Danielle Baum and Michael Hein for the assistance they provided in preparing the manuscript for publication.

Paris and Hamburg, May 1997

Paul Bélanger & Albert Tuijnman[2]

---

[1] *Information about the adult education participation instruments employed for this investigation is given in the companion volume,* The Emergence of Learning Societies: Who Participates in Adult Learning? *(edited by P. Bélanger and S. Valdivielso, Pergamon Press, Oxford 1997). Information about the survey design, data collection procedures and achieved coverage and response rates are provided in* The International Adult Literacy Survey: A Technical Report *(edited by T.S. Murray and I.S. Kirsch, National Center for Education Statistics, United States Department of Education, Washington, D.C. 1997). Conceptual issues and problems of measurement and assessment are discussed in* Adult Basic Skills: Advances in Measurement and Policy Analysis *(edited by A.C. Tuijnman, I.S. Kirsch and D.A. Wagner, Hampton Press, New York 1997).*

[2] *The views expressed in this volume by the editors are their own and do not necessarily reflect those of the United Nations Educational, Scientific and Cultural Organisation, the Organisation for Economic Co-operation and Development, or their Member countries.*

Chapter 1

The "Silent Explosion" of Adult Learning

Paul Bélanger and Albert Tuijnman

1.1 Introduction

Since the introduction by UNESCO and OECD of the idea of lifelong education in the early 1970s, and after nearly three decades of dispersed initiatives, it is now becoming possible to discern more precisely the empirical reality of adult learning, by mapping and analysing the high rates of participation of women and men in adult education and training and tracing the relations between initial and further education. Thus, one can observe the conflicting trends affecting adult education participation within national territories and between member states of the multilateral organizations. This analysis portrays the global trend through which countries are transiting in different ways and patterns towards fully fledged learning societies.

This chapter sets the scene for the rest of the volume. Section 1.2 looks at broad trends in economy, culture, and society, including globalization, demographic developments such as ageing and migration, the diffusion of information technologies, changes in industrial, occupational and qualification structures in segmented labour-markets, unemployment and underemployment, the changing work environment, newly evolving family structures, and indicators of cultural and linguistic diversity. The presentation is mainly descriptive; in broad strokes it paints a picture of the multiple forces of change that are currently at work around the world and that point to the opportunities but also considerable risks confronting the further development of adult education. Section 1.3 discusses the reasons why the developments highlighted previously inevitably put mounting pressure on the traditional ways of organizing adult education and training delivery. The changes evidently necessitate a response—the realization of lifelong learning for all. But the "silent explosion" in the demand and provision of adult learning opportunities over the past decades shows that such cultures of learning have been building for a long time, and that an inclusive learning economy cannot emerge overnight. Section 1.4 presents a reflection on some of the barriers and obstacles to the promotion of adult education and training in an broadened vision of lifelong learning for all. Section 1.5, finally, presents the conclusions and discusses the role of research into adult education participation.

1.2   Broad Trends in Economy, Culture and Society

The six countries studied in this volume share many economic, social, and cultural trends. The overarching trend is globalization. This is not a new or even a recent process. The contemporary scene, however, is new in its specific features. It has been broadened to encompass changes not only of investment capital, goods, and services, but also of people—their knowledge, ideas, dreams, and various ways of expression— and of socio-cultural movements across national and regional frontiers.

Compared to 1990, the share of foreigners and immigrants in the total population has increased in five of the six countries studied (Canada, the Netherlands, Poland, Sweden, Switzerland and the United States). The exception is Canada which experienced high levels of migration during the previous decades.However, There are large differences among the countries in the share of foreigners in the population, and there are also differences in the proportion of asylum-seekers admitted in recent years (OECD 1995). Despite these differences, encountering foreigners in the local environment is a common experience in all of the countries studied.

Foreign-born populations have to be integrated into the economy and society. In this, language barriers and cultural dialogue have to be taken into account, and an equilibrium must be found in combining new cultures with existing ones. Together with the objective of equality, recognition of differences is becoming a democratic value as more and more people with different value systems and cultural backgrounds interact in the community life and at the workplace. Second-language education and both general and vocational adult education are becoming an essential resource within the host-country populations as well as within the immigrant communities in addressing the challenges of economic regionalization and economic integration with respect for cultural diversity.

Globalization brings opportunities for economic and personal development, but it can also create vulnerability in the wake of rapid industrial transformation. As cultures mix, some of the traditional norms, values and cultural "maps" of communities and families no longer apply. One role of schooling has been to maintain the stability of society by socializing individuals with knowledge commonly accepted as being necessary for adult life. However, in a complex world characterized by changing values, skills and competencies, this traditional knowledge-base and the possibly ethno-centric belief systems of societies are increasingly being questioned—which presents another major challenge to communities, families and individuals. Increased emphasis on the benefits of adult learning is part of the response, because it provides countless micro-interaction opportunities for the expression and negotiation of differences.

Populations are ageing in all six countries. As the age ratios change, and with the emergence of two generations of senior citizens—the young-old and the old-old—there will be serious consequences for health care, social services and pensions' systems, as well as new opportunities available for societies to face the challenges ahead. These trends suggest that there will be a large and rising demand for adult and continuing education among older citizens. Providing adequate learning opportunities for older adults—who, as a group, are everywhere under-represented in adult education—is a priority for governments and local authorities, because such provision may help increase autonomy and will give this "new generation" the resources they need for their informed participation in community life. This new demand for adult education will be oriented towardss personal development as well as socio-economic goals in relation to the growing importance of the social economy and the role that older people will play within it.

The massive diffusion of new technologies—particularly information and telecommunication technology—influences the industrial, occupational and skill structures of labour markets. Today's growing industries are those involved in the creation, processing, and distribution of information and knowledge. The share in value-added by high-technology industries has increased in all OECD countries during the 1970s and 1980s, but in some countries more so than in others (OECD 1994a). Even though causality cannot be inferred, this points to a relationship between skills and technology, on the one hand, and innovation and productivity, on the other hand. Concomitantly with the deployment of new technologies, the share of white-collar jobs in total employment has tended to grow until now. Among the white-collar workers, the highly-skilled experienced the largest employment growth, indicating the continuing high demand for qualified workers. Growth in white-collar jobs contrasts with a continued decline in the number of jobs in low-technology manufacturing. For example, whereas blue-collar workers in manufacturing and transportation made up about 40 per cent of the United States work force in the 1950s, they accounted for less than 20 per cent in the early 1990s (OECD 1994a).

Many of those unemployed are not able to find work for sustained periods of time. Over 1995, long-term unemployment of one year and more (as a percentage of total unemployment) was 10 per cent in the United States, 14 per cent in Canada and 16 per cent in Sweden, compared with 32 per cent in Switzerland, and 43 per cent in the Netherlands (OECD 1996a). Unemployment is expected to remain at a high level throughout the remainder of the decade. This bleak prospect is bound to have consequences for the education systems.

Today, Canada and Sweden experience relatively high unemployment, with overall rates approaching 10 per cent (OECD 1996a). Rates are somewhat lower in the Netherlands, Switzerland and the United States. The data in Table 1.1 indicate that unemployment tends to be related, among different factors, to adult literacy performance, with those at a low level of skill being unemployed much more likely than those at a high skill level.

Many of the disappearing jobs are low-skilled, whereas most of the new jobs tend to demand intermediate and high-level skills. They require a good deal of formal education and training, and the ability to continuously acquire and apply analytical knowledge. The changes in occupational structures are reflected in the trends in long-term unemployment. Unemployment was generally low during the 1950s and 1960s; rates were in the range of 1.5 to 3 per cent (OECD 1994a). Since then these rates have progressively jacked up.

Table 1.1   Unemployment rates by literacy levels [1], 26 to 65-year-olds, 1994 (percentages)

	Level 1	Level 2	Level 3	Level 4/5
Canada	25.0	12.9	8.1	6.6
Netherlands	14.6	6.3	6.0	3.3
Poland	13.0	13.9	11.0	4.7
Sweden	18.3	9.2	6.0	4.4
Switzerland [2]	5.9	4.0	3.2	2.1
United States	8.7	4.0	3.1	2.6

1.   *Level 1 denotes low skill and level 4/5 high skill (see Chapter 7).*
2.   *Combined rates for French and German-speaking Switzerland.*
Source: OECD and Statistics Canada (1995).

Among the unemployed, youth and especially under-schooled youth are over-represented. Those whose schooling is incomplete are more liable to be out of work or in temporary posts. Workers, particularly older ones, thrown out of work by structural changes experience difficulty in finding alternative forms of employment if they possess no qualifications, or only low-level ones. Generally, the correlation between low attainment and unemployment shows no sign of weakening (OECD 1994b). If those who are out of a job and others who are socially deprived are to escape from poverty traps, new active labour-market policies will be required. In these, adult education will have an important part to play.

Work arrangements are changing not only with respect to the nature and content of jobs but also in terms of their organization and location. Until recently, lifetime employment with a single employer was by no means an exception. But conditions are changing, and so are the expectations and demands of both employers and employees. This results in part-time, temporary, multiple, or irregular jobs. Temporary work has become more common. As work environments change in response to technological innovation, conditions of work are altered. This is reflected in the differentiation of work arrangements, including alternative patterns like self-employment, but also, at times, in a new social stratification of working conditions and their application in strategies for the reduction of labour costs. In this context, and as a policy alternative, the internal flexibility (Piore & Sabel 1984) of the active population becomes crucial. Such flexibility depends on—presupposedly—the widespread capacity, willingness, and opportunity to continue learning. The development of the knowledge-intensive economy and the concomitant transition towards learning societies tend, in this new policy orientation, to be accommodated within the context of a broad, non-instrumental view of learning. Developing the creative and adaptive potential of all individuals has intrinsic value: contributing to social and economic adjustment is not the only imperative.

High-performance workplaces are on the increase. Such workplaces emphasize self-managing teams, study circles, flexible rather than narrow job design, flat organizational structures, employee problem-solving groups, information and office technologies, just-in-time learning and production, the ability to meet customer needs, and, particularly, innovation and total quality management. People's knowledge, skills, and qualifications are key to all these priorities. The move towards the high-performance and flexible workplace thus calls for a major adult education and training effort. But the nature of learning in the workplace is also changing. Self-directed and team learning have assumed greater importance, and instead of alternating work with occasional spells in formal adult education the emphasis is on learning while working and working while learning. Home-working and self-employment, and the increase in temporary and part-time employment, are further factors impinging upon the demand for and supply of opportunities for adult learning.

The long-term decline in working hours has resulted in an increase in the time available for other activities such as private life, education and training, travel, and leisure. In the United Kingdom which has long recorded time-keeping information, available non-work hours in the average lifetime increased from 118.000 in 1856 to 287.000 in 1981. Over the same period, average working hours fell from 124.000 to 64.000 (Ausubel and Grubler 1994). This trend is significant, because it indicates that the portion of a person's total lifetime spent at work has fallen from about 50 per cent in early industrial society to less than 20 per cent in late industrial society. The expectations are that this figure will drop even further in the post-industrial, knowledge-intensive economy. One-fifth of a person's total lifetime is nowadays spent on formal education and training before entering the world of work. Even this proportion is expected to grow as knowledge-intensive economies mature.

The decline in working hours, combined with the growing precariousness of employment, have changed the scope of the non-working life. In the future there may well be increased emphasis on the pursuit of leisure, personal development goals, and aesthetic and intellectual interests, as well as on new forms of associative life and social participation. However, the increase in time for non-work-related activities is distributed unevenly over the different life stages and between social groups. And the social divides in the availability of opportunities for improving the quality of life will pose new social and political challenges. "Postmaterialism" will involve a redefinition of values, cultural norms, institutional structures and communities, and interpersonal and social relationships. The indications are that countries and their education systems are in for a significant "cultural revolution" in this respect.

Cultures—a wide concept encompassing languages, traditions, values and belief systems, but also habits and the "art of living"—are being redefined and pluralized. As an increasing number of communities and families are linked by mainlines, cable and satellite, entrepreneurs rather than governments are setting the pace, and the choices are multiplying. Networks such as the Internet provide unprecedented supply of often diffuse information. Hence, more than ever people need the knowledge, literacy, and analytical skills to search for and select the information they need, and to put it into perspective. While the skills needed to operate personal computers and related equipment come almost naturally to some people, this is not true for many others. A literate and learning population is the key to unlocking the benefits while safeguarding cherished cultural values. At the same time, the aspiration of people to choose their own way of life among the different options now available for cultural expression, as well as the mix that will increasingly characterize such cultural forms, will require space for dialogue and for transforming inter-ethnic tensions into inter-cultural learning opportunities.

New ways of organizing family and private life relationships are also emerging (Stevens and Michalski 1994). Single-parent families can be vulnerable to economic upheaval. Such families are especially prevalent in the United States, where one-third of female-headed families are classified as poor (NCES 1994). Important social and economic issues are at stake because children living in poverty risk missing out on the social, cultural, and economic capital they need if they are to establish the foundations for success in lifelong learning and work. With poverty and unemployment continuing at high rates, social assistance remains important for large segments of the population.

Because knowledge, skills and educational and occupational qualifications are powerful factors in determining access to good jobs with adequate pay, initial and adult education are necessary components in any strategy for improving the quality of life of disadvantaged populations. Although educational policy cannot offer solutions on its own, there is a growing realization that education, training, and adult learning more generally have a major role to play in complementing existing social insurance provisions.

The above considerations represent a broad albeit patchy catalogue of explicit and implicit demands upon education systems and their adult learning components, implying higher levels of knowledge and skill for all citizens. The changing conditions signify large changes for the adult education and training providers: the demand for adult learning is increasing as well as diversifying, as are provisions.

1.3   The New Discourse in Adult Education and Training

In this new context, at the threshold of the 21st century, engagement in adult education or training activities has grown to a stage where more than half of the entire adult population of some countries is active over the course of a calendar year. The "silent explosion" of the demand for adult learning has to be understood against the backdrop of globalization and the profound changes in the economy mentioned above. Beyond that, high participation rates are the result of a series of quiet transformations in the conditions of people's non-working lives. Changes affecting the workplace, the community, and the private sphere of individuals and families have cumulated. As a result, organized adult learning has become an important factor in the biographies of many women and men.

Different chapters in this volume refer to the increasingly knowledge-intensive character of production in post-industrial societies. In these societies, the active population tends to demand access to adult education and training, and measures taken to promote the provision of organized learning opportunities over the entire lifespan of women and men are already increasingly in place. Policies for the promotion of adult learning are driven by a diagnosis common to analysts in many countries, ranging from the United States (Hudson Institute 1987) to the United Kingdom (1991) and from Australia (1988 and 1994) to Canada (1991). Moreover, this diagnosis is shared with international organizations, such as the OECD (1996b), the ILO (1996), the European Commission (1993), and, most recently, the World Bank. At heart, the diagnosis can be summed up as follows: "If we are to survive, develop and compete, the most critical resource is our people's talent and energy."

There is no denying that adult learning has once again become a prominent social and economic issue. This realization of the central position of adult learning and human resource development in the perspective of lifelong learning is now part of the official positions of UNESCO (1995) and the OECD (1996b).

Lifelong learning is promoted by governments as a strategy for meeting a range of social and economic policy objectives. It is considered a means for shaping the future of knowledge-intensive societies by emphasizing the personal development of the individual, thus countering the risks to social cohesion and promoting the democratic traditions in society, and responding to the challenges posed by an increasingly global and knowledge-intensive production system.

The discourse calls for more opportunities to learn, for more training within industry, and for more chances for people to acquire new skills, to learn a second or third language, and to improve their capacity to deal with increasingly complex information. Under the pressure of global competition, the knowledge-intensive economy, with its ongoing conversion and adaptation of the processes of production, is inducing a high demand for continuing education, leading to a growing number of skill development programs across *all* occupational strata.

Another force behind the increase in the demand for adult learning opportunities is the overwhelming impact—well-documented in the chapters to follow—of initial educational attainment on the rate of participation in adult education and training. Participation in adult education is a lifelong cumulative process. As the authors of the subsequent chapters will show in different ways, initial education is the strongest predictor of participation in organized adult learning. In every country, the longer people attend schools and the higher their level of initial educational attainment, the more they tend to participate in organized learning activities in adulthood. Thus, the rise in the level of educational attainment observed in all developed countries, with younger age groups having obtained more and better quality education than older age groups, coincides with the rise in the demand for adult learning opportunities. Accordingly, the steady rise in the level of initial educational attainment which is now a general phenomenon is likely to produce a substantial future increase in the demand for adult learning opportunities. However, this process works both ways. The documented 'positive' impact of accumulated education advantages works to the disadvantages of those who have had a limited or negative education experience early in their life.

This process of a silent but steady and cumulative growth in educational demand among the adult population is reinforced by the widespread deployment of information and communication technologies and the emergence of new, knowledge-intensive and print-related life and work contexts. Also, the previously mentioned increase in the portion of non-work time over the lifespan adds to the general trend. The more these contributing factors grow in strength, the more the demand for adult learning is expected to increase in the future.

Apart from the steady increase over the last three decades in the number of people participating in organized learning activities, a significant qualitative change is also taking place. The inner transformation of the factors at work in this, combined with the long-term processes creating the silent explosion in the demand for adult learning opportunities, are challenging the ways in which this demand is being defined, communicated, and eventually met.

There is considerable demand for "second-chance" education, expressed by numerous women and men who missed out on their initial schooling. In addition, there is need for skill upgrading in response, for example, to the introduction of new technologies in the workplace. But today the demand for adult learning goes far beyond the need for compensatory education and occasional occupational upskilling. The current transformation in the demand for learning opportunities can be described in relation to the emergence of "cognitive societies." But this notion has its drawbacks, it may lead to policies which are too narrowly defined. For example, it does not convey a sense of the profound changes that follow in the wake of the transformation of the production process and of parallel transformations in community life.

The emergence of the "post-taylorist" or "knowledge-intensive" economy with its requirements of "just-in-time" flexible production, the lost credibility of technocratic "top-down and quick-fix" solutions, and the increased unpredictability characterizing all spheres of modern life—all these related trends have led to the rediscovery of the paramount importance and centrality of the people themselves, of their knowledge, skills, initiatives, and creativity. The social and economic transformation induces individuals to enhance their competence and their ability to lead a creative life, and it induces public agencies to rely more on people's own initiative. Thus, we are at a turning point in history; what we witness in the present era is the emergence not only of "cognitive" or "knowledge-based" but also, and more profoundly, of "reflexive" societies (Beck, Giddens & Lash 1994). It refers to what the French sociologist Alain Touraine in 1989 called "le retour de l'acteur"—the comeback of the individual and the collective actors to the core of the workplaces and communities.

Two factors need to be taken into account in grasping more of this quiet revolution in adult learning. Firstly, the linear-adaptive learning paradigm generally adopted for the development of work skills is increasingly being called into question. Secondly, the necessity of increasing productivity is not restricted to the wage economy, but is felt in all spheres of life.

The response to the current transformation requires more than an occasional adaptation of the production system to new technologies and structures. Narrow skill-adjustment policies and practices are dysfunctional in the reflexive era of production. Alternative action will involve comprehensive education and training programmes that allow more flexibility within an occupational family and greater autonomy of learners. Adult education policies and practices are thus required to change radically. Having already been enlarged in terms of scope and time, they now have to be aligned with another perspective, namely that of human resource development for more inclusive and general sectors of specialization, rather than for narrowly defined occupations. This calls for a move from occasional training for skill-adjustment purposes to comprehensive and polyvalent adult education programmes for the empowerment of learners. This shift in perspective opens up new opportunities for those who are employed within the core of the formal economy, but poses new constraints and barriers for the growing number of people who are excluded from this core.

The high-skill and high-wage economy creates a huge demand for adult learning among regular employees. Those who work in the micro-enterprises of the knowledge-intensive sector may find themselves adequate learning opportunities through their "virtual networks". But the growing number of those employed in precarious jobs, and the many people who, while being confronted with redundancy as a result of new technologies (Rifkin 1996), try to cater for themselves and their family by means of initiatives undertaken within the informal or social economy, also belong to the economically "active" population. This second group is no less in need of expertise and therefore of adult education and training.

Moreover, the social activities and initiatives in which an increasing number of adults outside the formal economy are engaged, are of no less importance from an economic point of view. The informed participation of citizens in the monitoring and management of the environment, the involvement of local communities in intercultural exchanges, social dialogue, and tolerance building, the growing interest to take part in health prevention and promotion activities all create new learning demands. The apparent aspiration of people to increase their level of social and cultural participation makes it necessary to broaden our understanding of the concept of economic productivity and of the kind of investment required to make ends meet.

The material benefits resulting from increasing productivity, competence, and creativity of people should of course be analysed in terms of their effect on employment and wages, but analysis should not stop there. Benefits aside, there is a huge cost of *not* increasing the overall productive capacity of all citizens (Reich 1991), both in the developed countries (Benton and Noyelle 1991) and in the developing countries (see, for example, the "Jomtien Declaration", UNICEF 1990). In the reflexive society and in the post-industrial economy the benefits of the investment in people cannot be properly assessed without taking the opportunity costs into account. What will be the cost for future societies for not investing now in a prolonged basic education for all citizens and in the development of their capacity to be active in a print-oriented culture? What, if we do not recognize and support the ways in which many of the so-called non-participants learn? How will societies be able to bear the increasing curative and custodial costs if they do not invest on a long-term basis in preventive health education and in the rehabilitation of criminal offenders through education? What will be the future price for not investing, as Habermas would say, in the development of communicative skills to ensure further development of micro and macro negotiation processes as a prerequisite for tackling current social problems?

It is the broader understanding of the new demand for adult learning that makes the empirical analysis—across countries—of the patterns of adult education participation and of the gaps between the social demand and actual provision so crucial. It is the expanded vision of the role of people's creativity and learning in a new culture of productivity that makes the study of barriers to and determinants of participation in organized adult learning, as well as of the interplay between socio-cultural and the economic factors, so critical for education policy development in a framework for lifelong learning.

1.4 Inclusions and Exclusions in Adult Learning

The primary idea underpinning lifelong learning is that everyone is able and should be encouraged to learn and to continue doing so throughout life, whether the learning takes place in formal institutions of education and training or informally, at home, at work, or in the community. While this notion of lifelong learning is now widely accepted, and although it has already become a natural feature of everyday life for certain privileged groups, there remains the essential next step of making it a reality for all those as well who are currently excluded. Whatever the answers to this challenge, it is clear that at every step along the road from acceptance to design to realization, the diversity of the adult learners and settings for learning must be appreciated as a central characteristic.

The key problem faced by all countries is that the resources allocated to adult education, the processes of adult learning, and the uses people make of the opportunities on offer, all tend to discriminate against certain groups in society. Thus, the countries are faced with a policy paradox. On the one hand, adult education and training are the instruments of inclusion, of economic development and community building; they present the means of acquiring the knowledge, skills and experiences that can help people adjust and cope with change, including finding a new balance, whether in work, culture or family life. But at the same time adult education is also an instrument of exclusion. The research on adult education participation conducted to date shows consistent patterns of inclusions and exclusions. With the move towardss learning economies and societies, the cost of non-participation to individuals, their families and communities is expected to increase.

The obstacles to realizing the goals within the framework of lifelong learning are many; they include the divides across jurisdictions, the difficulty of obtaining a broad consensus of interests, and financial resources. Other, second-order problems are the lack of legal arrangements for study leave and lack of financial support during periods of learning.

The biggest obstacle is perhaps attitudinal: participation in organized adult learning results from educational expectations and aspirations. However, research studies show that it cannot be taken for granted that all citizens will have the same opportunity to build a positive attitude towardss adult learning, or to develop a positive image of one's capacity to succeed in an educational context. Similarly, it will not be true that all adults will be equally ready to make use of the available opportunities, or that all women and men will be equally aware of the available educational possibilities. Such critical dispositional and informational barriers are sociologically determined. The recognition and acceptance of a value—that an educated life is better than an uneducated one, is crucial, but such a value is also significantly embedded in the stratified representation of formal education. To overcome these obstacles, the new adult learning policies should tend to be more 'demand-focused,' overcoming the information barriers, creating contexts that can facilitate the expression of needs and aspirations among the different social groups.

Many adult education and training activities are subsidized by employers. But employers tend to support predominantly those activities that do not take much time, generally less than 60 hours. Many adult learning activities are thus financed through other means. Even though the shares of adult education and continuing vocational training in total public education spending have increased in most countries since the mid-1970s, public funding of adult education is still tiny compared with the allocation of public resources to initial formal education. Apparently individuals are required to pay a large share of the total costs for adult education and training, and there are large differences between individuals in their capacity to do so.

Barriers inherent to financial, social and educational institutions, and in deep-seated individual and social attitudes, require further analysis. It is clear, however, that the practices of adult learning are open-ended to an extend although the expression of the educational demand is not uniform across firms and economic sectors. It is more strongly supported in some areas than in others. It is also thwarted by a growing segmentation of labour markets. The probability of obtaining employer's support for training is higher at the supervisory levels then for line workers. But the evidence emanating from this international study shows that the tendency towards a reproduction of educational inequality over the life-span is neither linear nor absolute. If you are a less-skilled worker, the probability that you will have a chance to participate in adult education or training activities will be significantly reduced, but not if you are working in Sweden. Similarly, the impact of a lower initial education is reduced in economic sectors where, as in the personnel service sectors, the likelyhood of participation is higher.

The differentiated national adult learning scenes documented in this publication show that the factors influencing participation are complex and varied. The differences point to space for policy interventions. Neither is initial formal education the sole dispositional determinant, nor is the general economy of adult learning fixed and unresponsive to policy intervention. The cultural environments at home, in the community and at work tend to have a relatively autonomous influence on the disposition of the adult learners, stimulating or deterring curiosity, motivating or provoking resistance. Much less restricted and much more broadly diffused across the social milieus than formal schooling, these environments and the cultural practices like reading, radio listening and social participation constitute a new arena for policy intervention. They refer to less regulated spaces where people can express different learning aspirations and experience self-learning practices and informal education.

What seems clear, in this enlarged policy environment, is that cooperation between all the actors involved is essential if the different hurdles are to be surmounted. Perceptions of the role of governments and education institutions have shifted accordingly; it is now shared with others in a relationship of partnership with joint responsibility. "Partnership", "autonomy" and "choice" are keywords in educational debate. But partnership has to be developed, autonomy organized and managed, and choice cannot be absolute. How then should governments proceed? The tendency recently has been for the central authority to devolve more of its operational responsibilities for adult education to the other partners in the educational enterprise, whilst retaining overall strategic control. The governmental role, it is found, might best be 'steering' and 'supporting' ones. This entails greater autonomy for institutions, but lays upon them directly the duty of promoting "the public good" with high efficiency. For some individuals, but not for others, this vision opens up vistas of greater choice.

In the adult education sector, government is neither the sole provider of resources, nor necessarily the determiner of content of courses. Many other agencies are involved, most notably employers and the institutions themselves, and there are intermediary or "buffer" bodies. Nonetheless, the central authority is still called upon to act in a "steering" capacity, and to provide a legal framework and to correct inequalities and dysfunctions. In view of the expansion taking place in these sectors, which reaches certain groups but tends to leave others behind, the need to rethink policies is urgent. Dysfunction exists; as education and training systems have grown piecemeal, organizational frameworks have had to be imposed after the event. Mere tinkering with education systems in order to achieve reform will not suffice; coherence but also targeted interventions are both needed if policies are to support the transition to "learning societies", where learning in all forms and at all ages contributes to significant improvements in employment, social cohesion and the quality of life of all citizens.

Such a "learning society" cannot arise overnight, and strategies for realizing it are open-ended; they address learning in all its forms; they accept neither narrow demarcations between education and training, academic and vocational programmes, nor restrictions to learning opportunities in formal structures. Yet, it is this very breadth and diversity that call for a close examination of the directions that can be taken if lifelong learning is to be more than a chaotic, disconnected collection of structures and functions that benefit those who are included and punish those who are not.

1.5 Conclusions

This chapter has reviewed a number of broad trends affecting life in post-industrial countries, including demographic change and aging, globalization, the diffusion of new information and communication technologies, trends in employment and shifts in the distribution of occupations, qualifications and skills, and developments in the worlds of work, community and family life. Together, these trends and developments point to an array of gradual but profound changes. The symptoms of the ongoing transformation reveal both risks and opportunities. Despite continuing productivity gains and a gradual increase in overall standards of living, unemployment, poverty and social exclusion remain widespread, and the aspirations and needs of many are unfulfilled. The emerging high-skill, high-wage knowledge-intensive economy accommodates a growing share of the work force in some countries, but the divisions between those who are included and those who are excluded are sharp, and can deepen further. These inclusions and exclusions in the formal economy tend to correspond to inclusions and exclusions in lifelong learning.

Thus, the challenges clearly go beyond the mere noting of a growing demand for education and training among learners of all ages, and an increase in the diversity of providers. There is a need for a different quality and content of adult education, which signals a generic and paradigmatic shift from education to learning and from single to differentiated learning contexts. New information and communication technologies can change the way education is organized. Instead of a supply-led and heavily institutionalized system, the new conditions allow for a demand-led approach, where motivated learners can obtain the education they desire from diverse sources and in ways they themselves plan.

Building a democratic learning society is a long-term goal; achieving it will take major and sustained efforts over many years. There is no single, unified and hierarchically structured "system" of lifelong learning that suits all countries. Lifelong learning will need to build upon specific national and plural cultural heritages, and policies modified to suit particular conditions and needs. A "system" of lifelong learning cannot be imposed; it must depend and thrive on a great variety of initiatives taken by different actors in many spheres of life and work. Further, the role of government is not to "invent", manage and pay for a "system" of lifelong learning opportunities, but rather to monitor and steer developments, to create demand and to redistribute resources so that provision is inclusive, equitable, flexible and efficient.

The very nature of lifelong learning—diverse, pluralistic, and undertaken over a lifetime—calls for co-operation and co-ordination among many policy sectors, involving both macro-economic and structural policies. The policy environment of adult education and training is undergoing an important transformation. In sharp contrast to the organizational pattern of formal initial education, the provision of adult education is increasingly diffused over many different structures and arrangements. The trend towards a diversification of provision is taken place both within the public sector, where a growing number of ministries support adult learning activities and programmes (in health, in environment, in welfare), and within civil societies where, beyond the 'traditional' adult and nonformal education associations, many non-governmental institutions and organizations are offering in their specific fields of action a series of training and empowering initiatives.

In the post-industrial countries where the building blocks of the learning society have been increasingly put into place as the 20th century draws to a close, the challenge to reduce the exclusive tendencies in adult education, and to make it a common, even universal experience is becoming more urgent. The bleak messages contained in the cumulated research evidence on non-participation suggest that this goal cannot be accomplished under current conditions and modes of provision. Major reforms and outreach policies are called for if adult education is to become more inclusive. Unless some adjustment is made in current policies, unless more space is created for diversity in learning projects, and unless the main socio-cultural obstacles or barriers to participation in education are lifted, lifelong learning will still mean, for too many people, a continuous frustration of their aspirations and a repeated deprivation throughout their lifespan. For society, the loss will obviously be huge.

The design of successful strategies will depend crucially on the knowledge base of adult education. It is in improving this knowledge base that this book hopes to make its contribution to the field.

References

Australia.1988. *Industry Training in Australia. The Need for Change*. Canberra: Department of Employment, Education and Training.

Australia. 1994.W*orking Nation. The White Paper on Employment and Growth*. Canberra: Department of Employment, Education and Training.

Ausubel, J.H., and Grubler, A. 1994. *Working less and living longer: Long-term trends in working time and time budgets*. (mimeo) Paris: OECD.

Beck, U., Giddens, A., and Lash, S. 1994. *Reflexive Modernization*. Cambridge: Polity Press.

Benton, L., and Noyelle, T. 1991. *Adult Literacy and Economic Performance in Industrialized Countries*. Paris: OECD.

Canada. 1991. *The Road to Competence*. Ottawa: CEC.

European Commission. 1993. *Growth, Competitiveness, Employment: The Challenges and Ways forward into the 21st Century.* Brussels: Official Publications of the Commission of the European Communities.

Hudson Institute. 1988. *Opportunity 2000: Creative Affirmative Action Strategies for a Changing Workforce.* Washington D.C.: United States Department of Labor.

ILO. 1996. *Entreprise Strategy.* (Working paper) Geneva: International Labour Office.

NCES. 1994. *The Condition of Education.* Washington D.C.: National Center for Education Statistics, United States Department of Education.

OECD. 1994a. *The OECD Jobs Study: Facts, Analysis, Strategies.* Paris: OECD.

OECD. 1994b. *Labour Force Statistics 1972-1992.* Paris: OECD.

OECD. 1995. *Trends in International Migration. Annual Report 1994.* Paris: OECD.

OECD. 1996a. *Employment Outlook, June.* Paris: OECD.

OECD. 1996b. *Lifelong Learning for All: Meeting of the Education Committee at ministerial level, 16-17 January.* Paris: OECD.

OECD and Statistics Canada. 1995. *Literacy, Economy and Society: Results of the First International Adult Literacy Survey.* Paris and Ottawa.

Piore, M. and Sabel, C. 1984. *The Second Industrial Divide: Possibilities for Prosperity.* New York: Basic Book.

Reich, R. 1991. *The Works of Nations.* New York: Knopf.

Rifkin, J. 1996. *The End of Work.* New York: Tarcher Putnam.

Stevens, B., and Michalski, W. 1994. "Long-term prospects for work and social cohesion in OECD countries: An overview of the issues". In: *OECD Societies in Transition: The Future of Work and Leisure.* Paris: OECD.

Touraine, A. 1989. *Le retour de l'acteur.* Paris: Fayard.

UNESCO. 1995. *Mid-term Strategy 1996-2001.* Paris: UNESCO.

UNICEF and Inter-Agency Commission. 1990. *World Declaration on Education for All. Framework for Action to Meet Basic Learning Needs.* New York: UNICEF House.

United Kingdom. 1991. *Education and Training for the 21st Century.* London: Department of Education and Science and Department of Employment.

Chapter 2

Demand and Supply of Adult Education and Training

Willem Houtkoop and Hessel Oosterbeek

2.1 Introduction

In this chapter, the patterns of demand and supply of adult education and training are examined for six countries: Canada, the Netherlands, Poland, Sweden, Switzerland, and the United States. Following a more general introduction to the delivery systems in these countries, data collected as part of the International Adult Literacy Survey (IALS) are employed to describe and analyze national participation patterns, and demand and supply characteristics. Distinctions are made between work-related and leisure-related education and training. Special attention is devoted to the unfulfilled learning needs of people who considered they wanted to participate in adult education, but for one reason or another did not. Subsequently, the determinants of participation in work- and leisure-related adult education are explored in a multivariate model, and the relationships between the self-perceived usefulness of education or training and demand and supply characteristics are analyzed. Finally, the determinants of constraints felt in education or training choices are explored.

Most of the information analyzed in this chapter was provided by survey respondents who either participated in adult education or explicitly wished to do so. Although that information is quite detailed, it probably does not offer a complete picture of the complexity of the relationships between demand and supply characteristics, which in part determine the decision to participate in adult education and training programmes. Be that as it may, the analysis offered is among the most complete international comparisons of adult education participation available to date.

2.2   Delivery Systems

Sweden has an elaborate system of adult education and training provision. Characteristic of this system are the role of training as an integral part of active labour-market policy, a relatively open system of tertiary education, and ample opportunities for educational leave. Participation in education, including adult education, is high by international standards, and Sweden also has a leading position in terms of public education expenditure as a proportion of total public spending. Labour-market training is a tripartite responsibility and largely decentralized. Broad vocational and general adult education is mainly a responsibility of the municipalities. There is a separate system of adult basic education. Sociocultural adult education has a rich tradition in Sweden, with folk high schools and study circles as major providers. Most forms of adult education are free of charge, and participants are often entitled to some form of financial assistance (Houtkoop 1996).

Adult education is undergoing major changes in the *Netherlands*. Efforts are underway to create coherence in a fragmented system; money and authority are being transferred to local authorities, and the system is being adapted to the demands of the labour-market. Although public expenditure on adult education has risen substantially since the mid-1980s, participation as well as public expenditure are on an intermediate level compared to other Western European countries. Private vocational training is dominated by firm-based training, as it is in most industrialized countries. A peculiarity of the Dutch system is the strong position of private providers in the markets for work- and leisure-related education and training. The quality standards of private providers are governed by law. There is no legal arrangement for educational leave, but to an increasing extent it forms part of collective labour agreements. Although the training of the unemployed is subsidized by the government, it is the responsibility of the social partners, while the municipalities are responsible for general adult education and adult basic education. Adult basic education has been particularly successful in terms of participation and in attracting minority groups. Compared to other countries, institutions of tertiary education hardly play a role in adult education (Houtkoop 1996).

In *Canada*, adult education, like education more generally, is primarily a responsibility of the provinces. As a consequence, there can be large differences in policy—and in the ensuing participation patterns in the different provinces. The same applies to the *United States*, although there selective funding can have a major impact in specific areas, such as adult basic education and workplace literacy. In both countries, adult education is provided by a bewildering array of sponsors, including colleges and universities, community colleges, libraries, labour organizations, religious organizations, commercial organizations, business and industry, and the media. Most of them depend heavily on user fees for support. Adult education has been and continues to be essentially self-supporting with a few national priority programmes funded by government. The current emphasis in government-sponsored programmes in Canada and the United States is on workplace education (adjustment to changes in the workplace or job advancement) and to a lesser extent on programmes that enable people to (re)enter the labour-market. It is a familiar pattern: most adult education is taken up for job or career-related purposes, and participation tends to widen rather than narrow the gap between the most and the least educated (Griffith 1996).

Switzerland also has a highly decentralized political system. Continuing education is not regulated either at the national or regional level. As a consequence, there is no recognized right to training or educational leave. Another consequence is that there has been, until very recently, a dearth of statistical data about adult education and training in the country. According to a 1993/94 survey conducted by the Swiss Federal Office of Statistics (1996), 40 per cent of the adult population attended at least one course during the year preceding the survey—a share similar to that reported by other industrialized countries. The pattern of provision is dominated by private providers and courses given by employers. Educational policy in the fields of higher vocational and continuing education supports this pattern; there is a strong reliance on market forces to achieve an efficient qualification of the work force (OECD 1996).

Adult education has a long tradition in *Poland,* as in the other Central and East European countries, but after the communist take-over it was mostly restricted to vocational training and political adult education. Since the fall of the Berlin Wall in 1989, the economic, political, and social structures have undergone rapid change. Adult education has been expected to play a significant role in this process. Several nationwide projects have been initiated, such as sociocultural animation and study circles, civic education, and the establishment of a Network of Centres for Economic and Civic Education. There has been an explosive increase in adult education and training in the country, leading amongst other things to a proliferation of private adult education institutions, often filling the vacuum created by the demise of bankrupt Soviet-inspired institutions. The same applies to centres for management and business administration, often set up in cooperation with foreign tertiary education institutions. More than before, individuals are forced to invest in their own job-related training, as the state budget can no longer sustain the large expenditures required (Krajnc 1996).

2.3   The Dataset

The data used in this chapter were gathered in the context of the IALS—an international comparative project aimed at measuring the literacy and numeracy skills of the adult populations (ages 16-65) in a number of industrialized countries. The data were collected in Fall 1994 using a household survey approach. An open-ended test instrument was used for the direct measurement of adult literacy skills. An extensive background questionnaire was used to collect a range of variables useful for exploring the determinants as well as outcomes of skill levels. Because adult education and training are among the means of raising skill levels in the population, some of the countries gathered detailed information about participation in adult education and training. The instruments used for the data collection, as well as the collection procedures are described briefly in the appendix to this Volume.

The dataset employed for this study included information from Canada, the Netherlands, Poland, Sweden, Switzerland, and the United States. Unfortunately, in Sweden, many of the more detailed questions about participation were not asked. In the dataset, a distinction was made between the French- and German-speaking regions of Switzerland and the French- and English-speaking provinces in Canada. For the purposes of the data analysis reported in this chapter, the language groups in Switzerland and Canada are considered together.

The dataset thus assembled includes full information about participation in Canada, the Netherlands, Poland, Switzerland and the United States, and partial information about Sweden. The sample sizes are given in Table 2.1; all the analyses are based on weighed data.

Table 2.1.   Survey coverage, language of interview, and sample yields

Country	Survey coverage (population 16-65)	Language	Sample yield
Canada	13,676,612	English	3,130
	4,773,648	French	1,370
Netherlands	10,460,359	Dutch	2,837
Poland	24,475,649	Polish	3,000
Sweden	5,361,942	Swedish	2,645
Switzerland	1,008,275	French	1,435
	3,144,912	German	1,393
United States	161,121,972	English	3,053

One more restriction was made. To exclude young students, respondents who were younger than 25 and were studying at the time of the interview were omitted.[1]

2.4 Patterns of Participation

The major distinction is between participants and non-participants. The question put to the respondents was whether they had participated in any form of structured, organized adult education or training in the 12 months preceding the interview. This excludes much of the more informal forms of learning, commonly referred to as self-directed learning or—in a work context—on-the-job learning (Hiemstra 1996). Although there are national differences, there is a sizeable portion of the adult population of about 40 per cent who can be counted as participants (see Table 2.2).

Table 2.2. Percentage of the population participating in adult education

Country	Participating	Participating in job-related programmes	Participating in personal interest related programmes	Total
Sweden	52.9	–	–	N=2,147
United States	42.4	37.9	5.0	N=2,764
Switzerland	39.6	25.8	17.0	N=2,559
Canada	38.9	31.7	9.5	N=4,534
Netherlands	37.8	25.3	13.1	N=2,611
Poland	14.3	10.5	3.6	N=2,676

Sweden has an exceptionally high participation rate of more than 50 per cent. In comparison, the participation rate is relatively low in Poland. The other countries occupy the middle ground with participation rates around the 40 per cent mark.

There is an important distinction between participation for career or job-related purposes and participation for personal development and leisure interests. In this study, respondents were asked to make the distinction themselves.

---

[1] *It has been argued that respondents who participate less than 6 hours on a yearly basis in adult education should be excluded. This line was not fallowed here for three reasons. Firstly, because (very) short courses are also an interesting phenomenon to investigate; secondly, because the number of respondents involved is small (N=171 in the weighted sample); and thirdly, because strict application of the rule would result in loss of information, as not all the respondents gave enough information to calculate the total amount of time spent on adult education.*

People can take more than one course in a given year, and many did so. In Table 2.2, only the percentage of the population that took *a* course (one or more) for job-related or personal purposes is reported. The small number of people who took courses for other reasons (for example, legal obligations) are not taken into account. This explains why the percentages for participation in job-related and personal interest programmes do not add up to the percentage for total participation.[2]

It is clear that participation for job-related purposes is much more common in Canada and the United States than in Switzerland or the Netherlands. Switzerland stands out as a country were a relatively large proportion of the population participates in adult education for reasons of personal development and leisure interests—reasons that play only a modest role in the United States.

Although participation in job-related adult education is often correlated with participation in leisure activities (Houtkoop 1985), in the this study the two categories seem to an extent mutually exclusive. Only about 10 per cent of the people who participated in job-related courses also participated in courses taken for personal interest.

Participation in itself is a rather crude measure, because it can range from a one-day seminar to a part-time university course and because people can take only one course or several. The impact of adult education is probably more determined by the intensity of participation than by the occurrence of participation as such. Table 2.3 shows the average number of courses taken per country and the total amount of time spent. Separate figures are given for job-related and personal-interest courses. Again, the distinction is based on whether people took a job-related or a personal-interest course in the preceding year. Overlap between the two groups can occur.

---

[2]   *Because people often took more than one course, there are also people who took job-related as well as personal-interest courses. In the construction of the variable measuring whether people took a job-related course, we also included the group of people who took job-related as well as personal-interest courses. The following table depicts the participation pattern of people who took a job-related course. It is clear that they often took more than one job-related course, but in many instances took a personal-interest course as well.*

	Canada	Switzerland	United States	Netherlands	Poland
Per cent taking job-related course	159.7	146.7	167.3	143.3	135.9
Per cent taking personal interest course	13.4	20.0	5.2	13.9	4.3
Total	**N=1,438**	**N=658**	**N=1,047**	**N=659**	**N=282**

Table 2.3.   **Average number of courses taken and average amount of time spent on adult education in the preceding 12 months**

Country	Average number of courses taken	Average time spent on participation (hours)	Average time spent (work hours)	Average time spent (personal hours)
Canada	2.4	300	301	207
Switzerland	1.9	137	153	129
United States	2.7	161	151	123
Netherlands	1.6	239	283	163
Poland	1.4	149	128	200

There are significant differences in the average number of courses taken in the different countries, as well as in the average total amount of time spent on adult education and training. An important finding is that the range of total time spent is large. While the average total time spent on adult education is 217 hours for the countries in Table 2.3, the standard deviation is 419 hours. Although some respondents claim very substantial time investments, the exclusion of the upper ranges in the distribution hardly changes the overall picture.

Bearing in mind the magnitude of the standard deviations, people in Canada and the United States take more courses than people in Switzerland and the Netherlands, but Canada and the Netherlands lead the ranks as far as total time spent on adult education and training is concerned. In general, the duration of courses in the Netherlands and Canada seems to be twice as long as those in the United States. People also take more job-related than personal-interest courses, and they also spend more time on job-related courses, with the sole exception of Poland.

The findings appear to point to a distinct pattern. In Sweden, a large percentage of the population participates in adult education. The United States also demonstrates a relatively high participation rate, mainly spent on job-related courses that are of a relatively brief duration. Canada, the Netherlands, and Switzerland are in the middle range as far as participation is concerned, but patterns differ. People in Switzerland spend on average less time on adult education, and this applies to both job-related and personal-interest categories. But the Swiss are in a leading position with respect to participation in adult education for personal-interest reasons. Adults in Canada and the Netherlands spend the most time on adult education, especially that of a job-related nature. Poland is in an exceptional position, as can be expected from a country in a transitional stage. Participation in adult education is relatively low, but for those who participate the average time spent is in the same range as Switzerland and the United States. The volume of adult education participation is greatest in Canada, followed by the Netherlands, if both the share of the population that does participate and the total amount of time spent are taken into account.

2.5   Demand Characteristics

How can the people whose demand for learning translated into actual participation be characterized? In the countries investigated, men and women participated about equally; the countries with a slight over-representation of women amongst the participants are Sweden and the United States. However, a different pattern emerges if job-related and personal-interest courses are considered separately. On average, job-related courses are taken by 30.4 per cent of the men and 23.7 per cent of the women, and personal-interest courses by 6.4 per cent of the men and 12.5 per cent of the women (Swedish data excluded). This phenomenon is particularly marked in the Netherlands and, albeit to a lesser extent, Canada and Switzerland. The gender pattern in the United States and Poland is much more equal. By way of illustration, the situation in the Netherlands is compared with that of the United States in Table 2.4.

Table 2.4.   Participation in job-related and personal-interest adult education by gender in the Netherlands and the United States

| | Job-related (Percent) | | Personal-interest related (Percent) | |
	Netherlands	United States	Netherlands	United States
Man	30.9	39.4	8.1	3.4
Women	19.6	36.6	18.3	6.3
Total	**N=1,323**	**N=1,285**	**N=1,323**	**N=1,285**

Results showing participation by age are presented in Table 2.5. A general finding is that the rate of adult education participation tends to be lower in the older age groups. Leaving Poland aside for the moment, the highest participation rates for most countries are in the youngest age group (16-25), with the exception of Sweden. Canada is especially successful in attracting this group of young adults, many of whom have to make the transition from school to work.

In line with its high overall participation rate, Sweden's participation rate is higher in all the age groups above 25 years. The Swedish success in attracting relative large numbers of older adults is striking; about a third of the people aged 56-65 still participate in some form of adult education. The Netherlands and Canada are far less successful in this respect.

Table 2.5.   Percentage of participants in adult education in each age group

Age	Canada	Switzerland	United States	Netherlands	Poland	Sweden
16-25	57.7	49.5	46.9	49.1	17.4	47.0
26-35	41.9	46.6	46.5	45.9	17.4	57.2
36-45	41.7	42.2	44.9	40.4	18.4	61.0
46-55	33.4	35.8	43.8	30.6	11.4	57.3
56-65	14.7	20.6	26.8	17.0	2.8	34.8
Average participation	38.9	39.6	42.4	37.8	14.3	52.9
Total	N=4,534	N=2,557	N=2,764	N=2,610	N=2,676	N=2,146

In general, the best predictor of participation in adult education is the highest completed level of initial formal education (Houtkoop & van der Kamp 1992). For the purposes of comparative analysis, initial educational attainment is often measured using the levels specified in the International Standard Classification of Education (ISCED). The relationship between initial and adult education is presented in Tables 2.6 and 2.7.

Table 2.6.   Percentage of participants in adult education by level of educational attainment (ISCED)

ISCED level	Canada	Switzerland	United States	Netherlands	Poland	Sweden
0/1	15.5	9.7	12.3	17.8	2.7	27.0
2	27.0	19.1	23.1	29.5	10.3	47.2
3	35.5	42.9	33.5	44.5	20.8	53.4
5	53.6	56.0	57.8	–	33.2	67.0
6/7	59.7	55.2	67.1	52.7	36.0	70.2
Average participation	38.9	39.6	42.4	37.8	14.3	52.9
Total	N=4,471	N=2,420	N=2,760	N=2,594	N=2,762	N=2,064

There is a strong relationship between educational attainment and participation in adult education, with marked differences between education preceding and at the primary level (ISCED 1), lower secondary education (ISCED 2), and upper secondary education (ISCED 3). The differences are less marked between ISCED 5 and 6/7, which are all on the tertiary level but differ in the sense that level 5 does not lead to a university qualification while level 6/7 does. There is no level 5 equivalent educational programme in the Netherlands.

In line with its high overall participation rate, Sweden also attracts the most adult education students at all educational levels. Besides Sweden, the

Netherlands and Canada are also relatively successful in attracting participants with a lower educational background, whereas the United States draws a relatively large number of participants from the group with a university background.

The rate of participation in job-related courses is contrasted with educational attainment in Table 2.7. There is little variation in the capability of Canada, the Netherlands, and the United States to bring people with a low level of educational attainment into adult education. Only Switzerland lags behind in this respect. However, the capability of the United States to attract people with high levels of attainment stands out even more; 62 per cent of the adult population with a university background participated in job-related courses during the year preceding the interview.

Table 2.7.   Percentage of participants in job-related adult education by level of educational attainment (ISCED)

ISCED level	Canada	Switzerland	United States	Netherlands	Poland
0/1	11.2	4.0	9.8	9.9	2.1
2	18.8	7.5	14.8	18.0	7.6
3	29.5	28.5	29.7	29.1	16.4
5	44.6	39.8	52.0	–	20.3
6/7	51.0	39.0	62.0	40.9	26.0
Average participation	**31.5**	**26.1**	**37.9**	**25.3**	**10.6**
Total	**N=4,471**	**N=2,420**	**N=2,760**	**N=2,594**	**N=2,762**

In Table 2.8, the relationship between adult education participation and labour-market position is depicted. Because the category "student/work" is so small (about 1 per cent), it is omitted.

The distribution over the labour-market categories shows a similar pattern for the different countries, with an over-representation of participants amongst employed people and an under-representation amongst retired people and home workers. The large percentage of the employed in Sweden who participated in adult education (60 per cent) is striking. Although the unemployed participate less than the employed, there is still a sizeable share of this group that participates, amounting to around 40 per cent in Sweden and the Netherlands.

In line with the findings reported for previous research studies (Houtkoop & van der Kamp 1992), the employed population has the highest rate of participation in job-related courses, with a particularly high percentage for the United States. Still, the percentage of unemployed people taking job-related courses is also considerable, about a quarter of this group in most countries. Judged by the small percentage of home workers taking job-related courses, this group is only weakly attached to the labour-market. The courses they take are mostly motivated by personal interest.

Table 2.8. Percentage of participants in adult education by labour-market status

Labour-market status	Canada	Switzerland	United States	Netherlands	Sweden	Poland
Employed	44.8	43.3	49.6	44.4	59.5	20.6
Retired	10.8	17.3	12.6	13.1	16.1	2.0
Unemployed	32.3	31.6	28.4	37.8	44.0	9.4
Home worker	23.2	24.0	13.5	23.4	25.5	3.7
Other	23.7	27.2	17.6	22.1	25.7	8.1
Average participation	**38.9**	**39.6**	**42.4**	**37.8**	**52.9**	**14.3**
Total	**N=4,534**	**N=2,557**	**N=2,764**	**N=2,610**	**N=2,146**	**N=2,676**

The occupational categories with the highest participation rates are professionals and technicians. This holds for most of the countries. The agricultural professions have a relatively high participation rate in Switzerland, the United States, and Poland (based on the ISCO—International Standard Classification of Occupations). In all countries, the financial services sector has a high rate of participation in adult education. Community, social, and personal services is likewise a sector with a high incidence of adult education participation (based on the ISIC—International Standard Industrial Classification). Although the patterns differ in the various countries, the overall similarity in occupational and industrial sectors that have a high incidence of participation is striking.

The demand side, comprised of those who actually participated during the year preceding the interview, shows a distinct pattern. Men and women participate almost equally, but men take more job-related courses and women more personal-interest courses. The young participate more, as do people who already have a high level of educational attainment. In terms of labour-market status, those who are employed participate most in adult education and training.

There are national differences. The Swedes participate most, and that holds true for most of the demand classification variables investigated. Sweden is particularly successful in bringing older adults and unemployed people into adult education programmes. Besides Sweden, the Netherlands and Canada are also relatively successful in attracting people with a low level of initial educational attainment, whereas the United States (with Sweden) is particularly successful in attracting people with a university background. Adult education in the United States also attracts a large share of the employed population, so that recruitment there is concentrated more on the high end of the social continuum. Swedish adult education, in contrast, attracts people from the whole continuum, including a large percentage of those at the low end.

2.6   Supply Characteristics

Supply characteristics can be operationalized as characteristics of the courses that people take, such as course content, institutions, locations, and media used in the transfer of knowledge, as well as the conditions that influence participation, such as financial support and social stimuli. Information about these characteristics and conditions is gathered from the respondents who took part in adult education, and in that sense is filtered by the fact that these are people who were motivated to participate and know about the structure of provision (or that part that is relevant for them). Limited information about the people who did not participate but wished to do so is also available and is analyzed in a subsequent section. No information was collected for the group who did not participate and also had no wish to do so. Thus, with the data at hand, it is not possible to construct a completely inclusive picture of the ways in which characteristics of the supply side influence decisions about whether to participate.

As noted previously, participants often took more than one course. In the data collection instrument, questions about these different courses were asked, up to a maximum of three courses. In Tables 2.9-2.11, the people who participated in an adult education course constitute the base from which the percentage distributions are calculated. Hence, the figures may exceed 100 per cent in some cases.

The vast majority of adult education participants take a course that counts toward a professional qualification or skill upgrading. For most countries this holds for 90 per cent of the participants. When only job-related courses are considered, this figure rises to over 100 per cent, reflecting that people could have taken more than one course. University qualifications rank second in the United States and Canada (mentioned by 24 and 13 per cent of the participants), whereas vocational qualifications rank second in Switzerland (10 per cent), the Netherlands (9 per cent), and Poland (16 per cent). Compared with some European countries, the institutions for tertiary education play a markedly important role in provision in North America. In Canada, a relatively large number of people enrol in adult education in order to obtain a school diploma (10 per cent).

What institutions provide these courses? The data in Table 2.9 suggest that firms rank foremost in all the countries, whereas commercial providers also hold a strong position, especially in the Netherlands and Poland. Institutions for tertiary education also play an important role, especially in the United States. Further education colleges are also major providers, but this is a difficult category for comparative analysis because of the structural differences among education systems. The pattern does not change much if participation is restricted to only job-related courses, although in this case the share of firms in provision rises. It is somewhat surprising that the share of commercial providers does not rise accordingly. Such for-profit institutions apparently attract a sizable segment of their clientele from the leisure market as well.

Table 2.9.   Suppliers of adult education and training (percentage base=all participants in adult education and training)[1]

Supplier	Canada	Switzerland	United States	Netherlands	Poland
University or other					
tertiary institution	21.6	20.4	44.1	17.8	11.2
Further education colleges	25.7	–	9.5	22.6	22.0
Commercial provider	24.9	31.1	30.1	32.4	26.0
Producer or supplier of equipment	11.2	11.7	12.4	4.9	6.1
Non-profit organization	19.3	24.8	16.4	8.5	12.5
Firm or establishment	49.6	42.2	51.9	34.6	28.5
Other supplier	20.4	106.4	18.5	31.5	34.0
Total	**N=1,762**	**N=701**	**N=1,170**	**N=987**	**N=367**

1.   *In some cases, the respondents did not answer all the categories in a question. In Tables 2.9 to 2.11, those cases are marked with an asterisk, and the number given is the average number of respondents who answered the different categories.*

Table 2.10 indicates a striking similarity in the order of country rankings with respect to the medium of instruction. So-called "traditional" media such as classroom instruction and reading materials are by far the most important. Cassettes and tapes take third position and on-the-job training fourth. A "modern" medium such as educational software is in a modest fifth position. Little use seems to be made of this medium, especially in the United States. The picture does not change much if only job-related provision is considered, although on-the-job training then becomes more important.

Table 2.10.   Medium of instruction (percentage base=all participants in adult education and training)

Medium	Canada	Switzerland	United States	Netherlands	Poland
Classroom methods	147.4	134.4	148.2	109.1	113.4
Education software	31.4	33.3	17.7	32.1	19.4
Radio or television	6.0	8.9	3.1	19.4	10.0
Audio or video	62.3	41.5	30.4	49.4	38.7
Reading material	112.3	83.1	50.5	106.1	78.5
On-the-job training	46.1	33.8	30.4	33.3	54.8
Other methods	6.3	38.4	4.7	13.5	11.4
100% =	**N=1,747**	**N=761***	**N=1,170**	**N=987**	**N=382**

To what extent do people receive financial support for taking courses in adult education? Financial support—for example from employers or governments—can be a major stimulus to participation. In Table 2.11, an overview is given of different forms of financial support in the countries involved for participants in adult education in general.

The participants themselves and their employers are important sponsors. Moving the focus from financial support for participation in adult education in general to participation in job-related adult education, the role of employers increases and takes first rank in all the countries involved. Nonetheless, to a large extent the participants themselves are also willing to invest in job-related adult education. In the United States and the Netherlands, the employers have a predominant position. The role of financial support from the government differs, playing a larger role in Canada and Switzerland and a smaller role in the United States and the Netherlands.

Table 2.11.   Financial support for participation in adult education (percentage base = all participants in adult education and training)

Who shares in meeting the costs?	Canada	Switzerland	United States	Netherlands	Poland
Self	67.3	77.6	52.2	60.3	40.7
Employer	75.7	69.5	103.6	76.4	78.1
Government	31.8	21.1	15.1	13.6	7.4
Union or professional association	4.5	3.2	2.3	1.5	0.8
No fee	6.2	2.7	5.9	1.4	11.7
Other sponsor	2.1	4.0	4.9	5.6	7.0
Total	**N=1,762**	**N=1,008**	**N=1,176**	**N=987**	**N=373**

When asked who suggested or decided to participate in adult education or training, the respondents' own initiative ranks first, with the exception of the United States, where employers take first rank. In all other countries, employers are the second source of the initiative to participate. Legal requirements are also mentioned, but far less often. Poland is the only country where legal requirements or rules laid down in collective labour agreements play a relatively important role.

The predominance of job-related provision also manifests itself in the supply characteristics. Firms are the most important providers in all countries, and most courses taken lead to professional goals or skill upgrading. Employers are also mentioned most frequently as the financial sponsors of participation in general and of participation in job-related adult education in particular, especially in the United States and the Netherlands. The participants themselves are often the first to take the initiative to participate, however, and they are often willing to pay for it also.

2.7   Determinants of Participation

A model explaining participation in adult education and training is explored in this part of the chapter. The descriptive analyses in the previous sections already revealed that the factors influencing participation in job-related adult education and training and those influencing participation for personal development and leisure interests are quite different. The purpose of the data analysis is to distinguish these two types of participation. This implies that there are two dependent variables to be explained: participation in job-related courses and participation in leisure-related courses. Both variables are measured using a dichotomy which can take only two values: 1 (yes) or 0 (no). This type of dependent variable is commonly studied using a probit or logit model (see Cramer 1991). A model which takes account of the probability that the two dependent variables are interdependent—the bivariate probit model—is employed for the data analyses. The results are presented in Table 2.12.

The variables which were introduced previously in the descriptive parts are specified in the model as the explanatory variables: gender, age, level of educational attainment, and labour-market status. In the empirical training literature, it is usual to restrict the sample to those respondents who have a job, and to focus attention entirely on job-related training. Doing so allows the analyst also to include as regressors variables which are related to the job a person holds, such as information about industry, occupation, and firm size. The method applied here is different, as the focus is on different types of adult education and training.[3]

---

[3]   *For an analysis of the IALS data using only working respondents, we refer to Leuven and Oosterbeek (1996).*

Table 2.12.   Determinants of job-related and personal-interest or leisure-related adult education and training by country

Predicting variables	Bivariate probit estimates (t-values)				
	Canada	Netherlands	Poland	Switzerland	United States
Job-related adult education and training					
Female	-.12 (6.2)	-.13 (2.4)	-.17 (2.2)	-.01 (.2)	.07 (1.7)
Age 16-25	.58 (16.3)	.22 (3.0)	.03 (.2)	.13 (1.6)	.12 (1.8)
Age 26-35	.07 (2.7)	.04 (.6)	-.09 (1.0)	.11 (1.5)	.10 (1.7)
Age 36-45	reference	reference	reference	reference	reference
Age 46-55	.01 (0.4)	-.29 (3.6)	-.11 (1.0)	-.04 (.5)	.06 (.9)
Age 56-65	-.22 (5.7)	-.70 (4.6)	-.44 (2.2)	-.26 (2.5)	-.16 (2.0)
ISCED 0/1	-.37 (8.8)	-.49 (5.5)	-.97 (7.0)	-.92 (5.2)	-.48 (4.7)
ISCED 2	-.29 (8.3)	-.16 (2.4)	-.52 (5.5)	-.75 (8.6)	-.54 (4.4)
ISCED 3	reference	reference	reference	reference	reference
ISCED 5	.40 (16.2)	–	.14 (1.1)	.24 (3.0)	.54 (10.2)
ISCED 6/7	.64 (27.3)	.36 (5.2)	.29 (2.5)	.35 (3.9)	.86 (15.5)
Employed	reference	reference	reference	reference	reference
Retired	-1.56 (7.5)	-1.41 (3.0)	-1.14 (5.3)	-.94 (3.6)	-1.29 (7.7)
Unemployed	-.26 (6.3)	-.14 (1.2)	-.80 (5.0)	-.15 (1.2)	-.34 (2.9)
Student	.51 (8.8)	.72 (2.1)	–	.03 (.1)	.91 (2.5)
Home worker	-1.0 (22.3)	-1.03 (9.4)	-1.14 (3.8)	-1.02 (8.1)	-1.31 (12.0)
Other labour market status	-.40 (7.9)	-.62 (4.0)	-.65 (2.4)	-.83 (2.7)	-.69 (4.9)
Migrant	-.09 (4.2)	.33 (3.3)	–	-.30 (4.1)	-.40 (5.7)
Leisure-related adult education and training					
Female	.52 (12.8)	.52 (8.1)	.09 (.8)	.38 (6.4)	.29 (3.6)
Age 16-25	.03 (.6)	.01 (.1)	.46 (3.1)	.10 (1.1)	-.16 (1.1)
Age 26-35	-.18 (4.5)	.18 (2.1)	.02 (.1)	-.11 (1.5)	-.01 (.1)
Age 36-45	reference	reference	reference	reference	reference
Age 46-55	-.02 (.4)	.05 (.6)	-.24 (1.4)	-.18 (2.0)	.06 (.6)
Age 56-65	-.11 (8.0)	-.11 (1.0)	-.51 (1.8)	-.50 (4.3)	-.06 (.5)
ISCED 0/1	-.10 (1.5)	-.48 (4.8)	-.85 (3.7)	-.68 (4.3)	-.24 (1.1)
ISCED 2	-.16 (3.3)	-.30 (4.1)	-.35 (2.6)	-.40 (4.6)	.29 (1.6)
ISCED 3	reference	reference	reference	reference	reference
ISCED 5	.29 (6.6)	–	.48 (3.0)	.20 (2.2)	.23 (2.6)
ISCED 6/7	.44 (11.2)	.03 (.4)	.61 (4.1)	.19 (1.8)	.42 (4.8)
Employed	reference	reference	reference	reference	reference
Retired	1.03 (7.7)	.21 (1.1)	-.13 (.6)	.40 (2.3)	.27 (1.9)
Unemployed	.10 (1.6)	.10 (.7)	.16 (1.0)	-.35 (2.1)	-.21 (.7)
Student	-.10 (.6)	-.09 (.2)	–	.52 (2.1)	-.11 (.2)
Home worker	.33 (7.7)	.14 (1.6)	-.11 (.5)	.10 (1.1)	.15 (1.5)
Other labour market status	-.18 (1.6)	.39 (2.9)	.02 (.1)	-.10 (.4)	-.30 (.9)
Migrant	-.66 (15.9)	-.20 (1.5)	–	-.23 (3.0)	.18 (1.6)
Rho	.005 (.3)	-.028 (.7)	0	-.071 (1.9)	-.126 (2.4)
log-likelihood	-3,519.5	-2,357.5	-1,077.2	-2,365.0	-2,090.4
N cases	4,039	2,704	2,665	2,431	2,687

In Canada, the Netherlands, and Poland, the probability of participating in job-related adult education and training is lower for women than for men. In Switzerland, there is no significant gender difference, whereas in the United States women have higher job-related training probabilities. The latter result deviates from other findings for the United States. The difference can be attributed to the inclusion of both working and non-working respondents in the data analysis. Although significant, the gender differences in training probabilities are quite small. Evaluated at mean values of the other explanatory variables, the difference does not exceed 3 per cent. This issue is studied more in depth in Chapters 9 and 9.

The negative relationship between the incidence of job-related adult education and training and a person's age also shows up in the multivariate context. Older individuals show a lower chance of participating than younger persons. The relationship is strongest in Canada and the Netherlands. Again, evaluated at mean values of the other regressors, persons in the youngest age group (16-25 years) have about 25 per cent higher job-related adult education and training probabilities than persons in the oldest age group (56-65 years). In Switzerland and the United States, the age differential is about 10 per cent, and in Poland it is only 6 per cent.[4] The biggest effects on the probability of participating in job-related training are associated with initial level of educational attainment. Having the highest level of education (ISCED 6/7) instead of the lowest (ISCED 0/1) raises the training probability in the United States by 44 per cent. In Canada the difference is 35 per cent, in Switzerland 28 per cent, and in Poland and the Netherlands the education training gap is around 20 per cent. These percentages were obtained in a model that holds the other variables at their mean values. Strong effects are also found for the person's labour-market status. In Canada, the Netherlands and the United States, working persons have about a 30 per cent higher chance of engaging in job-related adult education or training than retired persons. In Switzerland this difference is 24 per cent, and in Poland it is 12 per cent.

With respect to the determinants of enrolment in leisure-related adult education, the effect of gender is again significantly different from zero, but has a sign opposite to that in the job-related training equation. Women are more likely to participate in this type of adult education than men. But although significant, the size of this effect is modest. The largest gender difference is found in the Netherlands, where women have 11 per cent more chance to enter a leisure-related course than men. In Switzerland the difference is 9 per cent, and in Canada and the United States it is 5 and 3 per cent, respectively.

---

[4]   *In Poland, however, the participation rate is also much lower.*

The relationship between leisure-related adult education probabilities and labour-market status is also different from the one found for job-related training. Here, non-working persons have similar or sometimes even higher probabilities of attending a leisure-related course. For instance, in Switzerland, retired persons have 13 per cent more chance to follow such a course than the employed.

For age and initial level of educational attainment, patterns are found similar to those observed for job-related training. Older and less-educated people have lower probabilities of engaging in leisure-related training than younger and more highly educated persons. In Switzerland, persons in the highest age bracket (56-65 years old) have on average a 13 per cent lower probability of attending leisure-related training than persons in the youngest group. In Canada the age difference is 5 per cent, in Poland it is 7 per cent, and in the Netherlands and the United States it is between 2 and 3 per cent. The effects of educational attainment are even larger. In Switzerland, the difference between the lowest and the highest education category amounts to 17 per cent; in Canada, Poland, and the Netherlands this is between 10 and 15 per cent, whereas in the United States it is only 4 per cent.

The results thus indicate that the probabilities of participating in job-related and leisure-related adult education have a similar relationship with age and level of educational attainment, but have an opposite relationship with gender and labour-market status. Given, however, that the magnitudes of the effects of age and level of educational attainment are much larger than those of gender and labour-market status, it can be expected that the two probabilities are positively correlated. Calculations show that this is indeed the case. The fitted probabilities of the two types of adult education were specified in a model for all respondents. For Canada, the model finds a simple correlation with a value of 0.49. For Poland and the United States, the correlations have a similar value (0.66 and 0.51, respectively). In Switzerland, the value of the correlation is 0.22, and only in the Netherlands is the correlation equal to zero (0.005).

2.8 Perceived Usefulness of Job-related Adult Education

The usefulness of job-related adult education and training is measured by the worker's perception of it. Literally, the question posed reads, "To what extent are you using the skills or knowledge acquired in this training or education at work?" As possible answers, respondents could choose between four response categories: (1) to a great extent, (2) somewhat, (3) very little, and (4) not at all. Since the nature of this measure is ordered, a so-called ordered probit model is applied that takes this feature into account. The model relates the perceived usefulness of job-related adult education to its source of finance, the source of provision, the initiator of the education or training, the modes of instruction, and the duration of the learning effort. In addition, gender, age, and level of educational attainment are specified as control variables. The results are presented in Table 2.13.

Table 2.13. Perceived usefulness of job-related adult education and training

Predictor variables	Estimates obtained in an ordered probit model (standard errors)				
	Canada	Netherlands	Poland	Switzerland	United States
Financed by worker	-.12 (.13)	-.02 (.22)	.42 (.33)	-.18 (.17)	.18 (.21)
Financed by employer	.11 (.14)	.18 (.24)	-.02 (.30)	-.14 (.18)	.72 (.22)
Financed by government	.01 (.11)	-.55 (.25)	-.48 (.46)	-.05 (.17)	.19 (.20)
Financed from other sources	.01 (.17)	-.04 (.37)	-.01 (.27)	.22 (.27)	0.30 (.25)
Provided by university	.08 (.20)	-.09 (.46)	-.30 (.48)	-.06 (.25)	.06 (.17)
Further education college	-.06 (.19)	.15 (.47)	-.29 (.38)	–	.10 (.24)
Commercial organization	.29 (.17)	.21 (.48)	-0.07 (.41)	-.60 (.27)	.06 (.16)
Producer/ supplier	.59 (.20)	.04 (.50)	.43 (.46)	.31 (.28)	-.14 (.19)
Non-profit organization	-.16 (.21)	-1.52 (.67)	.03 (.38)	.01 (.25)	.19 (.19)
Employer	.44 (.18)	.12 (.47)	-.00 (.37)	.01 (.21)	.18 (.16)
Other supplier	.13 (.20)	-.12 (.48)	-.01 (.38)	-.18 (.21)	.16 (.20)
Own initiative	-.10 (.11)	.09 (.18)	-.05 (.20)	.27 (.15)	.10 (.12)
Friend or family	-.01 (.13)	-.21 (.35)	-1.04 (.53)	-.30 (.33)	-.54 (.25)
Employer's initiative	-.03 (.12)	.27 (.18)	-.13 (.20)	.08 (.15)	.01 (.13)
Colleagues	-.32 (.31)	.25 (.45)	-.40 (.52)	.62 (.54)	-.79 (.64)
Other	-.02 (.23)	-.08 (.42)	.09 (.22)	.20 (.36)	.88 (.56)
Classroom	.03 (.12)	.01 (.13)	-.49 (.29)	.08 (.16)	-.26 (.16)
Education software	-.11 (.09)	-.05 (.13)	-.49 (.23)	.24 (.14)	.12 (.17)
Radio or television	.03 (.17)	-.01 (.18)	.29 (.38)	.05 (.33)	-.11 (.31)
Audio or video	.04 (.09)	-.11 (.12)	-.27 (.20)	-.04 (.15)	.07 (.13)
Reading material	-.15 (.10)	-.05 (.13)	.10 (.16)	-.01 (.12)	.03 (.12)
On-the-job training	.42 (.10)	.26 (.13)	.24 (.17)	.23 (.15)	.55 (.14)
Other methods	.07 (.20)	.30 (.25)	-.17 (.37)	-.22 (.21)	-.04 (.30)
Time/1000	.08 (.13)	-.03 (.20)	.40 (.52)	.47 (.36)	.49 (.19)
Log-likelihood	-991.7	-431.1	-264.4	-466.8	-751.3
N=cases	964	564	229	517	828

The source of finance seems unimportant for the perceived usefulness of the adult education or training course. There are two exceptions. In the United States financial contributions by employers are associated with higher levels of usefulness, and in the Netherlands adult education or training which is (co-) financed by the government is believed to be less useful. The first result may reflect that firms in the United States are only prepared to pay for adult education or training when it is useful for the worker's performance at the workplace. The second result may point to a low degree of monitoring of the effect of subsidies by the Dutch government.

The usefulness of a job-related adult education programme bears no strong relationship with the institute or organization providing that course. In Canada, commercial providers of adult education seem to perform above average, whereas in Switzerland the opposite holds. In Canada alone, education provided by the supplier or producer of equipment and by the employer is believed to be more useful than training provided by other sources.

Who initiated the decision to take part in an adult education course appears unimportant for perceptions of its usefulness. The only exceptions here are that in Switzerland courses are considered more useful when initiated by the workers, and both in Poland and the United States courses are felt to be less useful when initiated by family or friends.

Turning to the modes of instruction, the findings indicate that adult education is likely to be more useful when provided in the form of on-the-job training. This holds in Canada, the Netherlands, and the United States. The use of educational software has opposite effects on the perceived usefulness of training in Poland and Switzerland. In Poland this modern mode of instruction is associated with training that is believed less useful, whereas in Switzerland the use of such media leads to a higher level of perceived usefulness.

Finally, there is the remarkable outcome that, with the exception of the United States, there appears to be no relationship whatsoever between training duration and perceptions of its usefulness.

2.9   Summary and Conclusions

It is clear from the results presented in this chapter that there is a high level of participation in adult education and training in the countries under investigation. Some 40 per cent of the adult population in the Netherlands, the United States, and Switzerland participated during the year preceding the interview; in Sweden the percentage is even higher, whereas in Poland it is lower. The average yearly time commitment is over 200 hours. Most participants take courses for job-related purposes, although in Switzerland and the Netherlands personal development and leisure interests are also an important motivation.

The demand side shows a familiar pattern. Men and women participate almost equally, although men take more courses for job-related purposes, a tendency that is particularly marked in the Netherlands. Participation is mostly concentrated in the youngest age groups, with the exception of Sweden and Poland. Canada is particularly successful in attracting participants from the younger age group; Sweden is one of the few countries that also attracts relatively many older participants. The relationship between participation and educational attainment is strong, as adults with an initially poor education participate far less than those with higher levels of educational attainment. People who are employed participate more, but a sizeable minority of the unemployed take courses as well, especially when these are job-related.

On the supply side, the vast majority of courses that are taken count towards professional qualifications or skill upgrading. The desire to obtain a university qualification is mentioned relatively often by participants in the United States and Canada. Firms are the major providers and sponsors of adult education and training, but commercial institutions have a strong position in provision as well, especially in Poland and the Netherlands. It is striking that as far as the media of instruction are concerned, "traditional" media such as classroom instruction and the use of reading material have the upper hand in perceived usefulness. For job-related adult education, informal learning on-the-job is the preferred method. Firms are major financial sponsors of participation in adult education, and this is particularly marked for job-related courses. But the participants themselves are also major financial contributors. The financial role of government in job-related adult education is of some importance in Canada and Switzerland, less so in the United States and the Netherlands, and almost absent in Poland.

Although the overall participation figures are impressive, there are still large gaps in provision and participation. Between 20 and 30 per cent of all adults, with the exception of Poland, wanted to take a course in the year preceding the interview but did not do so. People who previously participated at least once in an adult education course are also those who most frequently expressed the (unfulfilled) wish to participate more. Lack of time and financial constraints are mentioned most often as reasons why people eventually did not participate.

The multivariate data analysis shows that women, older adults, and those with a low level of educational attainment have lower probabilities of participating in job-related adult education than men, young adults, and people with high educational qualifications. Educational level is the strongest predictor. The pattern is somewhat different in adult education for personal development or leisure interest. Here women and people outside the labour force have a higher probability of participation. However, the effect of educational attainment and age is the same as in job-related adult education.

Finally, the relationship between the characteristics of a job-related course and the respondent's perceptions of its usefulness was studied. The findings suggest that the type of characteristics used, such as the source of financing, type of provider, modes of instruction, and the initiator of the adult education, are poor predictors of the perception of the course's usefulness. The only robust result is that adult education and training are considered more useful when given on-the-job.

References

Cramer, J.S. 1991. *The Logit Model: An Introduction for Economists.* London: Edward Arnold.

Houtkoop, W. 1996. "Europe, Western and Southern". In: A.C. Tuijnman (ed.). *International Encyclopedia of Adult Education and Training.* (2nd ed.) Oxford: Pergamon Press.

Krajnc, A. 1996. "Europe, Central and Eastern". In: A.C. Tuijnman (ed.). *International Encyclopedia of Adult Education and Training.* (2nd ed.) Oxford: Pergamon Press.

Griffith, S. 1996. "North America". In: A.C. Tuijnman (ed.). *International Encyclopedia of Adult Education and Training.* (2nd ed.) Oxford: Pergamon Press.

Houtkoop, W., and van der Kamp, M. (1992). "Factors influencing participation in continuing education". In: *International Journal of Educational Research* 17 (6): 537-548.

OECD 1996. *Education at a Glance: OECD Indicators.* (4th ed.) Paris: Centre for Educational Research and Innovation.

Hiemstra, R. 1996. "Self-directed learning". In: A.C. Tuijnman (ed.). *International Encyclopedia of Adult Education and Training.* (2nd ed.) Oxford: Pergamon Press.

Houtkoop, W. 1985. "Volwasseneneducatie en de ongelijke verdeling van educatieve kansen". In: J.L. Peschar and A.A. Wesselingh (eds.). *Onderwijssociologie: Een inleiding.* Groningen: Wolters Noordhoff.

Leuven, E., and Oosterbeek, H. 1996. *Demand and supply of work-related training: Evidence from four countries.* (Discussion Paper no. 97-013) Rotterdam: Tinbergen Institute.

Switzerland: Federal Office of Statistics 1996. *Die lernende Gesellschaft - ein Mythos? Aus- und Weiterbildung in der Schweiz: Erste Resultate aus der Schweizerischen Arbeitskräfteerhebung.* Bern: Federal Office of Statistics.

Chapter 3

Patterns of Participation in Adult Education: Cross-national Comparisons

Pierre Doray and Stephen Arrowsmith[1]

3.1 Introduction

We live in a world where evolving economic and social structures influence many aspects of our daily lives, and where coping with change has become the norm. While the changes impact on all institutional practices, it is in the world of work that the impact on people is the most immediate. On-going restructuring in the workplace requires people to be flexible and to be able to adjust to change. A sound platform of knowledge and skills acquired through initial education provides a basis for flexibility, but even this platform needs on-going revision and updating through continuing education and training. For the worker of the 21st century, lifelong learning is not a luxury, but a necessity. The intertwined processes of social, economic, and political transition necessitate lifelong learning; acquiring new knowledge and updating and expanding skills are critical to the well-being of individuals, economies, and societies.

All members of a society must be motivated and enabled to access and use lifelong learning as a tool for acquiring the knowledge and skills needed for active participation in the processes that shape future society. If this future is to be prosperous and just, then it is essential that no-one be excluded because of a lack of access to lifelong learning opportunities. As Nordhaug (1987) observes:

> "Participation in adult education has consequences of both individual and collective character. Individuals, families, social groups, social classes, companies, organizations, communities, and nations are all units which in different ways benefit from adult education" (p. 113).

---

[1]   *The authors wish to thank Jean Pignal and Richard Porzuczek of Statistics Canada and André Demers of the University of Montréal for their helpful comments.*

Clearly, the consequences of participation cover a broad spectrum. It is for this reason that a better understanding is needed of the patterns of lifelong learning provision that currently exist. A first step in improving this understanding is to determine who actually participates in programmes of adult education and training. This is not a new question; it was first raised in research studies undertaken in the United States in the 1920s and 1930s. Other countries, such as Canada, France, Sweden, and the United Kingdom, also have a long tradition of analyzing the patterns of adult education participation. To date, however, few internationally comparable studies have been conducted in the field. International comparisons are particularly difficult to undertake with any degree of validity, because of the heterogeneity of organization which characterizes the field, with policies, structures, and functions of formal adult education and training varying from country to country.

A further problem is posed by the manner in which national statistics are collected; different definitions and methods of measurement will yield different estimates of the numbers of participants in a country. In Canada and the United States, for example, large training markets have emerged in which both public and private suppliers compete for customers. For both countries, the usual administrative statistics offer rough pictures of the level of participation in the public sector, but the estimates will not be comparable, nor do they provide a complete view of adult education participation, because of the lack of information about the nature and extent of the learning that goes on in private-sector institutions.[2]

Obligations vested in law also result in between-country differences; some countries are more dedicated than others to active labour-market policies, or force employers to invest a certain minimum in the education and training of their employees.[3] This is the case in France, for example, where in 1971 the French government endorsed a law requiring employers to invest the equivalent of one per cent of the payroll in continuing education and training. This kind of legislation was also introduced in Australia, although it was revoked after some years because of persisting doubts as to its effectiveness (OECD 1996). However this may be, because of its continuing education law, the French authorities require all employers of a certain minimum size to account for and declare their training investments. Consequently, France is one of the few countries where national

---

[2]   *In all countries, there exist major problems in measuring nonformal education and informal learning. Typically, learning can occur on the job or through reading or watching videos or demonstrations by co-workers. Because the learning is unstructured and not formalized, it is seldom recognized by respondents as training that counts towards labour-force qualifications, and it cannot be measured directly in large-scale social surveys.*
[3]   *There may be specific instances where an employer is required to invest in the education or training of an employee, but where there is no overarching legislation.*

statistics about workplace education and training have been published annually for decades. Unfortunately, very little information of this type exists in other OECD countries. Hence, because there is no exhaustive basis for common measurement, it has been impossible to undertake meaningful international comparisons of adult education participation (Murray 1996).

In this chapter, the determinants of adult education participation are studied for the OECD countries that participated in the first round of data collection for the International Adult Literacy Survey. The specific aim is to examine the common and divergent patterns of participation, using two different models. In the first, the effects of demographic, socioeconomic, and cultural variables on the level of participation of the adult population are examined. In the second model, the examination will focus on the relationships between workplace characteristics and adult education and training for the employed population only.

3.2   Theoretical Framework

Participation research has a long history in social science research. Courtney (1992) reviews some of the earliest studies conducted in the United States. The populations studied were usually locally or institutionally specific. Nationally representative surveys were undertaken only after the Second World War; Johnstone and Rivera's (1965) study is the most well-known example.

There are many good reasons for undertaking studies of adult education participation. The desire to somehow "Plant" the supply of adult education and to improve the match between supply and demand has been popular with administrators in both local and central levels of government. By examining the socioeconomic and cultural characteristics of the "typical" adult participant by types of institution, administrators essentially undertook an analysis of what may be termed "profiles of learning needs". This line of investigation is also commonly used by both public and private providers of adult education and training. The second reason researchers undertake studies of adult education participation has to do with the "fuzzy" boundaries between institutions mentioned previously. Adult education is highly heterogeneous, and this diversity not only characterizes the field but also constitutes major strengths and weaknesses. Analysts are interested in the study of this diversity and its consequences. A third perspective for the study of participation concerns the issue of "second-chance" education. For many analysts, adult education is supposed to work for equality of outcomes and "collective promotion"—offering a second or third chance to poorly educated participants is a way of achieving this. At issue, of course, is the extent to which adult education can do this, and how second-chance education can be made to work better in practice. A further element is contributed by sociological thought: if adult education is a means of achieving individual or collective upward mobility for the participants, then it serves a productive function for them but a reproductive function for non-participants. For all of these reasons, questions about adult education participation have been and still are important.

In his overview, Courtney (1992) notes the remarkable stability over time of the factors influencing participation. He found that variables such as age, gender, initial level of schooling, occupation, and place of residence consistently affect adult participation in terms of both access and choice of courses. Given the volume of the body of research carried out to date, and if year by year the same factors influence participation in the same ways, it may come as a surprise that the debate about the determinants of participation is still not settled.[4] Three reasons can be given for the current interest in the covariates of adult education participation:

- A "global" analysis of participation cannot be made with the use of administrative data sources only, because of the heterogeneity of the field;

- definitions of adult education participation have changed frequently in the past—today both participation and motivation to participate can be defined with somewhat greater precision; and

- there is a continuous need to understand how participation in adult education is being influenced by larger developments in social and economic conditions, political events, and educational policies.

As noted above, previous research studies have established certain stable and recurring patterns in the determinants of adult education participation. Recent contributions have proposed a theoretical framework combining socio-demographic variables such as educational attainment, gender, age, and occupation, and socio-psychological variables such as motivation, reasons, expectations, and goals. Examples are provided by Cookson (1986) and Henry and Basile (1994). In Cookson's INSTALL model, participation implies a sequence of four steps influencing participation in adult education through a filter of "situational" variables: external context—influencing social background; social roles—influencing socio-psychological variables; personality and intellectual capacity factors; and attitudinal dispositions and retained information. Henry and Basile (1994) propose a different model, in which decisions to take part in a course are influenced by an individual's personal characteristics but filtered in accordance

---

[4]　*But what is the meaning of the concept of "determinants" of participation? According to one view, a person's possession of certain demographic or socioeconomic characteristics, or psychological attributes, or experience of a specific social situation, can predict the likelihood of that person participating in adult education. Following this approach, an external observer would be able to predict behaviour based on the strength of observable characteristics or attributes.*

with a three-step sequence: reasons for enroling; sources of information; and institutional characteristics. In both models, the social, economic, and cultural background characteristics of the individual drive the decision-making process.

In previous research, a number of social factors have been identified as important in determining participation.[5] For instance, there has been a shift in participation trends by gender. For the United States, Courtney (1992) shows that between 1969 and 1984 the rate of participation of men decreased while that of women increased from 48 to 55 per cent of the total (p. 35). In France, men participate more than women, a trend that has remained stable from 1959 to 1970 (Dubar 1977) and well into the 1980s (Dubar 1996). In Canada, Deveraux (1984) found the reverse, that women participated more in adult education than men. Doray and Paris (1995) found that Canadian women had a higher general rate of participation than men, although this varied by type of activity, with women having higher rates in vocational activities, personal activities, and activities where the employer was not directly involved. Chicha (1994) indicates that women have less access to employers' training resources. The status of working women and the manpower policies of employers may explain a part of this inequality of access.

It is possible to describe the influence of each of the many variables that are known from the research literature to influence participation in adult education. Education level of the parents, age, initial educational attainment, and occupation are all variables which might influence adult education participation. Beyond the differences in rates of participation and the nature of participation, the main question of interest for analysts concerns the dimensions influencing participation. In this chapter, is examining the multiple effects on participation, an approach is taken whereby the factors influencing participation are grouped along five dimensions: cultural or "symbolic" attributes; social participation; time management; economic situation; and the supply of adult education.

Cultural or symbolic attributes refer to the socialization of individuals and their social construction of personality. Another way of describing this dimension is in terms of the cultural capital and educational background of the individual. The argument is that an individual's socialization lays the basis for personality and relation to culture, and consequently, for the person's relation to the institutions of society. Socialization is an element that cuts across several social and psychological dimensions, for example, in terms of motivation and how people perceive work, Plant projects, spend their leisure time, and envision the future. In this interpretation, differences in socialization account for much of

---

[5]   *Extensive information about motivation, goals, and the reasons for enroling in a course were not collected as part of the IALS endeavour. It is for this reason that the theoretical framework employed in this chapter emphasizes the influence of socioeconomic factors more than that of socio-psychological variables.*

the gender differences in the educational pathways taken by men and women. A similar logic holds that differences in the patterns of participation among age groups can be interpreted in terms of educational stratification; typically, older age groups have smaller proportions with higher levels of initial education than younger cohorts (Denton, Pinéo, & Spencer 1988). Occupational differences can be interpreted by the cultural attributes of class structures (Dubar 1977). Johnstone and Rivera (1965), for example, found that individuals from low SES backgrounds have a predominantly instrumental representation and motivation towards adult education. Individuals with high SES background, in contrast, think of adult education more frequently as a cultural or leisure-related activity. Variation on other indicators of participation are often interpreted by cultural attributes, SES or social class, parent's educational background, age, and initial educational experience.

Another dimension is *social participation*. The link between adult education and social participation is twofold. First, previous research has indicated that the "factors responsible for other forms of participation, particularly social and cultural, must also be responsible for voluntary educational participation" (Courtney 1992: 112). In other words, the social and cultural orientation and personality of those who participate in voluntary associations is similar in some respects to those who participate in adult education. Second, participation in voluntary associations is interpreted by some observers as a form of participation in adult education. Voluntary associations are viewed as nonformal or informal adult education "institutions". This view is found, for example, in Bélanger's (1980) concept of "counter-schools", which provide alternative educational resources for collective promotion. The issue of social participation is also raised in connection with leisure.[6] For instance, London et al. (as cited in Cookson 1986: 135) have distinguished active and passive leisure activities. They "discovered that people with broad and diverse leisure activities, particularly participants and members in formal organizations (except labour unions), were more likely to participate in adult education activities. In contrast, those whose social participation was limited to immediate surroundings, restricted friendship circles, and passive involvement in sports and the mass media were less likely to participate in adult education activities."

---

[6]   *It may be noted that for some observers a "society of leisure" is a condition for development in adult education.*

Social participation and leisure open up the larger question of the *management of time*. Time is not an infinite resource, and for many individuals free time is a scarce commodity. Consequently, the allocation of "free time" involves a series of decisions. In this situation, a decision to participate in adult education is also a decision about the use of time. Enrolment in formal adult education is a time-consuming proposition, whether it be the the time taken up by the course in evenings and weekends or the time spent on study and homework.

Continuous skill renewal and upgrading are important means for individuals to remain productive and competitive in the modern economy. In this respect, employers regard adult education and training as elements of their *economic strategy*. In larger firms, this strategy is given meaning through human resource management. However, policies and programmes for human resource development will vary by labour-market sector, the productivity and profitability of firms, and firm and employee characteristics (Doray & Paris 1995; Statistics Canada 1995; Dubar 1996). Current evidence indicates that firms competing in high technology sectors invest more in employee training than firms in other sectors of the labour-market. It is also evident that large firms with complex internal structures are more likely to provide training for their work force than small firms. Differences between primary and secondary labour-markets, and segmentation more generally, are reflected in the importance various employers attach to adult education and training in what Cookson (1986) refers to as the "resource opportunity structure". Since these structures vary across sectors of the labour-market, the educational opportunities and training resources available to various categories of workers will also vary. For example, the training advantage that managers and professionals have over other occupational groups is well documented in previous research studies (see Johnstone & Rivera 1965; Dubar 1977; Deverraux 1984; Dubar 1996). It is often argued that temporary or part-time workers tend to have less access to training than permanent and full-time workers, because firms prefer to invest in their "stable" or "core" workforce (Chicha 1994).

It follows from the above that crucial variables predicting participation in adult education andtraining are gender, age, and previous educational background (Johnstone & Rivera 1965; Chica 1994; Dubar 1996; Doray & Paris 1995; van der Kamp 1996). Clearly, the presence of gender differences in the amount, quality, and orientation of job-related training will raise problems for policy-makers and for society at large. Based on a review of the North American research literature, Knoke and Kalleberg (1994) suggest that, "it appears that many employers act as though training investments in women and minorities are less likely to be recaptured through future productivity, because these employees allegedly have weaker labour force attachments" (p. 539). Interestingly, the authors' own study did not support the hypothesis that, "establishments with work forces that are predominantly male and white provide more formal training than establishments with predominately female and minority workers" (ibid.).

Skill requirements in the evolving workplace are such that sound educational qualifications are required of new entrants into the labour force. Those without a completed upper-secondary education are penalized in the labour-market. Increasingly, even some post-secondary education experience is needed. This tendency can lead to the displacement of older, less qualified workers, and hence there is increased pressure on older and poorly qualified workers to renew and upgrade their skills base. This possibility calls attention to age and previous educational attainment as predictors of training incidence in the workplace. Current OECD data indicate that participation in job-related continuing education and training is closely related to the level of initial, formal schooling (see Borkowsky, Tuijnman & van der Heiden 1995). Consequently, those who are younger and have previously attained a higher level of educational qualifications are more likely than older and less qualified workers to receive additional education or training while working. It is possible that older workers choose voluntarily not to take training as they get close to retirement, possibly because they expect no benefits commensurate with the effort. But it may also be the case that employers prefer to target their scarce training resources towards younger employees who are expected to stay longer with the company and for whom the return on the training investment can be maximized.

But economic decisions do not only impact on the manpower strategies of firms. Differences in the participation rates of various occupational categories may also be due to individual strategic choices. For instance, Johnstone and Rivera (1965) observed that American blue-collar workers are more likely to emphasize an instrumentalist rather than cultural view of adult education and training compared with professionals, managers, or clerical staff. In this sense, blue-collar workers participate in adult education when the "virtues of continuing education can [...] be understood and appreciated [...] in the language of tangible benefits, concrete rewards, and practical gains" (p. 270). Dubar (1977) has found the situation to be more complex in France, because many blue-collar workers there took training even if no tangible private benefits resulted. More recently, Dubar (1996) identified five social orientations of participation, which affect categories of workers differently and can explain differences in participation rates (see Table 3.1).

The final dimension to be considered refers to the *supply of adult education*. This dimension concerns the opportunity structure of adult education as shaped by public policy and institutional choice. The strategic role of public policies in the organization of supply has been documented in numerous comparative studies (Titmus 1996; Tuijnman 1996). For instance, the movement towards a "new professionalism", which can be observed in many OECD countries, may explain the weight of professional activities in adult education. Henry and Basile (1994) analyzed institutional supply using "micro-sociological" indicators: "course attributes" such as duration, number of sessions, time the course is held, and course content; "institutional and situational deterrents" such as travel time to class, communications, course fees and method of registration; and "institutional perception", which refers to an individual's image and attitude towards the course, and the impression of the institution (p. 73).

Table 3.1. Social orientations of participation in adult education

Orientations of adult education	Social groups
● **Compensation; therapy:** adult education offers an opportunity for integration following a period of social exclusion or personal difficulty	● working-class home workers ● unskilled workers ● unemployed people ● failing young students (school drop-outs) ● immigrants
● **Internal mobility:** on-the-job or off-the-job vocational training in workplace specific skill domains	● unskilled or semi-skilled workers seeking advancement to jobs with higher skill content within the same work organization
● **Retraining:** vocational adult education as a means of acquiring a new set of workplace skills	● workers faced with redundancy ● unemployed people
● **External mobility:** academically oriented adult education as a means of acquiring new professional qualifications	● workers seeking 'academic' training programmes as a means of securing employment with higher social prestige and pay ● overeducated or underqualified workers
● **Upgrading:** adult education offers improved professional skills, such as in information technology, communications, new medical appliances or teaching methods	● managers ● professionals and technicians ● liberal professionals ● firm directors ● teachers

Source: Adapted from Dubar (1996)

In summary, five overarching dimensions influencing adult education participation are identified above. These dimensions are shown in Table 3.2, in which a set of indicators is proposed for each dimension. It will be seen that the framework poses theoretical and analytical difficulties, because a number of the indicators are included in more than one dimension. For example, age and gender are two determinants of participation, but it is not clear whether these variables refer to a social position in work, or cultural attributes, or time management. This poses an empirical question: Will it be possible to measure the direct and indirect effects of each indicator, and identify their weights separately? A second question is whether these effects are similar or different across countries.

Table 3.2. Five dimensions and associated indicators of participation in adult education

Cultural or symbolic attributes	Social participation	Economic situation	Management of time	Supply of adult education
• Gender • Age • Social class • Initial education • Parental educational background	• Participation in voluntary association • Use of leisure and free time	• Resource opportunity structure (job, employer, workplace organization, occupation, labour force status, socio-economic characteristics) • Strategic evaluation and usefulness of lifelong learning (occupation and socio-economic characteristics)	• Gender • Marital status • Age • Labour force status • Employment conditions (full or part-time; permanent or temporary work)	• Public policy • Public institutions • Private providers • Type and characteristics of course offerings

3.3 Methodology

Two traditions can be distinguished in cross-national comparative studies. In the first, one looks for similarities across two or more countries using a standardized dataset, an identical design, and the same method. In the second approach, the focus is more on a comparison of differences, and there is more scope for allowing variation in the applied methodology (Maurice, Sellier & Silvestre 1982). In this chapter, the first approach to comparative research methodology will be used, although some allowance is made for the fact that education systems vary by country and that this can lead to differences.

The Dataset

The dataset employed for the analysis is derived from information collected at the end of 1994 for the International Adult Literacy Survey (IALS). The instruments and survey methodology are described in Appendix A and B. The reference period with respect to questions about adult education participation was the 12 months preceding the interview.

It is necessary to define the term "adult". The IALS national study managers agreed on a common definition using three variables: age, enrolment in formal education, and duration of learning activity. For analytic purposes, the dataset was truncated across the three variables: first was an adjustment for age, so that only the population 16-64 remained in target. Second, students enrolled in formal education on a full-time basis were excluded from the in-scope population. Third, education or training activities that did not have a minimum duration of six hours were excluded. This procedure resulted in a data file containing 18,947 in-scope individual records, a figure that falls to 12,658 records when only employed persons are considered.[7] The purpose of the exclusions was to create a homogenous dataset. Full-time students aged 16-24 were excluded because they were deemed to be engaged in their initial, formal schooling, whereas individuals over the age of 64 were deemed to have exited from the active labour force. It was felt that a duration of six hours (typically one day) would be a meaningful cut-off for duration. Based on these truncations, the sample counts by country are as shown in Table 3.3.

Table 3.3.   In-scope records by country

	Whole population	Working population only
Canada	3,917	2,509
Switzerland - German	1,334	948
Switzerland - French	1,351	962
United States	2,703	1,955
Netherlands	2,665	1,790
Poland	2,657	1,571
Sweden	2,348	1,805

Description of Variables

A decision had to be made to maximize either the number of variables or the number of countries to be included in the analysis. For the purposes of this research, the second option was taken and only common variables were selected for use. There are instances where a country had to be excluded from a particular data run because a certain variable was either not available or because there were too few cases to yield statistically meaningful estimates. The dependent variable, participation in adult education, is a dichotomous measure for all countries. It is based on a simple response to the question:

"During the past 12 months, that is since August [October/November] 1993, did you receive any training or education including courses, private lessons, correspondence courses, workshops, on-the-job training, apprenticeship training, arts, crafts, recreation courses or any other training or education?"

---

[7]   *The "employed persons only" category thus excludes those individuals who reported themselves as being either unemployed, full-time student, retired, or home worker.*

Based on a review of the research literature and the explanatory dimensions outlined previously, a number of important predictor variables were selected for inclusion in the models. These are described in Table 3.4.

Table 3.4   Description of independent variables

Variables	Definition and specification
Socio-demographic	
• Gender	Male or female
• Age	People older than 64 and full-time students aged 24 and younger are excluded
• Household	The distinction is between people who live alone and people living with one or more other persons
• Community	The distinction is between rural and urban areas
Education	
• Parents' education	A generic variable that combines mother's and father's education is used because this reduces the possibly biasing effect of missing values in the original variables. The result is a dummy measure indicating whether one parent received some post-secondary education (1) or not (0)
• Respondent's education	The variable is based on four levels: primary school or less; lower secondary education; completed upper secondary education; and some education at post-secondary level
Social participation	
• Membership of association	The measure indicates whether the respondent participated in a voluntary or community-based association or organization. This is considered as a form of active leisure
• Hours watching television	The distinction is between people who watched television or videos for two or more hours each day (passive) and those who watched less(active)
Economic situation	
• Labour force status	Three categories are distinguished: employed; unemployed but looking for work; and outside the labour force or not looking for employment (retired, student, home worker).
• Occupation	Categories are: manager; professional; technician; clerk; services worker; skilled worker; Plant worker and low-skill worker
• Working time	The distinction is between full and part-time work
• Tenure	The distinction is between a permanent and temporary worker
• Position in workplace hierarchy	Categories are: worker without supervisory responsibility; worker with limited supervisory responsibility; worker with large supervisory responsibility; self-employed and self-employed with employees
• Labour-market sector	Categories include: primary manufacturing; public utilities and construction; trade; transportation; finance; public and private services

3.4   Findings

The purpose of the analysis presented in this section is to identify the common patterns in adult education participation across countries. Findings are presented in two stages. Bivariate relationships are presented first. Results obtained in a logistic multivariate analysis of the determinants of participation are presented in a subsequent section.[8] The results are presented separately for the whole population and for the more restricted group comprised only of employed people.

Covariates of Participation: General Population

At first glance, a review of the results indicates that adult education participation rates vary widely among the countries surveyed, ranging from 14 per cent in Poland to 53 per cent in Sweden. This large difference notwithstanding, there are many common trends in the patterns of adult education participation among the countries. Figure 3.1 shows that the participation rates are consistently higher for the employed population compared with the general adult population.

Figure 3.1.   Rate of adult education participation by country, general adult population and employed population 1994 (per cent)

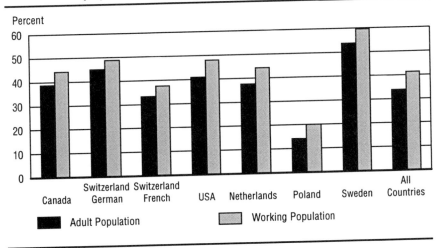

---

[8]   *The results are obtained in a logistic multivariate regression analysis. This method makes it possible to estimate the effects of an independent variable on the dependent variable while controlling for the influences of all other variables in the model. The regression coefficients indicate whether any of the variables has a statistically significant effect on the participation outcome. A coefficient with a value below one indicates a negative effect and signifies a deterrent to participation. A coefficient with a value exceeding one indicates a positive effect, increasing the likelihood of participation. The magnitude of a coefficient indicates the strength of the variable in influencing the outcome.*

It is often argued that the rate of participation in adult education declines with age. The results in Figure 3.2 bear this out clearly, even though the decline varies by country, with Canada, the French-speaking cantons of Switzerland, and the Netherlands showing a steeper decline in participation rates for those aged 45-54 than the other countries. This finding also holds for the employed population, although the rates remain higher than those for the general adult population.

Figure 3.2.   Rate of adult education participation by age and country, general population 1994

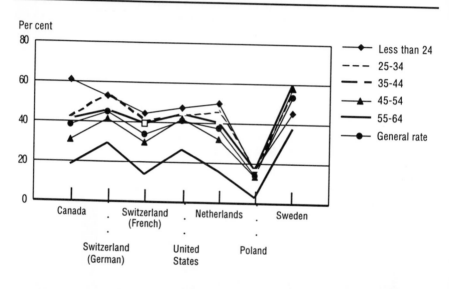

The common finding that "education begets education" is also supported by the evidence. The data in Table 3.5 show, for each country, that individuals with some post-secondary education experience have higher rates of adult education participation than those without such experience. In all countries but the Netherlands, which uses a somewhat different taxonomy for classifying non-university tertiary education (OECD 1995), the participation rate for those with post-secondary education is about 10 per cent higher than it is for the others. For most countries in the study, participation rates for the former group are in excess of 50 per cent.

Table 3.5.   Rates of participation in adult education by selected descriptors, general population 1994 (per cent)

	Canada	Switzerland (German)	Switzerland (French)	United States	Nether-lands	Poland	Sweden
Overall rate	**38.6**	**45.1**	**33.9**	**41.0**	**37.7**	**14.0**	**53.3**
Age							
24 or less	61.1	53.1	44.4	47.6	49.8	16.3	45.5
25-34	41.9	54.3	41.2	44.0	46.0	17.7	55.7
35-44	41.3	45.9	39.3	44.3	40.3	16.9	61.2
45-54	31.2	41.5	29.9	42.0	32.2	13.4	57.9
55-64	18.3	29.3	13.9	26.4	16.1	2.8	38.1
Gender							
Female	39.4	46.0	38.2	41.6	39.6	15.4	51.4
Male	37.9	44.2	29.7	40.6	35.8	12.6	55.2
Living single							
Yes	39.4	46.0	38.2	41.6	39.6	15.4	51.4
No	37.9	44.2	29.7	40.6	35.8	12.6	55.2
Parents' education							
No post-secondary level	34.7	43.6	31.0	37.1	36.9	13.0	52.2
With post-secondary level	59.5	52.2	47.3	58.6	47.5	34.2	60.3
Social participation							
Low television viewing	45.8	47.6	37.4	45.9	46.0	16.2	not specified
High television viewing	27.7	28.8	25.1	33.7	27.5	10.6	not specified
Member of association	49.0	52.4	42.4	50.9	41.1	19.9	45.9
No member of association	30.7	39.7	29.4	30.7	35.5	12.7	57.3
Educational attainment							
Primary or less	15.6	6.4	10.0	10.8	17.1	2.7	29.0
Lower secondary	26.8	23.3	14.8	22.3	29.1	10.0	47.1
Upper secondary	34.8	48.5	35.7	31.7	44.6	20.6	53.3
Some post secondary	56.1	58.9	52.0	62.4	51.8	33.5	67.0
Region							
Rural	32.9	38.5	32.0	33.8	36.3.	9.4	51.8
Urban	39.9	47.7	34.7	44.0	38.1	16.7	54.0
Labour force status							
Employed/self-employed	44.1	48.8	37.3	47.8	44.0	20.0	59.5
Unemployed-looking	31.8	37.1	24.5	27.3	37.5	9.4	44.8
Unemployed	24.1	29.7	21.8	16.7	23.1	3.1	28.2

Since an individual's own level of education is an important determinant of adult education participation, it will come as no surprise that parents' education also appears to be related with participation. Table 3.5 shows that in every country except Sweden and the German-speaking region of Switzerland[9], individuals who had a parent with a post-secondary level of education had higher participation rates than those without such a parent. It is also clear that employed individuals are much more likely to participate in adult education than those who are not employed. In every country, the participation rates are higher for the employed population than for the unemployed looking for work or the unemployed not looking for work. It is also evident that those who are unemployed but look for work have higher participation rates than those who do not seek work.

Urbanization is another interesting variable. In modern societies, the learning infrastructure is often of better quality in urban than in rural areas. Therefore, proximity to urban centres can be an important factor in determining whether a person will have access to adult education. Although the interpretation of the terms "urban" and "rural" will differ between countries such as Canada and Switzerland, the evidence clearly shows that the participation rates are higher in urban than in rural areas.

Social participation is measured by two non-exclusive indicators of how individuals spend their leisure time: television viewing and membership of a voluntary association. As might be expected, individuals with a higher propensity to watch television are much less likely to participate in adult education. This finding is consistent for all countries. However, the hypothesis that members of voluntary associations will have higher participation rates than non-members does not hold in all countries.

The above findings indicate a number of predictor variables which covary with who participates in adult education and who does not. The data also point to considerable cross-national similarity in participation patterns. But the predictor variables can be interdependent, and some may exert greater influence than others. For instance, in all likelihood there is a relationship between parents' education and an individual's education. Thus the interrelationships between the predictor variables must be accounted for if better understanding of the phenomenon of participation in adult education is to result.

---

[9]   *The education variable was collapsed into two categories only because of insufficient sample sizes in some countries. In the cases of Sweden and German-speaking Switzerland it is possible that respondents in apprenticeship programmes may not have identified theireducation as post-secondary and the resulting dichotomous variable may be too truncated.*

Determinants of Participation: General Population

The results obtained in a logistic regression of the dependent variable on all predictor variables are presented in Table 3.6. The reference group is the general population aged 16-64.

For Canada, it will be seen that living alone, living in an urban area, parental education, having a post-secondary level of education, being a member of a voluntary association, and having a job all have a positive effect on adult education participation. Age and passive leisure consumption also influence participation. Gender exerts a significant influence in German-speaking Switzerland, with women being more likely to participate than men. For Switzerland, living in an urban area, having a high level of education, membership in a voluntary association, and having a paid job are all positive predictors of participation. Negative influences on participation are associated with old age and passive leisure consumption.

In Switzerland, the specificity of the canton is important, and this is reflected in differences between the German- and French-speaking regions. In the French-speaking part of Switzerland, gender, living in an urban area, having a first level of secondary education, and participation in voluntary associations do not have a significant effect on participation. The only deterrent variable appears to be advanced age. This finding is consistent with the patterns observed for other countries. In the United States, only three variables do not appear to have a significant effect: gender, living alone, and lower secondary education. In contrast, being unemployed does have a significant effect on participation. Only one socio-demographic variable—advanced age—has a significant effect on participation in the Netherlands. Other significant indicators include parental education and labour force status. In Poland, as in the Netherlands, only one socio-demographic variable has a significant negative effect—old age. Parental education, respondent's education, and employment situation all have a positive effect. Social participation and leisure do not exert a significant influence. In Sweden, gender has a significant effect on participation, whereas age does not. This finding appears to be unique for Sweden; it is not observed for any of the other countries studied. Women participate more than men.

Table 3.6.   Regression estimates obtained in a logistic model specifying determinants of adult education participation, whole population aged 16-64

	Canada	Switzerland (German)	Switzerland (French)	United States	Nether-lands	Poland	Sweden
Socio-demographic characteristics							
Gender	0.98	1.32[1]	0.91	1.16	1.00	0.80	1.18[1]
Age	0.96[3]	0.97[3]	0.97[3]	0.98[3]	0.97[3]	0.97[3]	1.00
Single	1.37[1]	0.90	1.12	1.11	1.13	1.10	0.81
Urbanization	1.35[2]	1.40[1]	0.92	1.29[1]	1.05	1.16	1.00
Education							
Parents' education	1.79[3]	0.92	1.26	1.26[1]	0.99	1.48[1]	1.06
Respondent's education:							
– Primary or less							
– Lower secondary	1.25	4.23[1]	1.39	1.73	1.76[2]	2.50[3]	2.18[3]
– Upper secondary	1.29	11.07[3]	3.48[3]	2.74[3]	2.47[3]	6.09[3]	2.56[3]
Post-secondary	2.68[3]	17.61[3]	5.64[3]	7.62[3]	3.15[3]	10.25[3]	4.25[3]
Social participation							
Member of a voluntary association	1.81[3]	1.61[3]	1.45[2]	1.67[3]	1.22[1]	1.23	1.13[1]
Intensive television viewer	0.72[3]	0.78[1]	0.79	0.81[1]	0.55[3]	0.92	not specified
Labour force status							
– Not working							
– Not working but looking for work	1.32	1.41	0.74	2.10[2]	1.44	2.26[2]	2.01[3]
– Working	1.47[3]	1.93[3]	1.49[1]	3.52[3]	1.60[3]	4.70[3]	3.32[3]
N cases	**3,519**	**1,150**	**1,221**	**2,341**	**2,568**	**2,565**	**2,155**
Improvement	**671.6[3]**	**175.1[3]**	**158.5[3]**	**499.8[3]**	**292.4[3]**	**351.6[3]**	**210.64[3]**

1. $p < .05$.
2. $p < .01$.
3. $p < .001$.

There is remarkable stability in the effects of certain indicators across national borders. First, the magnitude of the negative influence of increasing age on participation is similar across countries, with each additional year exerting an effect with the same strength. Three other variables behave similarly: labour force status, experience of post-secondary education, and membership of a voluntary association. In each case, the probability of participation increases with possession of the attribute, even though the size of the influence is not always identical across the countries. For labour force status, there is an increase in participation when working; in Poland and the United States, however, being unemployed also exerts a positive influence. Lower levels of educational attainment do not always have a negative effect on participation. Membership of a voluntary association is related positively and with equal strength with participation in most countries. The effects of the other predictor variables vary across countries. Living alone has an influence only in Canada, while living in an urban area exerts influences on participation in Canada, the German-speaking regions of Switzerland, and the United States. The size and direction of the relationship is similar in these countries.

Covariates of Participation: Employed Population

In this second step of the multivariate analysis, the focus is on the adult working population. The results for the general population reviewed above show, for most countries, no great effect of gender on participation. For the employed population, however, the results for all countries except Francophone Canada and Switzerland show that somewhat more women than men obtain training, a finding that runs contrary to the popular idea that female participation rates are lower.[10] Why do the minority language sub-populations in both Canada and Switzerland show significantly reduced participation rates?

Age is a second variable of interest in a study of training participation in the work force. Typically, learning is concentrated in the earlier phases of one's life and decreases as one ages. Consequently, it can be expected that there should be a marked decrease in participation rates with the increasing age of the employed population. The data in Table 3.7 show that this general trend appears to hold. It was shown in a previous section that a greater proportion of the employed population participates in adult education or training than the general population, and this finding was consistent across all age groups studied. Interestingly, employed respondents aged 55-64 were 14 per cent more likely to receive training than the population at large.[11] However, if one only considers the proportion of employed respondents that received adult education, then it is clear that the 55-64-year-olds receive less than younger adults. This pattern is consistent with that observed for the general population and also across countries.

---

[10] *This finding, which contradicts the results of some previous research, is investigated and qualified in chapter 8 and 9, which are devoted entirely to the study of the gender factor in adult education participation. The results of these more in-depth analyses will show that the critical variables are not participation per se but training intensity and course orientation.*

[11] *The general population also includes employed people. As shown in Table 3.6, the employed population receives significantly more adult education and training than other groups. Age is the subject of a further chapter in this volume, in which participation patterns are studied also for the population over age 64. It will be seen that some of the findings reviewed here for the employed population are reversed for the non-active elderly population.*

Table 3.7.   Rates of participation in adult education by selected descriptors, employed population 1994 (per cent)

	Canada	Switzerland (German)	Switzerland (French)	United States	Nether-lands	Poland	Sweden
Participation rate	44.1	48.8	37.3	47.8	44.0	20.0	59.5
Age							
24 or less	62.7	52.7	47.4	52.7	51.4	20.6	53.0
25-34	44.5	56.4	42.6	47.4	49.3	22.2	60.6
35-44	44.0	49.4	44.7	49.6	43.8	20.9	63.6
45-54	34.5	43.3	31.4	49.0	37.7	18.2	60.9
55-64	36.0	37.1	13.3	37.7	22.8	9.5	51.3
Gender							
Female	45.3	52.3	33.6	48.7	44.1	20.5	63.1
Male	43.2	46.4	40.6	47.0	43.9	19.7	56.0
Education							
Primary or less	18.1	7.7	11.3	17.6	23.7	5.0	37.4
Lower secondary	32.4	25.5	13.7	29.6	34.0	12.5	53.9
Upper secondary	36.9	51.8	39.7	36.3	48.7	28.3	58.5
Post secondary	59.0	62.2	53.4	66.9	55.6	39.0	71.7
Working time							
Full time	40.5	48.7	37.1	47.5	46.6	19.2	59.2
Part time	52.0	45.0	35.4	44.8	36.3	12.1	53.3
Tenure							
Per-manent	43.1	48.1	36.7	47.4	44.6	20.0	not specified
Tem-porary	40.4	52.0	44.4	42.2	50.2	13.4	not specified
Position in workplace hierarchy							
No supervisory responsibility	37.9	45.8	32.2	39.9	42.5	17.5	not specified
Limited supervisory responsibility	53.1	61.4	47.0	61.0	39.4	26.0	not specified
Extensive supervisory responsibility	50.0	46.0	51.7	62.3	54.6	37.3	not specified
Self-employed, no employees	36.7	42.5	27.9	34.1	34.8	10.2	not specified
Self-employed with employees	49.2	50.9	33.3	31.1	32.9	10.0	not specified
Occupational status							
Manager	42.5	46.1	44.1	56.3	39.1	28.9	62.0
Professional	63.7	66.4	49.3	71.7	53.3	45.8	71.2
Technician	46.3	61.0	47.5	70.4	49.6	36.5	69.2
Clerk	47.6	49.0	32.6	54.3	47.0	26.2	54.2
Services worker	43.7	47.2	27.0	40.4	43.2	13.2	54.7
Skilled blue-collar worker	30.6	37.6	34.6	28.7	38.2	11.3	42.1
Plant and elementary worker	30.2	31.3	17.2	24.3	30.8	11.4	40.7

Table 3.7. **Rates of participation in adult education by selected descriptors, employed population 1994 (per cent) (Concluded)**

	Canada	Switzerland (German)	Switzerland (French)	United States	Nether-lands	Poland	Sweden
Labour-market sector							
Primary	36.2	35.0	26.8	22.7	25.0	7.2	47.1
Manufacturing	29.9	41.3	30.4	36.6	45.1	16.0	54.4
Public utilities and construction	24.2	40.2	32.6	34.4	32.2	20.3	45.8
Trade	36.0	40.6	23.4	40.2	37.2	19.1	47.8
Transportation	51.6	55.0	57.9	51.3	35.2	19.8	52.2
Finance	65.1	56.4	47.1	50.8	49.1	47.2	60.3
Public and private services	49.0	60.5	43.2	57.7	50.2	24.5	65.0

Education is another variable of interest. The results in Table 3.7 indicate that individuals with lower levels of educational attainment are much less likely to participate in adult education and training, while experience of post-secondary education is associated with higher participation rates. This result is consistent with earlier findings concerning the entire adult population. It is also in line with the findings regarding the distribution of continuing education and training that emerge from comparisons involving the common labour force surveys of OECD countries. The OECD (1995), for example, concludes that, "job-related continuing education and training seems to allow those who already have a good stock of skills to continue to develop their competence, thereby maintaining or furthering their advantage in the labour-market" (p. 157). A cursory review of the OECD evidence on training (see Hasan & Tuijnman, in: Bélanger & Valdivielso 1997: chapter 9) may lead one to suggest that most of the adult education and training is obtained by those who completed upper secondary education. This, however, speaks to numbers rather than distributions within the group comprising the sub-population. The IALS data clearly support the OECD finding, as can be seen in Table 3.7, but the differentiation is more according to experience of post-secondary education than to completed secondary education. This finding is consistent across all the countries investigated.

Certain types of occupation are more susceptible to adult education and training than others at given points in time. Consequently, one should expect to find variation in participation rates by occupation. Table 3.7 shows that this is indeed the case, with managers, professionals and technicians demonstrating higher participation rates than the others. Participation rates are also expected to vary with firm size and an individual's position in the hierarchical structure of the workplace, labour force sector of employment, and tenure. Typically, the larger the firm the more likely it is that the organization will be structured hierarchically. The relationship between firm size and the rate of participation in adult education and training is investigated in Table 3.8, for the pooled dataset.

The results confirm that participation rates increase with the size of establishments, with rates over 50 per cent in firms with more than 500 employees.

Table 3.8.   Size of establishment and rate of participation in adult education and training, by gender, pooled dataset (per cent)

N employees	Male	Female	Average
Less than 20 employees	26.7	33.2	29.7
20-99 employees	32.4	37.8	34.8
100-199 employees	29.7	29.8	29.8
200-499 employees	32.1	51.0	39.9
500 or more employees	55.1	55.7	55.4
All establishments	**39.8**	**43.9**	**41.6**

Table 3.8 presents the results for men and women separately. The data suggest that women (44 per cent) receive proportionately more training than men (40 per cent). The distributions by establishment size show that women have a higher representation in each cell than men. Generally, the differences are not large, but there is an exception: female participation rates significantly exceed those of males in establishments with between 200 and 499 employees. Why this is so cannot be determined from the data.

As mentioned, tenure might be another important determinant of training. Recent studies show clear growth in part-time work and temporary labour contracts. OECD figures suggest that the incidence of part-time employment is relatively high for men in the Netherlands, the United States, and Canada, and relatively low in Germany, Switzerland, and Poland. The incidence of part-time work tends to be higher for women in all countries, but there are large differences in this regard (OECD 1994). The research literature suggests that full-time and permanent employees are more likely to receive training than part-time and temporary employees. However, the IALS results shown previously in Table 3.7 indicate that the differences are mostly small, and that temporary workers demonstrate a somewhat higher participation rate than permanent workers.

Determinants of Participation: Employed Population

The previous section reviewed the important covariates of participation. In this section, the interrelationships among the variables are examined, for the employed population, in two different models. Occupation is specified in the first (Table 3.9) and position in the workplace hierarchy in the second (Table 3.10). The other variables specified in both models are the same as those used previously in the multivariate analysis of the determinants of participation for the entire adult population.

For Canada, negative and statistically significant effects are found for gender and age, with employed women and older age groups at a disadvantage. The gender effect thus appears to operate differently for the general and the employed population, although the influences are reversed with respect to urbanization. Living single appears to have a positive impact, as does the educational background of parents. The respondents' own educational background is also positively related to participation, whereas time spent watching television is related negatively. Of particular interest is the relationship with full-time work, which has a negative effect on participation compared with part-time work. The probability of adult education participation decreases for Plant and elementary workers. This is the only occupational category for which a significant effect on participation is found. The category labour-market sector of employment shows no clear pattern of influences either, although three sectors—manufacturing, public utilities and construction, and trade—influence adult education participation negatively, whereas the opposite effect is observed for transportation.

Table 3.9.   Regression estimates obtained in a logistic model specifying occupation and other determinants of adult education participation, employed population aged 16-64

	Canada	Switzerland (German)	Switzerland French)	United States	Nether- lands	Poland	Sweden
Socio-demographic characteristics							
Gender	0.74[2]	1.14	0.74	0.81	1.02	0.75[1]	1.00
Age	0.97[3]	0.96[3]	0.97[3]	0.99[3]	0.97[3]	0.98[2]	0.99
Single	1.81[3]	0.83	1.00	1.00	0.89	1.24	0.70[1]
Urbanization	1.13	1.77[2]	.85	1.16	1.05	0.93	0.94
Education							
Parental education	1.72[3]	.78	1.51	1.28[1]	0.94	1.28	0.83
Respondent's education							
– primary or less	reference	reference	reference	reference	reference	reference	reference
– lower secondary	1.46	1.98	0.47	1.47	1.47	1.87[1]	1.86[2]
– upper secondary	1.50[1]	4.49[2]	1.67	1.70[1]	1.98[2]	3.82	1.84[2]
– post-secondary	2.23[3]	7.75[3]	2.29	3.77[3]	2.35[3]	4.39	2.44[3]
Social participation							
Member of a voluntary association	1.69[3]	1.46[2]	1.31	1.59[3]	1.25*	1.21	1.19
Intensive television viewer	0.60[3]	0.83	0.93	0.91	0.60[3]	0.99	not specified
Work situation							
Full time work	0.41[3]	0.79	1.01	0.99	1.84[3]	1.25	1.44[1]

Table 3.9.   Regression estimates obtained in a logistic model specifying occupation and other determinants of adult education participation, employed population aged 16-64 (Concluded)

		Canada	Switzerland (German)	Switzerland French)	United States	Nether-lands	Poland	Sweden
Occupation								
– Manager	reference		reference	reference	reference	reference	reference	reference
– Professionnal	1.43		1.83	0.74	1.35	1.08	1.90	1.21
– Technician	0.88		1.41	0.91	1.81	1.20	1.58	1.30
– Clerk	1.26		1.26	0.60	1.35	1.38	1.12	0.74
– Services worker	1.16		1.23	0.54	0.78	1.33	0.59	0.78
– Skilled blue collar worker	0.75		1.06	0.66	0.58^2	1.09	0.79	0.40^2
– Plant and elementary worker	0.62^2		0.84	0.38^2	0.47^3	0.83	0.59	0.40^2
Labour-market sector								
– Primary	reference		reference	reference	reference	reference	reference	reference
– Manufacturing	0.64^1		0.69	1.21	2.20	2.65^2	2.04^2	0.79
– Public utilities and construction	0.43^2		0.68	1.35	2.13	1.63	2.63^2	0.55
– Trade	0.40^3		0.62	0.96	1.94	1.70	1.96	0.61
– Transportation	1.68^1		2.14	4.70^2	2.54^2	1.41	2.15^1	0.82
– Finance	1.03		0.95	1.67	2.47^1	2.87^2	4.24^2	0.72
– Public and private services	0.67		1.09	1.85	2.78^2	2.86^3	1.80^1	0.79
N cases	**2,260**		**743**	**724**	**1,734**	**1,728**	**1,510**	**1,647**
Improvement	**534.39³**		**115.91³**	**121.06³**	**331.73³**	**171.74³**	**205.18³**	**145.68³**

1. $p < .05$.
2. $p < .01$.
3. $p < .001$.

In the German-speaking region of Switzerland, age has a significant negative effect, while living in an urban area has a positive one. Having a completed upper secondary education or experience at the post-secondary level has a positive effect, but its magnitude is lower than for the general adult population. Hence, it can be concluded that the handicap posed by the lack of an advanced education is somewhat compensated for in working life. Indeed, there are significant effects for all labour-market-related variables. Social participation, as measured by membership in a voluntary association, also has a positive effect, whereas passive leisure behaviour has a significant negative effect for the working population. The patterns are somewhat different for French-speaking Switzerland, where older age has a significant negative effect. Contrary to the results for the German-speaking region, but consistent with the Canadian data, only one occupational category—Plant and elementary worker—shows a significant negative effect.

In the United States, urbanization and type of leisure do not exert significant influences for the working population, which contrasts with the results obtained for the general adult population. As in Canada, the effect of educational attainment is smaller for the working population than for the entire adult population. Part-time work does not affect the participation rate. The two blue-collar occupational categories both exert a significant negative influence, whereas three labour-market sectors—transportation, finance, and services—have a positive one.

The models estimated for the general and the employed population do not show any differences for the Netherlands. All indicators that exert significant influences on adult education participation in one model also do so in the other. It is interesting to note that in this country, which has a relatively high incidence of part-time work compared to the OECD average (OECD 1994), those who are employed on a full-time basis have a greater chance of participating in adult education and training. Occupation, on the other hand, does not exhibit a significant effect. Three labour-market sectors—manufacturing, finance, and services—contribute to an increase in the probability of participating in adult education or training.

In Poland, gender and increasing age are associated with a decrease in the probabilities of receiving training for the working population. Educational attainment has less predictive power for the employed population than for the general population. The finding that lower secondary education exerts a positive effect, while the higher levels do not, is consistent with Poland's lower overall level of educational attainment compared with the other countries (OECD 1995). Occupational categories do exert some influence, but these are conditional on the sector of employment. The evidence clearly indicates that the overall pattern of participation in Poland differs from that observed for the comparison countries included in this study.

Gender does not appear to influence the probability of adult education participation for the employed population in Sweden. Living single exerts a significant effect, which is unlike the finding for the general adult population. Educational background is less important as a determinant of participation for the employed than for the general population, except at the lower levels of attainment. Membership of a voluntary association has no effect for the employed population in Sweden. Full-time employment increases the probability of receiving training, while blue-collar employment has the opposite effect.

The overall, comparative patterns are as follows. Gender does not play a significant role in determining adult education participation except in Poland and Canada, where gender decreases the probability of participation. Age and living single have a similar effect, except in Sweden. The effect of urbanization disappears for the employed population in the United States and Canada. Parental education has the same, significant effect in all countries except Poland, where it exerts less influence compared with the effect size found for the general population. Initial educational attainment does not have a similar effect in all the countries. Generally, the magnitude of the effect of this variable on participation is lower in the model estimated for the employed population than in that for the entire adult population. The effect of membership in a voluntary association is independent of employment status, except in the French-speaking cantons of Switzerland. The effect of leisure behaviour, which was significant for the general population, mostly disappears in the model for the working population. The Netherlands is the exception in this respect.

The influences of work-related characteristics on participation do not show consistent patterns across the countries investigated. Full-time work has a significant effect in three countries: negative in the case of Canada, and positive in Sweden and the Netherlands. Labour-market sector of employment does not influence participation in any clear way. The models for two countries, Canada and Poland, indicate major differences across sectors, but no differences are apparent in Sweden and German-speaking Switzerland. A surprising result is the relative absence of significant effects of occupational status on participation. It seems that being employed is often a more important factor than type of occupation, although employment in blue-collar jobs can have a negative effect on adult education participation in some cases. The relatively weak association that exists between occupation and participation once employment is held which is constant across the models suggests that other employment-related factors may be implicated in the relationship. This hypothesis is explored in a second model, presented in Table 3.10, in which the occupation variable is replaced with a measure of the employed person's supervisory responsibilities as an indicator of the level or status of the job.[12]

---

[12]   *The assumption is made that workers who supervise other workers have more responsibility, a higher job level, and more status in the hierarchy of the workplace organization than workers without supervisory duties. Moreover, both job level and status are assumed to rise with an increase in the number of workers supervised.*

Table 3.10. Regression estimates obtained in a logistic model specifying position in the workplace hierarchy and other determinants of adult education participation, employed population aged 16-64

	Canada	Switzerland (German)	Switzerland French)	United States	Netherlands	Poland
Socio-demographic characteristics						
Gender	0.92	1.23	0.75	0.96	1.10	0.85
Age	0.97[3]	0.97[3]	0.96[3]	0.99[2]	0.97	0.98[2]
Living single	1.75[3]	0.86	1.05	0.96	0.89	1.24
Urbanization	1.15	1.80[3]	0.81	1.21	1.00	0.99
Education						
Parental education	1.77[3]	0.86	1.52[1]	1.37[2]	0.94	1.40
Respondent's educational attainment						
– Primary or less	reference	reference	reference	reference	reference	reference
– Lower secondary	1.53	1.82	0.72	1.49	1.54[1]	1.82[1]
– Upper-secondary	1.53[1]	4.96[2]	1.99	1.90[1]	2.09[3]	4.66[3]
– Post-secondary	2.57[3]	9.65[3]	2.89[1]	4.54[3]	2.50[3]	6.59[3]
Social participation						
Member of a voluntary association	1.69[3]	1.46[1]	1.19	1.70[3]	1.27[1]	1.19
Intensive television viewer	0.61[3]	0.92	0.96	0.89	0.60[3]	0.91
Work situation						
Full-time work	0.38[3]	0.70	0.75	0.98	1.85[3]	1.27
Position in workplace hierarchy						
– Employee without supervisory duties	reference	reference	reference	reference	reference	reference
– Employee with limited supervisory duties	1.51[3]	1.60[1]	1.81[2]	1.70[3]	1.08	1.32
– Employee with extensive supervisory duties	1.81[3]	0.87	2.97[3]	1.83[3]	1.34[1]	1.74
Self-employed without employees	0.60[2]	0.92	0.98	0.71	0.77	0.76
Self-employed with employee(s)	1.68[1]	1.08	1.09	0.52[1]	0.65[1]	0.29[2]

Table 3.10. Regression estimates obtained in a logistic model specifying position in the workplace hierarchy and other determinants of adult education participation, employed population aged 16-64 (Concluded)

	Canada	Switzerland (German)	Switzerland French)	United States	Netherlands	Poland
Labour-market sector						
– Primary	reference	reference	reference	reference	reference	1.68
– Manufacturing	0.62[1]	0.80	1.03	1.61	2.21[2]	2.35[2]
– Public utilities and construction	0.44[2]	0.81	1.32	1.61	1.53	1.80
– Trade	0.46[3]	0.74	0.87	1.58	1.67	1.80
– Transportation	1.76[1]	2.47	4.40[1]	2.13	1.30	4.53[3]
finance	1.43	1.17	1.82	2.39[1]	2.63	1.98[2]
Public and private services	0.84	1.43	1.78	2.66[1]	2.59	
N cases	2,261	741	765	1,734	1,737	1,469
Improvement	548.65[3]	116.72[3]	136.53[3]	333.13[3]	176.93[3]	193.39[3]

1. $p < .05$.
2. $p < .01$.
3. $p < .001$.

The variables measuring position in the workplace hierarchy do not change the effects of other indicators in the models estimated for Canada, German-speaking Switzerland, and the United States. However, a few interesting modifications occur in the models of the other countries. The first change is that the effect of initial educational attainment increases when examined in the context of supervisory responsibilities instead of occupation. A second change occurs in the model for Poland, where the specification of job status makes the gender effect disappear.

The effect of the new indicator on adult education participation is different in each country. In Canada, all categories have a significant effect. To be employed and to have supervisory responsibilities increases the probability of participation. Self-employed people without employees have reduced chances of participation. In German-speaking Switzerland, it is only the employees with limited responsibilities who have a significantly higher training probability. Employees with both limited and extensive responsibilities have a greater chance of participating in adult education in French-speaking Switzerland. In the United States, the training probabilities also increase with an increase in responsibility. In Poland, the self-employed have less chance of participating.

3.5   Implications for Theory

The first dimension of the model examined refers to the *cultural attributes* that influence adult education participation. Individuals can be studied in terms of cultural and symbolic attributes, which define a relationship between culture, on the one hand, and initial and adult education on the other. Initial educational attainment is the most robust predictor of participation in adult education, but this effect is not identical in each country. In Sweden, the Netherlands, Poland, and German-speaking Switzerland, there is a progressive effect, with each higher level of educational attainment showing an increase in adult education participation. In the United States and French-speaking Switzerland, only those with at least an upper secondary or tertiary education show higher participation rates. In Canada, this is the case only for tertiary education.

Differences in participation rates by gender and age are often explained in terms of differences in initial educational attainment between men and women and between age groups. The analysis presented in this chapter shows no significant relationship between gender and participation, except for Sweden and German-speaking Switzerland. In both countries, however, these gender effects disappear when only the labour force is considered. Another exception with respect to gender is that it has a significant effect on the participation rates of the employed population in Canada and Poland. This effect disappears, however, if position in the workplace hierarchy is substituted for occupation. This leads one to assume that women in these countries have less access to resource opportunities because of their position in the workplace. Further analyses of the gender factor are presented in subsequent chapters.

Age has a significant effect on participation in all countries except Sweden, where many older people are attracted to remain active learners by the social and cultural attributes of the popular study circles. Older people and older workers participate less, in part because they received less formal education initially. The age factor can be explained in two ways. A first explanation is that older adults participate less because they are less attracted than young adults by the predominantly work-oriented structures of adult education and the credentialism this brings. A second reason may be that with increasing age, adults tend to shift their priorities from work-oriented learning to forms of cultural consumption.

Parental educational attainment is an important indicator of home background, which in turn is an element in social stratification and cultural reproduction. Previous research indicates that the effects of home background do not come to an end when the offspring leaves the initial system of education. Rather, parental educational attainment continues to exert an influence on educational choice and learning behaviour well into adulthood. This relationship is confirmed by the results obtained for Canada, the United States, and Poland. In conclusion, the main finding with respect to cultural attributes is the weight that must be given to the educational background of respondents and their parents.

The second dimension investigated in the model concerns *social participation and time management*. The results tend to confirm current theories about social participation and adult education. In all countries except Poland, there is a significant association between membership in voluntary associations and participation in adult education. The effects of different leisure time behaviours are well noted in the North American research literature. People with an active leisure lifestyle have a higher tendency to participate in adult education than people with a more passive leisure orientation. The analysis of data employing hours spent watching television as an indicator of leisure orientation confirms the relevance of this dimension for four countries. The effect is less strong for the active population than for the general adult population.[13] Differences in leisure behaviour can be attributed to personality traits, but it is also possible that other factors come into play, for example, the structure of adult education supply. There are many types of adult education, and various ways of obtaining it. Motivation is another factor that enters into a person's decision to participate in adult education. Although adult education represents a leisureactivity and a social meeting place for some people, for others it is a strain and anything but leisure. Consequently, the notion of adult education as a useful leisure activity is not pervasive.

Time management is linked with social participation and leisure time behaviour. But the results show that this factor does not play a significant role in predicting participation in adult education in most countries, because many individuals are apparently capable of negotiating and organizing the time they spend on work, family, leisure, training, and other activities. Living alone was found to have a significant effect only in Canada. Being employed rather than unemployed or having another labour force status was found to have a positive effect on adult education participation.

A third dimension of the model concerns the *economic situation* of the adult population. Previous research studies have shown how the economic situation in which adults find themselves provides an opportunity structure for accessing scarce resources. Access to these resources can enhance an individual's chances of securing occupational or social mobility. The empirical results presented in this chapter are of interest in this respect: in the first step of the data analysis, the relationship between labour force status and participation was examined for the entire adult population. It was found that the employed have a significantly higher chance of receiving adult education or training than people who do not work. The difference between these two groups is particularly pronounced in Poland. Active labour-market policies appear to have a significant effect on participation

---

[13]   *Possibly this finding is explained by the fact that working people tend to watch television for fewer hours than the adult population in general.*

in the United States, Poland, and Sweden. In these countries, the unemployed have a higher probability to participate than those outside the labour force. The second step of the data analysis examined the patterns of participation specifically for the working population. A surprising finding is the relatively weak weight of occupation. There are large differences in participation rates between occupational groups as such, but their significance as a major determinant was reduced once the effects of other variables were held constant in the model. Being a "blue-collar" worker was the only occupational category that reduced the probability to participate in adult education or training. Perhaps the explanation is that in the current climate of workplace restructuring, all occupational groups are being trained and retrained, with the notable exception of blue-collar workers. A further noteworthy result occurred when the occupation variable was replaced in the model by another indicator of labour force status, namely, a person's position in the workplace hierarchy measured by "supervisory position". This variable was shown to have only a weak link with educational attainment. Yet, the variable was positively associated with adult education participation in all countries except Poland.

Economic theory suggests that employers prefer to invest in the training of their permanent, full-time workers. The evidence presented in this chapter provides no support for this assumption. The distinction between permanent and temporary work status is not associated with the determination of participation in adult education and training. In most countries, the relationship was not significant statistically, and in those cases where an effect was observed it manifested itself differently. In Canada, full-time workers have less chance of participating, whereas the opposite appears to hold in the Netherlands and Sweden. Why might this be the case? In Canada, the boundaries between youth status and adulthood have become blurred. Many young people combine studies with part-time work. Alternately, many employees work part-time and study on the side. For the Netherlands, the explanation might be the relative abundance of part-time jobs, requiring more training initially.

A further economic variable investigated in this study concerns the impact of labour-market organization, particularly the industrial structure, on access to opportunity resources. There is a significant difference in participation rates among labour-market sectors in Canada, the United States, the Netherlands, and Poland, but not in Sweden and Switzerland. An explanation for this may be found in the public regulation of adult education. Vocational training in Switzerland, specifically in the German-speaking cantons, is organized in accordance with the principles of the dual system. The return to vocational training subsequent to serving a few years in employment is common practice in all sectors of the labour-market. In Sweden, there are many programmes for adult education and training, and as a result access may have been equalized between sectors. Another explanation might be that in Sweden only 40 per cent of all participants take courses for job-related reasons, a figure that is much lower than in the comparison countries.

3.6   National Participation Patterns

The model investigated in this chapter does not predict participation in adult education equally well in all the countries. This calls into focus the question of the relationship between socials tratification and participation. Even though there is no evidence of real convergence among the countries studied, there are some noteworthy similar trends:

- Initial educational attainment is the most significant determinant of participation in adult education. However, this effect is not uniform across countries.

- For all countries in the study, being employed increases participation rates. The workplace evidently plays a role in improving the opportunity structure.

- With the notable exception of Sweden, participation tends to decrease with increasing age.

- There are few gender differences in overall participation rates, but social stratification does have an effect everywhere.

The specific weight of indicators differs from country to country. Differences between French- and German-speaking Switzerland provide glimpses of the influences of cultural factors on both opportunity structures and the pattern of actual adult education participation. There is evidence for what Maurice, Sellier, and Silvestre (1982) call "societal efficacy", in that participation is consistently influenced by stratification criteria. For instance, the Canadian participation model shows the largest number of statistically significant relationships, and these account for more of the variance in participation than in the models estimated for the other countries, but the specific patterns observed are not necessarily the same as those found for other countries. The nature of a "societal effect" on adult education participation requires future analysis. Several issues should be considered in this respect:

- Firstly, how does a society deal with issues of social stratification? There is evidence of cross-national variation in the relationships of gender, educational attainment, age, and social engagement with adult education participation. This suggests that there are country-specific social structures which influence the learning pathways taken by individual people.

- A second set of issues concerns the nature of human capital investment policies in the workplace, and the need to examine more profoundly how firms manage their human resources.

● A third area for further exploration focuses on the structures of adult education and training. Characteristics of supply are clearly associated with national patterns of adult education participation. Tables 3.11, 3.12, and 3.13 show that the differences among the countries are important in this respect.

Table 3.11. Summary indicators of the determinants of participation by country, based on an analysis of data for the entire adult population

	Positive effect	Negative effect
Canada	● Living single ● Living in urban area ● Parental education ● Respondent's education ● Voluntary association member ● Labour force status (employed)	● Age ● Intensive television viewing
Switzerland (German-speaking)	● Gender ● Living in urban area ● Respondent's education ● Voluntary association member ● Labour force status (employed)	● Age ● Intensive television viewing
Switzerland (French-speaking)	● Educational attainment ● Voluntary association member ● Labour force status	● Age
United States	● Living in urban area ● Parental education ● Respondent's education ● Voluntary association member ● Being unemployed ● Working full-time	● Age ● Intensive television viewing
Netherlands	● Respondent's education ● Voluntary association member ● Working full-time	● Age ● Intensive television viewing
Poland	● Respondent's education ● Voluntary association member ● Being unemployed ● Working full-time	● Age
Sweden	● Gender ● Respondent's education ● Voluntary association member ● Being unemployed ● Working full-time	

Table 3.12.   Summary indicators of the determinants of participation by country, based on an analysis of data for the employed population

	Positive effect	Negative effect
Canada	• Living single • Parental education • Respondent's education • Voluntary association member • Supervisory responsibilities • Transportation	• Gender • Age • Intensive television viewing • Full-time employment • Unskilled blue-collar worker • Self-employed • Industrial sectors
Switzerland (German-speaking)	• Living in urban area • Respondent's education • Voluntary association member	• Age
Switzerland (French-speaking)	• Parental education • Respondent's education • Supervisory responsibilities • Transportation	• Age • Unskilled blue-collar worker
United States	• Respondent's education • Voluntary association member • Supervisory responsibilities • Industrial sector	• Age • Blue-collar worker
Netherlands	• Respondent's education • Voluntary association member • Full-time employment • Supervisory responsibilities • Industrial sectors	• Age • Self-employed with supervision of employees • Intensive television viewing
Poland	• Respondent's education • Industrial sectors	• Gender • Age • Self-employed with supervision of employees
Sweden	• Respondent's education • Full-time employment	• Living single • Blue-collar worker

Table 3.13. Variation in national patterns of adult education participation (per cent)

	Per cent in job-related courses	Share of education system in provision (3)	Share of employers in provision (4)	Share of for-profit institutions in provision (5)	Other suppliers (6)	Total (3+4+5+6)
Canada	79.2	33.8	21.7	1.4	43.1	100.0
Switzerland (German)	58.9	9.0	9.7	10.4	61.9	100.0
Switzerland (French)	64.4	14.5	15.6	12.3	42.4	84.8
United States	87.6	33.9	29.1	1.9	35.1	100.0
Netherlands	64.3	—	14.3	—	85.7	100.0
Poland	75.6	14.4	25.1	0.6	59.9	100.0
Sweden	38.9	—	—	—	—	—

3.7 Conclusions for Policy

It is imperative for countries to have a better understanding of the role and weight of adult education and training in the provision of lifelong learning. To date, there has been little cross-national empirical research that could provide policy-makers with insights into the determinants of adult education participation. The IALS dataset offers a unique opportunity for examining the similarities and differences in national patterns of adult education participation, albeit for a small number of countries and a limited number of explanatory variables. In this study, several factors have been found to be associated with participation. Those who are working and those with higher levels of formal educational attainment are most likely to participate.

These findings serve as an illustration of the importance of formal schooling for building an inclusive learning society. They also raise the more difficult question of how to bring the non-participants on board. Alternatively, the question is how one might perceive adult education differently, in such ways that large segments of society are not excluded. Policy-makers will need to focus on the fact that those not working are less likely to receive adult education or training, even though they probably require the training to secure a job. The evidence moreover shows that in the United States and Sweden, there is a high likelihood that those not working but looking for work will participate in adult education. This raises the issue of how social welfare policies can contribute to meeting the education and training needs of those outside the world of work.

In conclusion, the IALS dataset has provided a first opportunity to overcome some of the deficit in comparative research on adult education participation. Clearly, more work on the determinants and barriers to participation is called for. Subsequent chapters will examine the subject matter orientation and duration of the courses or programmes; intensity of learning effort; individual reasons for participating; and the structures of adult education supply.

References

Bélanger, P. 1980. "Une pratique de contre-école : Une expérience éducative du mouvement en Guinée-Bissau". In: *Sociologie et Sociétés* XII (1): 155-167.

Borkowsky, A., Tuijnman, A.C., and van der Heiden, M. 1995. "Indicators of Continuing Education and Training". In: OECD. *Education and Employment.* Paris: Centre for Educational Research and Innovation.

Chicha, M.-T. 1994. *La participation des travailleuses à la formation en entreprise et l'accès à l'égalité: Une jonction intéressante mais peu explorée.* Montréal: Ecole de Relations Industrielles, Université de Montréal.

Cookson, P.S. 1986. "A Framework for Theory and Research on Adult Education Participation". In: *Adult Education Quarterly* 46 (Spring): 130-141.

Courtney, S. 1992. *Why Adults Learn? Towards a Theory of Participation in Adult Education.* London, New York: Routledge.

Denton, F.T., Pinéo, P.C., and Spencer, B.G. 1988. "Participation in Adult Education by the Elderly: A Multivariate Analysis and Some Implications for the Future". In: *Canadian Journal of Ageing* 7 (1): 4-16.

Deveraux, M. S. 1984. *Une personne sur cinq. Enquête sur l'éducation des adultes au Canada.* Ottawa: Statistique Canada et Direction générale de l'aide à l'éducation du Secrétariat d'Etat, Gouvernement du Canada.

Doray, P., Paris, L., and Institut canadien d'éducation des adultes. 1995. *La participation des adultes à l'éducation au Québec.* Montréal: Université du Québec and Institut canadien d'éducation des adultes.

Dubar, C. 1977. Formation continue et différenciations sociales. In: *Revue française de sociologie* XVIII: 543-575

Dubar, C. 1996. *La formation continue.* Paris: La Découverte.

Hasan, A., and Tuijnman, A.C. 1997. "Methodologies for Monitoring Adult Education Participation". In: P. Bélanger and S. Valdivielso (eds.). *The Emergence of Learning Societies: Who Participates in Adult Learning?* Oxford: Pergamon Press.

Henry, G.T., and Basile, K.C. 1994. Understanding the decision to participate in formal adult education. In: *Adult Education Quarterly* 44 (2): 64-82.

Johnstone, J., and Rivera, R. 1965. *Volunteers for Learning: A Study of the Educational Pursuits of American Adults.* Chicago: Aldine.

Knoke, D., and Kalleberg, A.L. 1994. "Job-Training in US Organizations". In: *American Sociological Review* 59: 537-546.

Maurice, M., Sellier, F., and Silvestre, J.J. 1982. *Politiques éducatives et organisation du travail en France et en Allemagne.* Paris: Presses Universitaires de France.

Murray, T.S. 1996. "Measurement of adult education". In: A.C. Tuijnman (ed.). *The International Encyclopedia of Adult Education and Training.* (2nd ed.) Oxford: Pergamon Press.

Nordhaug, O. 1987. "Outcomes of adult education: Economic and sociological approaches". In: *Scandinavian Journal of Educational Research* 31: 113-122.

OECD. 1994. *Employment Outlook.* Paris: Organisation for Economic Co-operation and Development.

OECD. 1995. *Education at a Glance: OECD Indicators.* (3rd ed.) Paris: Centre for Educational Research and Innovation.

OECD. 1996. *Lifelong Learning for All: Report of the Meeting of the Education Committee at Ministerial Level, 16-17 January 1996.* Paris: Organisation for Economic Co-operation and Development.

OECD and Statistics Canada. 1995. *Literacy, Economy and Society.* Paris and Ottawa: Organistion for Economic Co-operation and Development and Statistics Canada.

Therrien, R. 1996 "Elements de reflexion sur le champ de l'education des adultes a l'université". In Pierre Chenard. *L'evolution de la population edutiants a l'universit de Québec.* pp105-118.

Titmus, C.J. 1996. "Comparative Studies of Adult Education". In: A.C. Tuijnman (ed.). *The International Encyclopedia of Adult Education and Training.* (2nd ed.) Oxford: Pergamon Press.

Tuijnman, A.C. 1996. "Providers of Adult Education: An Overview". In: A.C. Tuijnman (ed.). *The International Encyclopedia of Adult Education and Training.* (2nd ed.) Oxford: Pergamon Press.

van der Kamp, M. 1996. "Participation: Antecedent factors". In: A.C. Tuijnman (ed.). *The International Encyclopedia of Adult Education and Training.* (2nd ed.) Oxford: Pergamon Press.

Chapter 4

Barriers to Participation in Adult Education and Training: Towards a New Understanding

Kjell Rubenson and Gongli Xu

4.1 Introduction

In 1994, UNESCO chose *Basic Education for All* for its Mid-term Strategy covering the period 1996-2001. Similarly, the fourth meeting of the OECD Education Committee at Ministerial level in 1996 proposed that making lifelong learning a reality for all should be a priority for Member countries for the next five-year period. The declaration from the OECD meeting reflects the new challenges facing policy-makers (OECD 1996). Today, governments are faced with the causes and consequences of severe unemployment, along with public demands for a response. Likewise, there are concerns about the skills base and quality of the workforce and the mounting disparities in society which threaten the cohesiveness of the social fabric. This is the context in which adult education and training are being promoted strongly in public policy documents as important instruments in tackling the problems facing society.

It is not only in policy discussions that opportunities and barriers to adult education and training in a framework for lifelong learning are taking central stage. The same is happening in various scholarly debates. The neoclassical approach to the analysis of innovation and technological change is being criticized and challenged by an evolutionary approach, in which the economy is viewed more as a process of learning, as are technological, organizational, and institutional change (Hommen, in press). Lundwall (1997) talks about "learning by interacting" to describe how product innovations occur via the experiences of customers and suppliers. The learning perspective is also prominent in those theories of industrial restructuring, flexible specialization, regulation, and the "techno-economic paradigm" that are trying to replace the dominant Fordist paradigm (Hommen 1994). Nonaka (1994) argues that the traditional focus on the input-process-output sequence results in a static view of organizations. This does not give due consideration to what the organization produces in terms of creating information and knowledge.

The economic imperative, although dominant, is not the only force driving interest in lifelong learning. In the former Eastern European countries there is a struggle to build a new system after the collapse of the old order. This involves finding a new identity, establishing democratic institutions, and recreating civil society. Touraine (1995) notes that while it is understandable that Eastern Europe places all its hope on the market, this is not enough to build a future. In the West, the status of civil society and democracy, the ecological crisis, and the status of women and minorities are being debated. Giddens (1994) notes that in the post-traditional order, individuals more or less have to engage with the wider world if they are to survive. He continues:

> "Information produced by specialists (including scientific knowledge) can no longer be wholly confined to specific groups, but becomes routinely interpreted and acted on by lay individuals in the course of their everyday actions." (p.7)

In the same spirit, the audit report from the Swedish Democracy Council (Rothstein 1995) adopted a broad definition of democracy and chose to talk about it as dialogue. This concept relates to Habermas's (1983) notion of the public sphere as an arena for debate, reflection, action, and moral-political change. The Council, like Putnam (1993), notes that voluntary associations providing a public arena are central for the development of the solidarity and trust on which civil society is built. It is in connection with this that the Council refers to the importance of the Swedish study circle tradition with its links to the social movements. Similarly, in the critique of modernity and the search to establish a new order of life, the role of learning in social movements, new and old, is receiving serious attention in social theory (see, for example, Giddens 1994; Lyman 1995; Touraine 1995).

Thus, it is understandable that there is a growing interest from various levels of government, intergovernmental organizations, and the social partners in the role of adult education and training within a broader context of lifelong learning. In most countries, this is a very recent phenomenon. As is evident from the OECD's reviews of national education policies, the main focus is still very much on "front-end" education. This is in stark contrast to the promotion of lifelong learning in national and intergovernmental policy documents or in statements from the private sector and the educational establishment. As the examiners state in the Irish review of national policies in education:

> "There has been much reference to the ideal of lifelong learning and the importance of second-chance education notably in the report of the Commission of Adult Education but, as in nearly all other countries, there is no evidence of any concerted efforts to render it a reality." (OECD 1991: 31)

It is of crucial importance for a cohesive strategy for lifelong learning for all to come to grips with the inequalities in participation in adult education and training. The general conclusion arrived at by Johnstone and Rivera in their comprehensive 1965 study is as true today as it was thirty-two years ago:

> "One of the most persistent findings emerging from the inquiry is that a great disparity exists in the involvement in continuing education of segments of the population situated at different levels of the social hierarchy."
> (p. 231)

In this chapter, we will take a closer look at why people do not participate in adult education and training. Research on barriers has focused on participation in formal and non-formal forms of adult education and training, which has resulted in a narrowing of the concept of lifelong learning. However, at the very core of lifelong learning is the informal or "everyday" learning, positive or negative, which occurs in day-to-day life (Dohmen 1996: 46). Here, the issue is the nature and structure of everyday experience and the consequences for a person's learning processes, way of thinking, and competences. Although the IALS survey measures barriers in the more restrictive sense, an attempt will be made to address everyday learning. The analysis will start with a more theoretical discussion on research on barriers and then proceed to an analysis of the IALS data.

4.2   Theoretical Approaches to Research on Barriers

The literature contains little or no theoretical discussion on barriers as such but tends to treat the issue as part of theories on participation, to which we now turn.

As Courtney's (1992) historical review of research on participation and barriers reveals, early studies were instigated not only out of "selfish" institutional motives but also due to social concern. The issue of participation in adult education was related to participation in society in general. Further, although this was relatively undeveloped, there existed an embryo of a sociological perspective. This line of research, which had totally dominated the scene in the early years, started to decline in the mid-1960s, although resurfacing now and then.

Fueled by concern regarding the lack of scholarly progress in adult education, theoretical concerns came to supersede preoccupations with traditional participation surveys. Looking at articles in *Adult Education Quarterly* from 1970 to 1995, there are three times as many papers addressing motivation as studies more directly addressing differences between participants and non-participants. This suggests that the social awareness of earlier studies has been replaced by a concern for theoretical development. In this process, the non-participants seem to have faded away.

The preoccupation with motivation research resulted in an emphasis on the individual and on psychological theory. Cross's (1980: 122-24) conclusion about common elements in existing theories still holds true today:

- all are interactions;
- all build on Kurt Lewin's field-force analysis;
- all are "cognetivist";
- all refer to reference group theory;
- all apply the concepts of incongruity and dissonance;
- all directly or indirectly build on Maslow's model of needs hierarchy.

Societal aspects are not ignored. On the contrary, all theories are, as Cross (1980) points out, interactionist. Participation is understood in terms of interaction between an individual and his or her environment. However, the focus and conceptual apparatus is clearly psychologically oriented. Structural factors or public policy decisions are not directly addressed but are at best treated as a vague background when explaining whether or not an individual will participate. An understanding of how these factors might constitute barriers is commonly ignored. Further, the societal processes that govern these structures are not part of theories on participation.

Knowledge about how the individual interprets the world cannot by itself give an understanding of barriers. Only when structural factors are also included and the interaction between them and the individual conceptual apparatus is analyzed does an interpretation become possible. Participation in adult education and the barriers preventing it—in their broadest interpretation—can be understood in terms of societal processes and structures, institutional processes and structures, and individual consciousness and activity.

Applying this to the "expectancy-valence" paradigm (Figure 4.1), one has to take into account the crucial "circumstances" in which expectancy and value are socially constructed. In accordance with Gidden's theories of society, these structural factors are not deterministic (see Giddens 1984: xxi). Instead, there is a dualism between structure and agent, and it is important to focus also on processes through which a human being as an active agent governs his or her relationship with adult education.

Figure 4.1. The expectancy-valence theory (after Rubenson 1988)

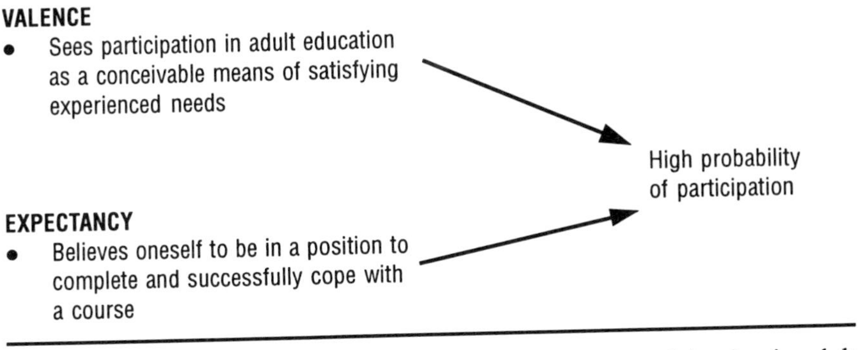

VALENCE
- Sees participation in adult education as a conceivable means of satisfying experienced needs

High probability of participation

EXPECTANCY
- Believes oneself to be in a position to complete and successfully cope with a course

According to Figure 4.1, persons who do not see participation in adult education as a means of satisfying needs, or who do not believe themselves capable of completing their studies, will probably not participate unless forced to do so. The latter can sometimes be the case as a result of "active labour-market policy", which can require training as a prerequisite to receive unemployment insurance. Further, it is sometimes the case that education and training at work is mandatory.

The link between societal processes and structures and institutional processes as they relate to adult education and training depends to a large extent on the possibilities and limits of the state. Carnoy (1995: 3) argues that there are crucial differences in what adult education attempts to do and can do in different socio-political structures. Korpi (1978) maintains that it is the difference in power resources between major collectives or classes in a society, particularly capital and organized labour, that regulates the distribution of life chances, social consciousness, conflicts on the labour-market, public institutions, and so on. In this perspective, the funding regimes and provision of adult education as well as eventual regulations around private sector adult education and training will depend on the political strength of the various collectives.

Public policy on funding regimes and provision of adult education can be understood in terms of various forms of the welfare state (see Esping-Andersen 1989). The liberal welfare state with its means-tested assistance and modest universal transfers caters mainly to a clientele of low-income dependents and would perceive adult education mainly as way of getting people off welfare. Participation would mainly be left to market forces, and entitlements are strict and often associated with stigma. The social-democratic welfare state, according to Esping-Andersen, rather than tolerate a dualism between state and market, between working class and middle class, promotes an equality of the highest standard, not an equality of minimal needs. The state would take a more active role in adult education and be more concerned about inequalities in participation. Thus, the Swedish situation in adult education, both in terms of what is good and what is deteriorating, can be understood in this broader context. It is argued here that what has been and is occurring in the area of adult education mirrors the status and transition of the Swedish social-democratic welfare state (see Stephens 1996; Rubenson 1997).

In terms of institutional barriers, we have to look at "the politics of adult education and training opportunities", including financial support. From this perspective, the fact that adult education and training are only slowly being recognized as important and integral components of a strategy for lifelong learning for all can be seen as a major barrier. For close to ten years, OECD reports, as well as other policy literature, have stressed the vital importance of adult education and training. One therefore has to wonder about the limited attention this emphasis has received in national education policy. In part, the explanation for this limited attention might be that some adult education activities fall under the auspices of other ministries, primarily labour, or are totally outside the public policy arena. Also, those parts of adult education that fall within ministries of education frequently carry a marginal status within the organization.

One vital policy issue is how the existing funding regime affects the recruitment of those who traditionally do not participate. In a market-driven system, it is obvious that advantaged groups will strongly influence the patterns of provision. However, there is also evidence to suggest that even organizations with pronounced ambitions to reach disadvantaged groups actually provide a provision that corresponds best to the demands of the advantaged (Nordhaug 1991). This is a result of the failure of existing funding regimes to compensate for the increased costs involved in recruiting the underprivileged. In a time when government policies seek to increase efficiency through the adoption of both a more market-oriented approach and outcomes-based funding, there is a growing likelihood that the organization goes after those easiest to recruit and more likely to succeed (see McIntyre 1996). Swedish adult education policies over the last · 25 years shed some light on the influence of the funding regime on recruitment effects. The experience has shown that general policies are not effective when it comes to recruiting disadvantaged groups, because traditionally strong groups consume most of the available resources. Instead, what has been effective is earmarked funding for targeted strategies, such as outreach, special study aid, and the broad dissemination of information about the supply of learning opportunities (Rubenson 1996).

The changing economy, with its demand for a better skilled work force, has created new conditions for adult education. This amplifies the old question of the division of responsibilities between the public and private sectors for educating and training adults. The issue for the state is the extent to which it should interfere in the "training market". So far, governments, regardless of political colour, have been cautious about intervention in this market. However, it is becoming clear that private-sector involvement is increasingly crucial for human resources development and is central in a strategy for lifelong learning for all. Of particular interest here is the link between, on the one hand, educational credential stratification, and, on the other hand, the way in which the work role encourages or discourages participation in adult education.

Educational credentials are the strongest predictor of occupational status. The former can to a large extent be explained by the influence of the family and the circumstances under which a person grew up. The point here is that valence and expectancy are reinforced by the link between initial educational attainment and the nature of an individual's work. Thus, the allocation of work roles influences participation and learning directly in at least two ways. Firstly, certain roles provide more opportunities to take part in adult education than others. Available data show that it is those who are already well educated at the time of entrance into the labour force and who are in management positions that receive employer-sponsored education and training (OECD 1996; Bélanger & Valdivielso 1997). With increased employer emphasis on an individual's competences and learning potential, adult education and training tend to increase the value of investment in the former (OECD 1996: 152). Secondly, those in higher positions also have by far the best chances to learn new things on the job itself (Rubenson 1996). From this it follows that the nature of the work position acts as both an incentive and a barrier to lifelong learning.

From the perspective of individual consciousness and activity, valence and expectancy can partly be understood in terms of Bourdieu's concept of habitus. The latter is a system of dispositions that allows and governs how persons act, think, and orient themselves in the social world. This system of dispositions is a result of social experience, collective memories, and ways of thinking that have been engraved in peoples' minds. Bourdieu's theory rests on the idea that a people's habitus, formed by the life they have lived, governs their conceptions and practice and in this way contributes to the reproduction of the social world, and sometimes—if there is no correspondence between peoples' habitus and the social world—to change (Broady 1991: 228). A given habitus facilitates a certain distinct set of strategies that, in relation to the social situation, provides the individual with a certain room to act. In this respect, the behaviour is seen as a result of human agency. Through socialization within the family, in the school, and, later on, in working life, a positive disposition toward adult education becomes a part of some groups' habitus but not of others. This is in accordance with findings from longitudinal studies which have revealed a strong link between cultural-oriented processes in the home—educational experiences—and cultural behaviour in adulthood (see Härnqvist 1989). The relationship between habitus and conceptions of adult education is also evident in studies conducted by Larsson et al. (1986). They found that unskilled workers who had a brief formal education, and who were occupied in work that offered limited possibilities for growth, were characterized by a very restricted notion of adult education. According to this restricted view, it is only when participation in adult education results in better and higher paying work that it is meaningful. The extent to which "objective" institutional and situational factors come to act as barriers will consequently depend on what habitus a person has come to develop and how this results in a certain interpretation of the value and expectancy of the outcome of engaging in adult education. This is important to observe when measuring barriers.

4.3   Measuring Barriers to Participation

Cross (1980: 98) in her seminal work *Adults as Learners* classifies obstacles to participate under three headings:

- situational barriers (those arising from one's situation in life— e.g. lack of time, because of work, family responsibilities, etc.);
- institutional barriers (practices and procedures hindering participation— e.g. fees, lack of evening courses, entrance requirements, limited course offerings, etc.); and
- dispositional barriers (attitudes and dispositions towards learning).

The IALS survey, like similar large-scale data collections, almost exclusively concentrates on situational and institutional barriers. Initially, people were asked whether there had been some education and training they wanted to take for work- or non-work-related reasons, but for some reason or other did not. Those responding "yes" to this question were then given a list of reasons for not having participated.

By proceeding this way, the focus will be on those indicating an interest that they have not been able to fulfill. The implicit assumption seems to be that there are no dispositional barriers, because the respondent has indicated an interest in participating. Hence, the barrier, if present, will be situational or institutional in nature. Barriers become of interest only when there is an expressed wish to participate, and the role of the research is to find out what prevents its realization. To ask those who did not express any interest in participation about barriers is often seen as irrelevant and not applicable, as without an interest there can be no barriers.

There are several problems connected with this approach to the study of barriers. The expression of interest is not such a straightforward indication of willingness and desire to participate as one is led to believe. With participation rates starting to approach 50 per cent in several industrialized societies, and constant talk about the importance of engaging in lifelong learning, it is obvious that the socially accepted thing to do is to express a positive disposition towards adult education and training. Longitudinal research has shown that it is very difficult to predict participation based on expression of interest (Rubenson 1996). Not surprisingly, actual participation was a much better predictor of later enrolment than was interest. More revealing in this study is that just over a third of those who at the first data collection indicated that they had not participated and had no interest in doing so came to participate at least one time during the following eight years. The figure for those who had participated but were not interested in further participation was 70 per cent, whereas about half of the non-participants interested in taking a course actually came to do so. Thus, it is clear that a large group indicating no interest most likely will become participants, whereas a smaller but still substantial number of interested people will never show up. It is previous behaviour rather than expressed interest that predicts whether or not a person will come to participate.

4.4 An Ethical Dilemma in Ascribing Barriers

In discussions around lifelong learning, it is often stressed that this should not be equated with lifelong schooling, and that participation should not be seen as being more or less obligatory. Instead, it is a voluntary act and we have to accept that people have different interests and avoid moralizing about whether a person participates. It is easy to sympathize with the position that middle-class values should not be imposed on everyone and that an individual's will and disposition has to be respected. However, this line of reasoning is not that straightforward.

A close look at different forms of adult education indicates that the better an education pays off in terms of income, status, occupation, political efficacy, cultural competence, and similar matters, the greater the differences in socio-economic status between participants and non-participants. With increased emphasis on the need for people to engage in lifelong learning, policy-makers face the dilemma that participation in adult education and learning is increasingly important for the opportunity structure in society. A "system" of adult education that implicitly takes for granted that the adult is a conscious, self-directed individual in possession of the instruments vital to making use of the available possibilities for adult education, and that relies on self-selection to recruit the participants, will by necessity widen, not narrow, the educational and cultural gaps in society.

From the perspective of social equality and cohesiveness, adult education and training can be promoted as instruments to create the resources (money, property, knowledge, psychological and physical energy, social relations, and security) which individuals can use to control and consciously govern their living conditions. For this to occur it is necessary that those with limited resources be recruited and that the education, directly or indirectly, promotes the creation of these resources.

After this more theoretical discussion on barriers, we turn to the IALS dataset to look at the reasons for not engaging in studies as well as the structural situation under which these decisions were made. The analysis begins with the reasons given for not having taken the training or education that one was interested in pursuing.

4.5   Analysis of IALS Data

Reasons for not having taken education and training

The responses to the list of reasons for not having taken the education and training wanted for work- and/or non-work-related reasons are presented in Table 4.1. An attempt has been made to group the barriers in accordance with Cross's classification of situational, institutional, and dispositional barriers. Unfortunately, as discussed previously, the survey design was such that the items do not really cover dispositional barriers. It was possible to mention more than one reason for not having participated. However, the great majority, 70 per cent, gave only one reason for not enrolling, and no more than 10 per cent mentioned three or more barriers. The picture that emerges from Table 4.1 corresponds well to what has been found in previous investigations of barriers to adult education participation (see, for example, Cross 1980; Jonsson & Gähler 1995).

Table 4.1.   **Reasons for not taking training or education respondent needed or wanted (n[1]; percentages)**

	Canada		Netherlands		Poland		Switzerland[2]		United States	
	Work-related n=1,324	Non-work related n=1,381	Work-related n=488	Non-work related n=539	Work-related n=318	Non-work related n=186	Work-related n=681	Non-work related n=793	Work-related n=645	Non-work related n=490
Situational	**63.9**	**77.5**	**61.4**	**72.4**	**53.8**	**58.8**	**62.1**	**75.5**	**68.1**	**76.6**
Lack of time	44.0	62.6	44.5	65.6	31.6	46.0	42.1	58.6	45.3	60.6
Too busy at work	12.2	15.5	12.0	7.0	13.8	14.6	15.5	21.6	17.3	15.8
Family responsibility	18.1	15.0	6.2	8.3	15.8	15.0	10.1	13.1	17.9	16.6
Lack of employer support	3.7	0.4	6.6	0.2	10.1	3.2	7.2	0.6	6.2	0.0
Institutional	**46.5**	**31.4**	**32.2**	**22.4**	**46.6**	**50.3**	**32.1**	**24.1**	**45.8**	**33.6**
No money	31.8	22.2	17.9	16.3	29.2	35.2	16.6	12.2	33.2	26.0
Course not offered	9.3	4.3	6.9	3.2	14.8	14.1	12.2	4.7	4.9	2.4
Lack of qualification	2.9	0.2	2.5	0.7	1.4	1.5	2.5	1.1	1.5	0.2
Inconvenient time	9.7	6.7	6.2	3.3	6.3	4.6	6.0	8.7	8.7	6.6
Dispositional	**3.0**	**3.5**	**4.3**	**3.7**	**4.3**	**4.6**	**5.3**	**6.2**	**2.9**	**4.0**
Language reasons	0.9	0.1	0.6	0.2	0.3	0.6	1.0	0.9	0.9	0.4
Health	2.1	3.4	3.7	3.7	4.0	4.0	4.3	5.3	1.9	3.6
Other	**12.8**	**6.2**	**12.3**	**11.3**	**16.1**	**14.1**	**16.6**	**11.5**	**8.4**	**4.2**

Notes:
1. *N is number of respondents who provided valid answers to the questions regarding reasons for not taking training or education either needed for career, job purposes or wanted for personal interest or other reasons.*
2. *Combined sample for French- and German-speaking Switzerland.*

As shown in Table 4.1, the situation is quite similar in all countries except Poland, which differs markedly from the others. It was more common to state situational barriers than institutional. This was particularly true for non-work-related education. In Poland, 59 per cent mentioned at least one situational barrier, whereas in the other countries the figure was around 75 per cent. With the exception of Poland, institutional barriers were somewhat more prevalent in connection with work-related than non-work-related education. Institutional barriers were cited less often in Switzerland and the Netherlands.

Looking at individual barriers, a general lack of time was the major reason for not having started a course one had needed or wanted to take. Around 60 per cent of the respondents in Canada, the Netherlands, Switzerland, and the United States gave this as the reason for not having started a non-work-related education programme. For work-related education and training, the figure in these countries was around 45 per cent. It was less common to refer to a specific situation, such as being too busy at work or family responsibilities. The latter was particularly absent in the Netherlands. Very few thought that a lack of employer support was the reason they had not started.

Among institutional barriers, financial reasons (too expensive/no money) was by far the most prevalent response. In Canada, Poland, and the United States, around one in three gave financial reasons for not having enrolled in work-related education. In Switzerland and the Netherlands, the figure was just over 15 per cent. It is worth noting that in Canada and the United States, financial reasons were more frequently mentioned as impediments to work-related education and training. Inconvenient time and courses not offered were, with the exception of Poland, rarely seen as a hindrance to engaging in non-work-related education. In Canada and Switzerland, a lack of appropriate courses was mentioned by around 10 per cent as a reason for not having engaged in work-related education. Health and language problems, which are regarded as dispositional barriers, were seldom brought up.

Closer inspection of the data on stated barriers reveals that general lack of time strongly dominated for both sexes. However, with the exception of the United States, it was somewhat more common among men (e.g. 67 per cent, versus 60 per cent in Canada). Women, on the other hand, were more prone to refer to family responsibilities. In the United States, 21.5 per cent of the women pointed to the family as a reason for not pursuing work-related studies, but only 8 per cent of the males. The situation was quite similar in the other countries. The gender inequalities as regards family responsibilities are also evident when it comes to work-related education and training. The gender differences were particularly noticeable in the United States and Poland.

Financial barriers to both work-related and non-work-related education were more pronounced among women than men in Switzerland. In the Netherlands and the United States, no such differences appeared, while Canadian women who had wanted to take work-related education mentioned a lack of money more often than men. Not surprisingly, those in higher income brackets (US$ 31,000 and above) mentioned financial barriers less often.

There were no clear relationships between age and barriers across countries. In Canada, Switzerland, and the United States, those up to 24 years of age mentioned situational barriers somewhat less than those 25 and over. The opposite was true for institutional barriers, which decreased with age in these countries as well as in Poland.

It is problematic to interpret the implications of the figures in Table 4.1 for a policy on lifelong learning for all. Lack of time, which emerges as the dominant barrier not only here but in almost all studies of this nature, is a vague concept. Time is not an endless resource but people have to make choices regarding how they want to spend their spare time. This is not to deny that because of work and family, some people may have very little time left over which they can use freely. Referring to the simple model in Figure 4.1, for many people mentioning "lack of time" is mainly a statement of the value they ascribe to adult education and training and the expected outcome of engaging in such a learning activity. Thus, it is of interest to note that participants and non-participants mentioned situational barriers to about the same extent. This was also the case with institutional barriers; in fact, there was a tendency for participants to slightly more often report these as the reason for not having taken other courses they were interested in. These findings are in line with Jonsson and Gähler (1996), who found that there were as many people with "objective" barriers in terms of various handicaps (having young children, long working hours, etc.) who participated in adult education as did not participate. They therefore conclude:

> "Instead of barriers, that might have to do with cost, lack of time, it is probably differences in expected rewards that can explain why some choose to participate while others remain outside" (Jonsson & Gähler 1996: 38).

We, of course, do not want to deny that some people face major barriers, like lack of childcare or high cost, that prevent them from participating. So, for example, the fact that fewer people in upper income brackets mentioned financial reasons is an indication that the answers not only reflect the willingness to pay but also the ability to do so. However, when Cross states that, "it is just as important to know why adults do not participate as why they do" (Cross 1980: 97), it is doubtful to what extent answers to questions regarding barriers do indeed shed light on the processes of non-participation. In light of the theoretical perspective presented above, we also have to look at the structural situation as a form of barrier that affects the usefulness a person ascribes to education and training.

Situational structures as barriers

The motive to participate is often discussed in terms of investment and consumption. To this should be added social mobilization. Here we are referring to the tradition within popular adult education connected to social movements to organize studies aimed at collective action. In some countries, particularly the Nordic ones, this has historically been a large and crucial component of the adult education scene. Official statistics and research reports (Bélanger & Valdivielso 1997; OECD 1996; Rubenson 1996; Skaalvik & Engesbak 1996) reveal the increased importance of adult education and training as investment, and document two important trends altering the "traditional" scene of adult education:

- publicly funded adult education is increasingly related to work; and

- employer-sponsored adult education is growing rapidly and is by far the largest sector of adult education provision.

The IALS data on participation presented in Tables 4.2 and 4.3 confirm a situation perhaps best characterized as "the long arm of the job".

Table 4.2.   Courses taken for career or personal reasons by country and by employer support (percentages)

	Career-or job-related	Personal or other	Total
Canada			
n	2,304	600	2,904
Employer supported	62.1	28.7	55.2
Non-employer supported	37.9	71.3	44.8
Switzerland (combined sample)			
n	973	615	1,588
Employer supported	64	32.7	51.9
Non-employer supported	36	67.3	48.1
United States			
n	1,753	243	1,996
Employer supported	71.8	30	66.7
Non-employer supported	28.2	70	33.3
Netherlands			
n	950	525	1,475
Employer supported	69.5	32.4	56.3
Non-employer supported	30.5	67.6	43.7
Poland			
n	383	123	506
Employer supported	74.9	20.3	61.7
Non-employer supported	25.1	79.7	38.3

Table 4.3. Courses supported by employers by country and motive (percentages)

	Employer supported	Non-employer supported	Total
Canada			
n	1,603	1,301	2,904
Career-or-job related	89.3	67.1	79.3
Personal or other	10.7	32.9	20.7
Switzerland (combined sample)			
n	824	764	1,588
Career-or-job related	75.6	45.8	61.3
Personal or other	24.4	54.2	38.7
United States			
n	1,331	665	1,996
Career-or-job related	94.5	74.4	87.8
Personal or other	5.5	25.6	12.2
Netherlands			
n	830	645	1475
Career-or-job related	79.5	45	64.4
Personal or other	20.5	55	35.6
Poland			
n	312	194	506
Career-or-job related	92	49.5	75.7
Personal or other	8	50.5	24.3

Table 4.2 shows that in all countries, at least half and in the case of the United States even two thirds of all participants received some support from their employer. Table 4.3 indicates that the strong influence of the world of work is also evident in the reasons for engaging in adult education or training. This was particularly the case in the United States, where 88 per cent of the participants had a career or job-related motive, and in Canada, where the figure was 79 per cent. Participation for non-job-related reasons was a bit more common in the Netherlands and Switzerland, where around 35 per cent had personal motives. The figures in Table 4.3 suggest that this might be because in these countries the employers were more willing to pay for courses people took for personal reasons. Thus, whereas US employers only supported 5.5 per cent of the courses taken for personal reasons, 24.4 per cent of Swiss employers supported the participants in these kinds of learning activity.

The data on financial support shown in Table 4.4 provide further support for the crucial role work plays in participation. The figures are based on all adults aged 16-64. Of particular interest is the extent of support from government in comparison to the support provided by employers. In the United States, only 4.5 per cent of adults reported that they had received financial support for education and training from the government, while as many as 26 per cent had received support from their employers. The smallest difference was in Canada, where the ratio was about 1 to 2 in favour of employer financial support. Self-financing also played a major role and was reported to about the same extent as employer support in Canada and the Netherlands. It was less frequent in the United States and somewhat more prevalent in Switzerland. In Poland, very few people received any form of financial support.

Table 4.4. Percentage of adults who received financial support from employers, governments and others

Country	n	Self or family	Employer	Government	Union or professional organization	Other	No fees
Canada	4,471	19.6	18.4	9.1	1.4	0.8	2.2
Netherlands	2,580	17.7	19.4	4.5	0.5	1.6	0.4
Poland	2,678	5.0	8.2	1.0	0.1	0.7	1.2
Switzerland	2,667	21.7	18.1	6.2	1.1	1.3	1.0
United States	2,831	14.6	26.0	4.5	0.7	1.2	2.0

1. *Sample includes all adults 16-64.*

The data in Tables 4.2, 4.3, and 4.4 raise the question of what work context provides employer- supported education and training and/or stimulates a search for non-employer-supported education for career and job-related reasons. As was shown in the preceding chapter, those most likely to receive employer-supported adult education and training were in the following occupations: professionals, senior officials and managers, and technicians and associate professionals. Further, they typically had a post-secondary education, often from a university, and were more likely to work in a large than in a small company. It is also interesting that they were in jobs that made substantial demands on their literacy skills. This finding is illustrated in Table 4.5. The figures are based on an analysis of pooled data, so national differences are not accounted for. However, a further chapter will show that the pattern is almost identical in the various countries, although the odds may differ somewhat.

Table 4.5 Likelihood of receiving employer support for training by demanded use of literacy skills at work, literacy competence, background characteristics, Country and occupation levels

Table 4.5. Likelihood of receiving employer support for training by demanded use of literacy skills at work, literacy competence, background characteristics, and occupation levels

	n	Percentage	Likelihood of receiving employer support Unadjusted	Adjusted
Canada	3,104	25.7	1.00	1.00
Switzerland	1,987	23.4	0.90	0.70^2
United States	2,142	32.7	1.44^2	1.58^2
Netherlands	1,726	28.4	1.14^1	1.32^1
Poland	1,612	13.4	0.45^2	1.59^2
Gender (Male)	5,931	26.2	1.00	1.00
Female	4,639	24.1	0.90^*	0.85
Age (17-24)	1,354	16.3	1.00	1.00
25-34 years	2,911	28.8	2.07^2	2.46^2
35-44 years	3,042	27.3	1.92^2	2.63^2
45-54 years	2,273	25.3	1.73^2	2.79^2
55-64 years	989	20.9	1.35^2	3.37^2
Education (Lower secondary or less)	979	8.8	1.00	1.00
Upper secondary	6,209	20.9	2.75^2	1.31
Non-university tertiary	1,350	33.9	5.32^2	1.07
University	1,922	41.6	7.41^2	0.97
Employment Status (Full-time)	8,788	26.7	1.00	1.00
Part-time	1,754	18.2	0.61^2	0.67^2
Income (US$18,000 or less)	1,188	11.2	1.00	1.00
No Income	256	11.0	0.99	1.08
$18,001 to $31,000	1,708	22.0	2.23^2	2.33^2
$31,001 to $47,000	2,185	29.4	3.30^2	3.14^2
$47,001 to $67,000	1,846	33.7	4.03^2	2.49^2
$67,001 or over	1,712	35.8	4.42^2	3.04^2
Type of Occupation (Elementary Occupation)	621	9.8	1.00	1.00
Senior Officials and Managers, Legislators	1,061	32.3	4.40^2	0.67
Professionals	1,636	41.5	6.54^2	0.74
Technicians, Associate Professionals	1,483	32.5	4.44^2	0.76
Clerks	1,352	28.3	3.65^2	0.57
Service workers, Shop Sales, etc.	1,517	17.8	2.00^2	0.10^1
Skilled Agricultural and Fishery	427	2.3	0.22^2	0.83
Craft Trades	1,324	19.6	2.25^2	0.88
Plant Operators and Assemblers	1,031	15.2	1.65^2	0.54

Table 4.5. **Likelihood of receiving employer support for training training by demanded use of literacy skills at work, literacy competence, background characteristics, and occupation levels (Concluded)**

			Likelihood of receiving employer support	
	n	Percentage	Unadjusted	Adjusted
Demand of Reading Skills (Level 1)[1]	**2,476**	**6.9**	**1.00**	**1.00**
Level 2 (next lowest demand quartile)	2,729	19.3	3.22[2]	1.24
Level 3 (next to highest demand quartile)	2,499	33.0	6.64[2]	1.77[2]
Level 4/5 (highest demand quartile)	2,745	41.4	9.53[2]	1.94[2]
Demand of Writing Skills (Level 1)	**2,607**	**7.8**	**1.00**	**1.00**
Level 2	2,570	22.3	3.38[2]	1.42[1]
Level 3	2,606	33.1	5.84[2]	1.47[2]
Level 4/5	2,720	37.8	7.16[2]	1.43[1]
Demand of Numerical Skills (Level 1)	**3,355**	**19.1**	**1.00**	**1.00**
Level 2	1,416	29.7	1.79[2]	1.02
Level 3	2,596	27.2	1.59[2]	0.93
Level 4/5	3,121	28.7	1.71[2]	0.74[2]
Reading Skills (Level 1)	**1,771**	**10.5**	**1.00**	**1.00**
Level 2	2,776	19.2	2.02[2]	1.10
Level 3	3,753	28.5	3.40[2]	1.40
Level 4/5	2,271	38.8	5.39[2]	1.42
Writing Skills (Level 1)	**1,720**	**10.5**	**1.00**	**1.00**
Level 2	3,073	19.9	2.12[2]	0.98
Level 3	3,862	28.1	3.35[2]	0.69
Level 4/5	1,915	41.4	6.04[2]	0.91
Quantitative Skills (Level 1)	**1,542**	**10.7**	**1.00**	**1.00**
Level 2	2,665	18.5	1.89[2]	0.77
Level 3	3,927	27.3	3.14[2]	0.74
Level 4/5	2,436	38.6	5.26[2]	0.82

1. Based on data for the 16-64 year-olds who were employed.
2. The term quartile refers to a separation of selected population into fourths based on the accumulated scores on variables related to demand of literacy use at work.

Table 4.5 looks at the likelihood of receiving employer support for adult education and training by country, use of literacy skills at work, background characteristics, and occupation. It provides estimates for the likelihood of adults receiving any kind of employer-supported education and training. These estimates derive from a logistic regression (Hosmer & Lemeshow 1978), where an odds ratio of 1 represents equal odds of a respondent receiving or not receiving training. Coefficients with a value less than 1 indicate less chance of receiving training, while coefficients with values greater than 1 represent an increased chance of receiving training, per one-unit increase in the independent or predictor variable.[1] So for example, according to Table 4.5, the likelihood (odds) of a Canadian receiving employer support was set at 1. From the results, it can be seen that the likelihood of a Pole receiving this kind of support was only 0.45 times that of a Canadian. However, the adjusted odds coefficient shows that when we take into account and control for the other factors included in the data analysis, Poles were 1.59 times more likely to receive employer support for training.

From Table 4.5, it is worth pointing out that there were only minor gender differences. What is not shown here is that, because women had a lower labour force participation rate, there were fewer women in total that received financial support from an employer, 14 per cent, versus 21 per cent of the men. Women, therefore, more often came to pay themselves for education and training, i.e. 18 per cent, versus 15 per cent of the men. As discussed more extensively in the next chapter on non-participation, there were major disparities with regard to type of occupation and level of education. However, these differences disappear when other variables were held constant in the model, which is explained by the close link between level of initial education and type of occupation.

It is interesting to note that the largest discrepancies for an individual variable (highest odds) can be observed for demand on reading skills at work. The higher the demand, the more likely it is for a person to receive some form of employer support. We can also see that when demands on literacy skills as well as other factors in the model are held constant, the adjusted odds coefficients for actual literacy levels are not significant. However, when reading skills and other factors are controlled for, those with jobs demanding the highest level of reading skills were still almost twice as likely to have received support as those with the jobs making the lowest demand (adjusted odds = 1.94).

The low relationships between demand for numerical skills and employer support is a bit puzzling and may have to do with the fact that many highly qualified jobs make relatively little demand on these skills.

---

[1]   *In multiple linear regression, coefficients are interpreted as the change in the dependent variable for a one-unit change in the predictor variable, given other variables in the model are held constant. Thus, the interpretation of an "effect" depends on which variables are included in the model. With logistic regression, a transformation of the coefficients, exp.(B), enables them to be interpreted in a similar way. The transformed logistic regression coefficient represents the change in the "odds ratio" [i.e., the Prob.(event)/Prob.(No event)] for a one-unit change in the predictor variable, given other variables in the model are held constant. In these analyses, the predictor variables have been coded as dummy variables, with an arbitrary reference category. The coefficients therefore can be interpreted as the odds of receiving training for the specified category compared with the reference category.*

The data in Table 4.5 shift the discussion on a strategy for lifelong learning for all from a supply to a demand issue. As regards the theoretical framework, it can be argued that to a large extent "valence" and "expectancy" are strongly influenced by the actual demand the job makes on literacy skills. Persons totally outside the labour-market or in jobs making little or no demands find themselves in a context that constitutes a major barrier to participation.

While work may be the foremost context regulating an individual's relationship to adult education and training, there is also the non-work aspect of everyday life. Unfortunately, the design constraints that applied to the IALS survey, particularly interview length and cost, made it impossible to collect much information about literacy demands connected with civil society and other aspects of everyday life. However, previous research has clearly demonstrated that those who participate in adult education are more often active in volunteer and political organizations (Jonsson & Gähler 1995; Rubenson 1996). Some support for this finding was offered in the previous chapter. Participants are also more likely to make use of literacy skills in the kind of hobbies and interests that they take up. Thus, not only may the demand for and practice of literacy skills at work be limited, but for the very same groups this can also be true of everyday life outside of work. These differences in demand for literacy point to major structural barriers and create a problematic situation for a policy on lifelong learning for all.

4.6   Policy Dilemmas

The crucial policy question is to what extent the state can and is willing to intervene in the societal and institutional processes and structures that create barriers to participation in adult education and training.

Judging from recent OECD *Reviews of National Policies for Education*, there is an unwillingness in policy circles to directly address the implications of "the long arm of the job", and in particular the increasing importance of employer-sponsored education and training for the distribution of learning opportunities. The common position seems to be to point out that it is not feasible to expect the public purse to cover the new demands and that ways must be found where the private sector and the individual contribute. As the IALS data on financial support and on who receives employer-sponsored education and training show, this will not be sufficient if one takes learning for *all* seriously. A polarization in demands made on literacy skills at work results in a polarization in learning opportunities.

A further complication is that employers, particularly in North America, seldom contribute to the general education of those with limited literacy skills. This leaves the public sector with the task of providing the foundation for lifelong learning to a large segment of the adult population with inadequate literacy skills. The cost scenarios for doing this are staggering. According to some estimates, the financial resources for educating those with low literacy proficiency in Germany would be 5.7 or 11.8 per cent of GDP, depending on whether the estimates are based on unit cost for secondary education or labour-market training. The same estimates for Sweden are 4.8 and 3.7 per cent of GDP (OECD 1996: 265). The situation for the United States and Canada, with their large numbers of citizens with low literacy levels, is even more severe. Thus, the discrepancy between available public funds, present funding regimes, and the extent of the task is a major barrier for lifelong learning for all.

As far as possible, government action must be concentrated not only on responding to demands but also on creating demand among those who see little value in education and training. In this context, it is of interest to compare the level of inequality in participation in adult education and training in Canada, the Netherlands, Sweden, Switzerland, and the United States. Sweden is also included in Table 4.6. This was not possible in the previous tables, as several questions were not asked in the Swedish survey.

The participation rates of around 40 per cent are quite similar in all countries except Sweden, where it is substantially higher (53 per cent). Not surprisingly, the data confirm the strong link between level of education and participation in adult education—the higher the level, the more likely a person is to participate. Of more interest are the differing levels of inequality between countries: in the Netherlands and Sweden, the differences appear to be substantially smaller than in the United States and Switzerland; Canada lies somewhere in-between. In Sweden, the high level of participation and comparatively low degree of inequality might be explained by the importance attributed to adult education and training by the social partners and government. Also important is the existence of a large, publicly funded voluntary sector, ear-marked funding for recruiting groups with low participation, and the tradition of industrial relations. These data provide some insights into how public policy on funding regimes and provision of adult education as well as strategies within industry affect the pattern of participation.

Using a broad interpretation of lifelong learning, which includes everyday learning, it is interesting that Sweden has a relatively high level of literacy in comparison to the other countries included in Table 4.6 (see OECD & Statistics Canada 1991). Further a Sweden's high levels of literacy and participation in adult education are accompanied by an extensive practice of literacy at work and, to the extent it is possible to judge from previous research, in civil society. This can be seen as a reflection of the active learning-demands the society makes not only on its elite but also, more importantly, on broad segments of the population. However, despite these positive features, there still exists in Sweden a large group of middle-aged persons living in a low literacy context and with no interest in adult education and training.

Table 4.6. Participation by educational attainment and country (Percentages and odds, 1994)

Level of Education	Canada			Netherlands			Sweden			Switzerland			United States		
	n	Part. %	Odds %	n	Part. %	Odds %	n	Part. %	Odds %	n	Part. %	Odds %	n	Part. %	Odds %
Primary or less	544	15.7	1	371	17.5	1	272	29.0	1	157	8.5	1	253	12.1	1
Some secondary	818	27.9	2.08[2]	718	29.4	1.92[2]	238	47.0	2.17[2]	346	21.7	2.95[2]	159	23.5	2.76[2]
Secondary completed	1,510	35.8	3.00[2]	984	44.7	3.79[2]	984	53.2	2.82[2]	1438	46.1	9.07[2]	126	33.7	3.79[2]
Tertiary non-university	803	53.7	6.24[2]	N.A.	N.A.	N.A.	288	66.6	4.83[2]	256	57.6	14.47[2]	418	58.0	9.88[2]
University	740	59.8	8.00[2]	493	53.2	5.33[2]	257	70.1	5.78[2]	237	59.3	15.53[2]	643	67.0	14.60[2]
Total	**4,415**	**39.4**		**2,566**	**38.1**		**2,039**	**53.3**		**2,434**	**42.7**		**2,739**	**42.6**	

N.A. Category not applicable.
1 p<.05.
2 p<.01.

Looking at the provision of adult education, several *Reviews of National Policies for Education* have sent a strong message about the present and future importance of the role played by the voluntary sector in delivering adult education (OECD 1990 and 1996). These reviews found that this sector is more flexible and adapts to new demands more quickly than the formal system. Also, it seems to reach adults who otherwise would not enrol in adult education. In addition, as the team examining Norway points out, this form of adult education could be of potential importance not only for civil society but also in the economic sector. However, the integration of the voluntary sector into a comprehensive adult education and training policy can be successful only if direct state intervention is avoided. As long as the goals for which state funding is received are fulfilled, the sector must be left to itself. However, this "hands-off" requirement might be perceived as a threat by the state bureaucracy, which seems to deter funding and acts as a barrier.

References

Bélanger, P. 1997. "The extent and the diversity of adult learning - an overview of adult education participation in industrialized countries". In: P. Bélanger and S. Valdivielso (eds.). *The Emergence of Learning Societies: Who Participates in Adult Learning?* Oxford: Pergamon Press.

Broady, D. 1991. *Sociologi och Epistemologi.* Stockholm: HLS Förlag.

Carnoy, M. 1995. "Foreword: How should we study adult education". In: C.A. Torres *The Politics of Nonformal Education in Latin America.* New York: Praeger.

Cross, K.P. 1981. *Adults as Learners.* San Francisco: Jossey-Bass.

Dohmen, G. 1996. *Lifelong Learning. Guidelines for a Modern Education Policy.* Bonn: Federal Ministry of Education, Science, Research, and Technology.

Esping-Andersen, G. 1989. "The three political economies of the welfare state". In: *Canadian Review of Sociology and Anthropology* (26): 10-36.

Eyerman, R. and Jamison, A. 1991. *Social Movements. A Cognitive Approach.* University Park, Philadelphia/ PA: Pennyslvania State University Press.

Giddens, A. 1984. *The Constitution of Society.* Berkely, CA: University of California Press.

Giddens, A. 1994. *Beyond Left and Right.* Stanford/CA: Stanford University Press.

Habermas, J. 1983. *Borgerlig Offentlighet.* Lund: Arkiv.

Härnqvist, K. 1989. *Background. Education and Work as Predictors of Adult Skills.* (Report No. 1989:01) Göteborg: Department of Educational Research, Göteborg University.

Hommen, L. 1997. "The British Columbia Labour Force Development Board delivering consensus". In: R. Haddow (ed.). *The Emergence of Labour Force Development Boards in Canada.* Toronto: Toronto University Press.

Hommen, L. 1994. *Setting Patterns: Technological Change, Labour Adjustment, and Training in British Columbia's Lumber Manufacturing Industry.* (Ph. D. Dissertation) Vancouver: University of British Columbia.

Hosmer, D.W., and Lemeshow, S. 1989. *Applied Logistic Regression.* New York: John Wiley and Sons.

Johnstone, J., and Rivera, R. 1965. *Volunteers for Learning.* Hawthorne, N.Y: Aldine.

Jonsson, J., and Gähler, M. 1995. "Folkbildning och Vuxenstudier. Rekrytering. Omfattning. Erfarenheter". In: *Statens Offentliga Utredningar* (141). Stockholm: Fritzes.

Jonsson, J., and Gähler. M. 1996. "Folkbildning och vuxenstudier: rekrytering, omfattning, erfarenheter-sammanfattning". In: *Statens Offentliga Utredningar* (159). Stockholm: Fritzes.

Korpi, W. 1978. *Arbetarklassen i Välfärdskapitalismen.* Stockholm: Prisma.

Larsson, S. et al. 1986. *Arbetsupplevelse och Utbildningssyn hos Icke Facklärda.* (Göteborg Studies in Educational Sciences). Göteborg: University of Göteborg.

Lundwall, B.-A. 1991. " Explaining inter firm co-operation and innovation: The limits of the transaction cost approach". In: G. Grahber (ed.). The *Embedded Firm: On the Socio-Economics of Industrial Networks.* London: Mansell.

Lyman, S.M. 1995. *Social Movements: Critiques, Concepts, Case-studies.* New York: NewYork University Press.

McIntyre, J., Brown, A., and Ferrier, F. 1996. *The Economics of ACE Delivery.* Sydney: BACE.

Nonaka, I. 1994. "A dynamic theory of organizational knowledge creation". In: *Organizational Science* 51: 15-37.

Nordhaug, D. 1991. *The Shadow Educational System: Adult Resource Development.* Oslo: Universitetsförlaget.

OECD. 1991. *Reviews of National Policies for Education - Norway.* Paris: Organisation for Economic Co-operation and Development.

OECD and Statistics Canada. 1995a. *Literacy, Economy and Society: Results of the First International Adult Literacy Survey.* Paris and Ottawa: Organisation for Economic Co-operation and Development and Statistics Canada.

OECD. 1995b. *Reviews of National Policies for Education - Hungary.* Paris: Organisation for Economic Co-operation and Development.

OECD. 1996. *Lifelong Learning for All.* (Report of the meeting of the Education Committee at ministerial level, 16-17 January 1996). Paris: Organisation for Economic Co-operation and Development.

Putnam, R. D. 1993. *Making Democracy Work: Civic Traditons in Modern Italy.* Princeton, N.J.: Princeton University Press.

Rothstein, B. (ed.). 1995. *Demokratirådets Rapport 1995. Demokrati som Dialog* Stockholm: SNS Förlag.

Rubenson, K. 1988.

Rubenson, K. 1997. "Sweden: the impact of the politics of participation". In: P. Bélanger and S. Valdivielso (eds.). *The Emergence of Learning Societies: Who Participates in Adult Learning?* Oxford: Pergamon Press.

Rubenson, K. 1996. " Studieförbundens roll i vuxenutbildningen". In: *Statens Offentliga Utredningar* (154). Stockholm: Fritzes.

Skaalvik, E.M., and Engesbak, H. 1996. "Selvrealisering og kompetanseutvikling. Rekruttering til voksenopplaering i et tjugarsperspektiv". In: S. Tosse (ed.). *Fra lov til Reform.* Trondheim: NVI.

Stephens, J.D. 1996. "The Scandinavian welfare states: Achievements, crisis and prospects". In: G. Esping-Andersen (ed.). *Welfare States in Transition.* London: Sage Publications.

Touraine, A. 1995. *Critique of Modernity.* Oxford: Blackwell.

Chapter 5

The Non-participation of Undereducated Adults

B. Allan Quigley and Stephen Arrowsmith

5.1 Introduction

In industrialized countries, it often seems that "lifelong learning" is conceptualized as a sort of "parade", with endless columns of citizens marching forward. We see them confidently passing the checkpoints of normative knowledge: kindergarten, public school, vocational education and training, tertiary education, and onward to boundless adult education opportunities. If this metaphor of modernity holds up, then those adult basic and literacy educators who work with society's undereducated may be pictured as beneath the surface of the parade route, working with those who have "fallen through the cracks". As the parade metaphor becomes the "information superhighway" involving exponentially higher levels of reliance on electronic and other technologies, the normative knowledge employed in industrialized countries is seen as moving further and further from the reach of the undereducated in society. As Shohet (1993) put it:

> "We mouth platitudes about living in an age when access to, and control over, information constitute a new form of capital. [...but] we are in the process of creating a new underclass of the dispossessed and the exploited in all those adults who lack the skills to accept, choose and use the information that is multiplying faster than the most literate among us can comprehend." (as cited in Hautecoeur 1994b: 346)

After failing to "eradicate" low literacy in America through most of the 20th century (Cook 1977; Quigley 1997), and following decades of literacy campaigns which rarely met their stated objectives (Arnove & Graff 1987; Carron & Bordia 1985; Gayfer 1987), it is surely time to ask what it is policy-makers and adult educators are realistically hoping to achieve with the undereducated who remain present in large numbers in the industrialized countries. Exacerbating matters, study after study reveals that a large proportion of the undereducated do not—possibly will not—participate in the adult education and training programmes provided. Ironically, it is the best educated, not the least, who benefit most from public and private investment in adult education. As Rubenson noted:

> "A close look at different forms of adult education reveals that the better an education pays off in terms of income, status, occupation, political efficacy, cultural competence, and similar matters, the greater the differences in socioeconomic status between participants and non-participants." (1989: 64)

Clearly there is a need to reconsider what the role of adult education should be—and realistically can be—with the undereducated in the coming years. Perhaps the greatest challenge facing educators and policy-makers concerns the question, "How can we learn from others", rather than, "How can we teach others"? Instead of asking, "What are the answers to the problem of the undereducated", the question ought to be, "What are the appropriate questions and who should we be listening to"? Bourdieu (1971) has stated: "Reality is not an absolute [...] it differs with the group to which one belongs" (p. 195). If history tells us anything in the area of undereducation, ultimately the question of "Whose reality" is pivotal both for the educational future of large numbers of undereducated adults and for the value of public expenditure on adult basic education in industrialized countries.

Unfortunately, to raise the issue of those who have obtained less than a complete high school or upper secondary education (the "undereducated") and the fact that they participate far less frequently in adult education than those with higher levels of educational attainment is to invite a range of value-laden assumptions and speculations. According to Fingeret (1983), these assumptions are socially hegemonic and deeply ingrained: "Educators believe that literacy is fundamental to competence and independence in modern society; it is difficult for us to conceptualize life without reading and writing as anything other than a limited, dull, dependent existence" (1983: 133). The literature reveals that it has also been difficult for educators and policy-makers to conceptualize low participation rates of the undereducated as much more than the aberrant behaviour of those in a condition of individual deficit (Fingeret 1984). The exceptions, however, have been during times of national crises—perceived or real. Typically, during such times low levels of education and their attendant low participation rates have been decried as the pathology of an invisible enemy threatening the economy, the well-being and safety of citizens, even democracy itself (Arnove & Graff 1987; Quigley 1997).

How we see the undereducated is no insignificant issue for policy, research, or practice. In the recent *National Adult Literacy Survey* (Kirsch et al. 1993) in the United States, considered the most comprehensive and reliable US study of the latter half of the 20th century, it was found that, "The approximately 90 million adults who performed in Levels 1 and 2 [lowest literacy levels] *did not necessarily perceive themselves as being 'at risk'*" [emphasis added] (p. xv). What does this mean for adult educators and policy-makers? For the authors of this study, it evidently meant that no less than 40 per cent of the 191 million adults in the United States (census population estimates) are too undereducated to fully realize what they are doing: "Even if adults who perform in the lowest literacy levels are not experiencing difficulties at present, they *may* be at risk as the nation's economy and social fabric continue to change" [emphasis added] (1983, p. xix). Is it possible that the educational solutions being offered in society are in fact "answers" to those problems which are selected on purpose?

The four arguments pursued in this chapter are intended to compel the field to reconsider some of the most socially sacred and, otherwise, most professionally self-serving assumptions:

- It is impossible to address the issues which arise out of the non-participation of the undereducated or build access to a basic education with inappropriate tools. The theories and research which have informed mainstream adult education on participation should not always be accepted as the appropriate research models for the undereducated, nor should the questions these have traditionally sought to investigate be assumed to be those of the undereducated;

- Questions relating to the participation of the undereducated would be more meaningfully researched if understood as a phenomenon of *non-participation*—not an aberration of the unaware, but one with meaning rich in implications, as examples of successful research and practice will show;

- The phenomenon of non-participation needs to be understood through sociological frameworks, not merely functional psychological ones, as will be discussed;

- The policy and research implications arising from the large non-participant group in the six industrialized societies studied in this chapter might be more meaningful if "adult education" in this context were not so distinctly divided into a participation/non-participation duality, and if the focus in our understanding of the issues were less on formal/non-formal types of education and training.

Rather, if *lifelong learning* were the true point of reference, then one might begin to draw a map where "undereducated" adults were seen to engage in multiple types of adult learning through self-directed, informal, and incidental learning throughout their lives. Rather than concentrating on normative education provided in formal institutions, the focus ought to be on the wider concept of lifelong learning—defined as "the process of *learning* which occurs throughout the lifespan" (Jarvis 1990). "For research and policy, as Fingeret posed it in 1991 to a UNESCO literacy seminar, it might be time to shift the central question [...] from "How many" to "How does change happen"? "(p. 17)

5.2   The Wrong End of the Telescope? Adult Basic Education and Participation Theory

Non-participation is clearly the uncomfortable side of the participation construct. Many educators and governments would rather consider the glass to be half full than half empty. The language of modernity is that of "progress"—for example, progress in closing the participation gaps. Government reports and research studies still carry euphemisms such as "retention" (not attrition) and "participation" (not non-participation). Even those who disagree with the lexicon of deficit must use the language given—such as the terms "undereducation" and "basic education" employed in this chapter. Thus, one ends up speaking about the "disadvantaged" and the "marginalized" when referring to those with lower levels of formal schooling. The literacy research shows that some of society's wealthiest (Clark 1990; Manning 1983) and most stalwart citizens (Eberle & Robinson 1980; Fingeret 1983; Manning 1983) are presented as being "marginalized" to one another.

Moving out of a history of social deficit and a singular societal expectation that remediation is the sole purpose of adult basic education (Arnove & Graff 1987; Fingeret 1983; Quigley 1987), the literacy field has frequently turned to school-based teaching methods, school-oriented curricula, classroom management practices, and schooling perceptions to provide what, not surprisingly, often ends up as remediation (Cook 1977; Fingeret & Danin 1991; Quigley 1989). Uncritical borrowing has been shown to hold the potential for compounding certain problems experienced by minorities, women, single parents, and those with learning difficulties (Horsman 1991; Kazemak 1988; O'Brien 1979). It is only fairly recently that many borrowed schooling models have been called into doubt in adult basic education (Fingeret & Jurmo 1989; Gowen 1992; Street 1987; Stuckey 1991). As Bohnenn described changes in literacy practices in the Netherlands: "The methods used in school for reading and writing, which failed these adults, cannot be used again" (1987: 27).

There is a slow but deliberate move towards what Wikelund, Reder, and Hart-Landsberg (1992) found in a meta-analysis of research studies on literacy participation in the United States: "Programmes will be most effective when they 'situate' instruction within the activities, lives, values and cultures of their individual learners" (1992: 4). The many calls for an education based on the lived experiences and needs of learners is beginning to be heard (e.g. International Development Research Center 1979; Haggis 1991; Hautecoeur 1994a). However, much remains to be accomplished before research and practice can be successfully "situated" within the lives of both participants and non-participants.

Participation research and mainstream adult education

Participation has been a major research issue in adult education for decades. But often the realities of the "undereducated" were studied through the wrong end of the telescope. The fact is that only a small proportion of adults without completed upper secondary education return to the adult basic or literacy programmes that are on offer in a society—in the United States, for example, it is only about 8 per cent of the identified population (Beder 1994), and less than 5 per cent by other counts (Cain & Whalen 1979). As will be discussed, the average participation rate of undereducated adults aged 25-65 in both formal and non-formal adult education in the Netherlands, Poland, Switzerland, Canada, the United States, and Sweden is shown to be only 13.5 per cent. A discussion of the involvement of undereducated people in traditional adult education initiated by others—not by the learners themselves—surely needs to be focused on the large majority. Unfortunately, however, the research on non-participation still tends to be dominated by the concepts and methods derived from the mainstream of the adult education literature.

Mainstream adult education embraced participation as one of its "big research questions" as early as 1964 in the United States (Courtney 1989) and did so partly out of the politics of forming adult education as a field of academic study. In *Adult Education: Outlines of an Emerging Field of Practice* (Hallenbeck 1964), which was seminal in establishing an academic discipline of adult education in the American university setting, a case was made for the "general acceptance of adult education" (p. 13). Hallenbeck made an argument, to be echoed through the decades, pointing to "increased participation in adult educational activities on the part of adults in the United States", and adding: "the number of facets of society in which adult education has come to have a place, and the vast amount of money being spent for adult education testif[ies] to [...] its important role in American life" (p. 13). These are not the dynamics or the history of the creation of the much older field of adult basic and literacy education (Cook 1977; Grattan 1955; Quigley 1997; Verner 1973).

Adult basic and literacy education early on became a sub-field of mainstream adult education. In the late 1950s, for example, adult basic education activities were categorized in the US literature as "remedial, assimilative, mobility-promoting, and compensatory" (Floud & Halsey 1958). This categorization was accepted widely, and it has since been in use essentially unchanged (e.g. Schroeder 1970). Despite its different history and the unique policy and social issues addressed, adult basic education has become part of the traditional mainstream. With its "subaltern status", the field of adult basic and literacy education has unfortunately either uncritically inherited or uncritically borrowed many of the paradigms and research models developed in the larger field, including traditional participation models and theories. Even though the fallacy that all adults are somehow "alike" is forcefully denied in the mainstream literature (e.g. Merriam & Caffarella 1991; Brookfield 1986), it often seems that certain dimensions of educational, motivational, and socioeconomic homogeneity are taken for granted when the issue of the participation of the undereducated arises.

The logic of non-participation by undereducated adults

No area of adult education research and policy is more myth-laden than that of the undereducated. First, those who do not participate in the programmes provided do not necessarily "lack motivation" or "lack opportunity". It has been shown that many undereducated adults cannot responsibly attend adult education programmes and still care for their children, hold jobs, deal with health or income problems, and cope with a host of situational barriers (Taylor & Draper 1989). Research studies as well as earnings and employment statistics indicate that situational barriers are often far more problematic for the undereducated than for adults with higher levels of educational attainment. There is a difference in quality, if not in kind, when educators speak of "access". For many undereducated women, for instance, Horsman (1989) found:

> "Whether they were able to attend or wished to attend was bound up with the relationships in their lives: social agencies required it of them, men were opposed to their attendance or supported them, and the needs of children might either provide a barrier to attendance or be the main focus for their desire to improve their literacy skills." (p. 373)

There are significant differences of response among older undereducated adults when "compensatory education" is offered. Beder (1989) found in his state-side research that "older adults are considerably less likely to perceive the need [for adult basic education]" (p. 93). Differences of lived experiences and their effects on the undereducated when perceiving the value of "remedial" education has just begun to be researched, as will be discussed, but it cannot be assumed that the theories which apply to the decisions to attend higher education (e.g. Cross 1982) are interchangeable with those facing undereducated adults who are to be "assimilated" and "compensated" through adult education.

On an institutional level, it has been documented that institutions carry inherent problems for the undereducated—tuition costs, scheduling, and access issues, to name but a few (Beder 1991; Fingeret 1984). Again, whereas institutional barriers are not unique to the undereducated—college students face situational and institutional barriers, too—frequently, issues of tuition, scheduling and accessibility are exacerbated for the undereducated. The impact of similar issues on dissimilar groups needs comparative research, but perhaps the most significant difference needing further study is the impact of the common experience of early leaving among those with less than an upper secondary or high-school education, and the common impact of persisting in school among those who enter mainstream adult education. Past educational experiences may be assumed to have been positive for those with completed upper secondary or some post-secondary education (Johnstone & Rivera 1965). In contrast, Cervero & Fitzpatrick (1990) found through a longitudinal study of 18,000 students from 1,200 US schools that adults who were school dropouts typically had very ambiguous feelings about past schooling experiences and re-entered formal and non-formal adult education at far lower rates. As the authors concluded, those who quit school early are "shaped [...] by a powerful set of social circumstances" (p. 92), including the profoundly negative effects of schooling. The conclusion the authors reached in their longitudinal study was that "officials, educators and *other researchers* [emphasis added] must better understand the long-standing and enduring nature of the factors in which a decision to participate is embedded before they decry the low participation rates [... in] adult basic education and job retraining" (p. 92). Wikelund, Reder, and Hart-Landsberg, following a meta-analysis of the literature, observed that "undereducated participants and potential participants tend to perceive and experience the adult education programmes [...] as extensions or continuations of the school programmes in which they have previously experienced failure, loss of self-esteem, and lack of responsiveness to their personal needs and goals" (1992: 4).

Despite such complexities, which would suggest that adult basic education needs its own body of participation research, the field has inherited mainstream participation models and assumptions. Darkenwald (1986) observed that the mainstream participation models introduced by Boshier (1973) and Rubenson and Hoghielm (1978) should be used in all participation research, claiming that "the quality of adult basic education research on participation and dropout would be vastly improved" (p. 12). More recently, Beder (1991) dedicated two chapters of his book *Adult Literacy: Issues for Policy and Practice* to participation, motivation, and non-participation, beginning with a summary of the adult motivation models and mainstream participation research. These included Miller's force field analysis model (1967), Boshier's congruence model (1973 1977), the expectancy-valence model of motivation proposed by Rubenson (1977), and the chain-of-response model developed by Cross (1982). Some of these theories and models have been infrequently applied to adult basic education research in the United States, such as expectancy-valence theory (e.g. van Tilburg & DuBois 1989; Quigley 1993b), but most have not.

The undereducated have been found to have much in common with people with more privileged backgrounds. It appears, for instance, that the reasons for participation mentioned by the undereducated are similar to those given by highly educated adults, based on those who do participate in forms of adult education. In his review of the participation literature, which included research studies concerned with undereducated adults, Beder (1991) reached the conclusion that among those who participate, "it can be inferred that in respect to kinds of motivations exhibited, students in adult basic education differ very little from the general population" (p. 65). He found that there were 10 consistent sets of motivation for participation among the undereducated and the general population:

"Self-improvement, family responsibilities, diversion, literacy development, community/church involvement, job advancement, launching [into better quality of life situations], economic need, educational advancement, and urging of others" (pp. 59-60). It should be noted, however, that this finding is based on the minority—between 5 and 8 per cent of the adult population in the United States—who choose to participate in adult basic education programmes (Beder 1994). Can the participating minority be considered representative of the vast majority not participating with any research credibility? Hayes (1988) studied deterrents to literacy participation by investigating participants in adult basic education programmes in the United States. She was criticized by Beder, who noted that, "Hayes' subjects were enrolled in adult literacy programmes; they were not non-participants. Thus [Hayes'] [...] study on deterrents to participation was conducted on the basis of a sample of adults who, by enrolling in literacy education, had demonstrated that they were not deterred" (1991: 89).

As Thomas (1983) put it: "The level and commitment to research activity in adult basic education [...] is not very great and is related to the small number of faculty members working in the field" (p. 107). It is important, therefore, that the few who do research such issues in industrialized countries work on the questions which are most relevant to the undereducated, do so within appropriate populations, and employ appropriate methods and relevant theoretical frameworks.

5.3   The Emergence of Alternative Research Paradigms

The early "deterrents" research literature

At the risk of truncating research history, in North America the research on adult basic and literacy education prior to 1970 was mostly descriptive, typically anecdotal, and highly influenced by psychological paradigms and deficit assumptions (Anderson & Niemi 1970). Fingeret (1984) found that these trends had continued into the 1980s. She categorized the research on adult basic education into "informal accounts of experiences" working with adult learners, "how-to-manuals and guides", and a limited number of "theoretical and philosophical articles exploring some of the underlying assumptions, values, and beliefs about literacy" (p. 3). It is safe to say that the "participation research" prior to the early 1980s was based on the "lack of participation" concept. It was largely based on the identification of internal and external deterrents, such as undereducated adults' allegedly unstable and transitory lives, the internal deviancies of the undereducated themselves, or the problems encountered in attempts to reach out to the "hard-to-reach".

Often school-based and psychological studies have helped to engrain a deficit perspective in society's understanding of the undereducated. Studies such as that by Reissman (1962) reached the conclusion that, among the least educated, "there is practically no interest in knowledge for its own sake [...] Nor is education seen as an opportunity for the development of self-expression, self-realization growth or the like" (p. 12). Reissman's 30-year-old assertions are carried quite uncritically in major adult education textbooks, such as *Adults as Learners* (see Cross 1982: 55-56). References also continue to appear to other early studies which stereotyped undereducated adults as being deficient in some ways. Anderson & Niemi's (1970) meta-analysis of the findings of pre-1970s research in Canada and the United States provided a list of incredible attributes of low-literate adults, including reports that low-literates: "often did not talk with their children at meal time [...] Hence, such children were ill prepared for entry into a middle-class school" (p. 27). They were "authoritarian and resort to physical rather than verbal dominance" (p. 21). It was claimed, in addition, that low-literate adults were "markedly reactionary in socio-political areas but somewhat favourable to economic liberalism" (p. 21). Although these assertions would assuredly have been challenged had they been about racial minority groups in industrialized countries (Beder 1991), as recently as 1980, Irish (1980) nevertheless framed her recruitment recommendations around Anderson and Niemi's (1970) stereotypes, asserting that the psychological characteristics of low-literate people include "insecurity, distrust, fatalism, low aspirations, limited time perspective, dependency, localism, and lack of empathy" (p. 41).

During the same period, however, a more complex and promising body of research studies on adult education participation began to emerge. One award-winning report, which has provided many insights relevant for both mainstream adult education and adult basic education, was that by Johnstone and Rivera (1965). Concerning the undereducated, they found that just as the well-educated have learned to embrace educational opportunities, those who have rejected or feel they have been rejected by school systems do not seek such opportunities to the same extent:

> "Lower-class resistance to adult education [...] does not appear to stem from feelings that education cannot do anything for a person, nor from a belief that one does not need an education to get ahead in the world. The feelings, rather, seem to be of a more diffuse nature and are undoubtedly a carry-over from [...] school and education which develops one's earliest contacts with the formal educational system" (p. 241).

Pursuing this logic of non-participation, some researchers in North America and elsewhere began to establish an area of studies in adult basic and literacy education built around the perceptions of reluctant adult participants, dropouts of traditional adult education, and undereducated non-participants who have chosen to question schooling, adult education, and the normative assumptions they are perceived to contain (e.g. Beder 1989 1991; Fingeret 1984; Gowen 1992; Hayes 1988; Darkenwald & Valentine 1985; Cervero & Fitzpatrick 1990; Horsman 1991; Martindale & Drake 1989; Quigley 1997; Scanlan & Darkenwald 1984; Stuckey 1991; Ziegahn 1992). This body of research explicitly seeks the inclusion of a non-participant perspective which is not assumed to be deviant, irresponsible, and poor.

The evolution of the non-participation research literature

Research on the undereducated with respect to their participation in adult basic education has evolved through three major phases since the mid-1970s. Firstly, participation research benefited from the adoption of theories and models derived from sociology. Accordingly, studies began to investigate factors arising from socio-economic differences, cultural diversity, gender and, albeit to a lesser extent, ethnicity and race. More sophisticated psychological and reading research studies were also added to the field (Scribner & Cole 1978). Studies in reading provided new knowledge on, for instance, learning disabilities (e.g. Bowren 1981), cognitive processes (Uhland 1995), field dependence and independence (Quigley 1987), ethnic differences (e.g. Heisel & Larson 1984), intrinsic motivation (Csikszentmihalyi 1990), as well as on different adult reading strategies (Boraks & Richardson 1981; Boraks & Schumacher 1981; Daneman 1991; Danis 1988; Green 1980).

Secondly, there has been a distinct move towards defining, interpreting, and addressing the issues of non-participation itself. This second, nascent thrust has been "situated" in the lives and perceptions of the non-participating adults themselves. Wikelund, Reder, and Hart-Landsberg (1992), for example, concluded in a review of the participation and non-participation literature that researchers working in the field of adult basic education "must recognize the wide range of perspectives that may exist regarding something so seemingly positive as literacy or education" (p. 23) and that we need to "understand the powerful influence of culture in shaping those perspectives" (p. 23).

Thirdly, although Benseman (1989) has cautioned against the substitution of barriers for theory, in adult basic education there has been a move away from a focus on singular deterrents to a more robust conceptualization of the multiple barriers affecting undereducated adults' decisions to participate or not. As will be seen, the sheer diversity of the barriers under investigation has led researchers to begin to consider theories unique to the undereducated adults who do not participate in the formal and non-formal programmes offered to them.

The introduction of sociological theory

Rubenson has observed that if the wider field of adult education "takes for granted that the adult is a conscious, self-directed individual in possession of the instruments vital to making use of the available possibilities for adult education— a system that relies on self-selection to recruit participants—[it] will by necessity widen, not narrow the educational [...] gaps in society" (1989: 65). Theories of reproduction (e.g. Bowles & Gintis 1977; Willis 1977) have long argued that human agency is limited by the restrictions and hegemonies of society. As early as 1940, C. Wright Mills explained that the construct "motivation" must be considered in a wider sociological frame, not merely in an individualistic or subjective frame: "Motives vary in context and character with historical epochs and societal structures" (1940: 904).

For critical educators, many of whom were informed by the New Sociology of Education, the main purpose of public education was seen to be social integration, by preparing youth for an unequal future (Willis 1977). The inclusion of reproduction theory in the education literature has, however, had only a modest impact on adult education. Rubenson (1989) has discussed reproduction theories and their applications to adult education, and introduced the theory of structuration (Giddens 1984) to adult education. He and others (e.g. Jarvis 1983; Griffin 1987) have argued that choices made by adult learners are not as "voluntary" as policy-makers and educators would like to think. Participant choices and learners' human agency, it has been argued, are affected by the lived situation and the learned frames of cultures and societies. As a consequence, "context and structure become critical" (Rubenson 1989: 39) to any understanding of adult education and adults' participation in it.

The recent trend has been to accommodate the analysis and interpretation of non-participation from a macro-sociological rather than an individualistic micro-psychological perspective (Quigley 1990; Beder 1991). In Britain, Willis (1977) used ethnography to study resistant working class "lads" in Midlands high schools. Fine (1982) investigated the resistance of young females who quit school not, as Giroux (1983) put it, out of "deviance and learned helplessness" but out of "moral and political indignation" (p. 289). Informed by the economic, political, and cultural reproduction literature (e.g. Bourdieu 1971; Bourdieu & Passeron 1977; Giroux 1983; Apple 1991;), research into adult basic education began to consider theories of resistance as "expressions of counter-hegemony" in the late 1980s (e.g. Quigley 1990; Stuckey 1991; Gowen 1992). Even more recently, resistance to "dominant culture literacy" has been documented in Spain (Carrasco 1994); and among the Maori in New Zealand (Yates 1996); and issues of "cultural survival" have been documented among indigenous peoples in Canada (Fogwill 1994), in minority cultures such as in Quebec (Dionne & Horth 1994), and in the State of Tennessee (Bingham & White 1994). Accordingly, the reluctance and resistance of some undereducated adults to participate has been termed to have its own "logic" in the adult basic education research literature (Quigley 1990; Gowen 1992). Hence, what may be seen as a vast array of educational opportunities by the educated elite can also be seen as irrelevant, even alien, terrain to others whose educational and cultural experiences have taught them negative lessons about the rules of "dominant" culture.

Current non-participation themes and emerging directions

What themes and directions appear to be emerging? In the North American literature, Valentine and Darkenwald (1990) provided one of the earliest quantitative studies on adults who chose not to participate in adult education. Although it was a questionnaire-based study set in one of the wealthiest regions of the United States, nevertheless 37 per cent of the total included had not finished upper secondary education. They grouped the reasons for non-participation into "external deterrents" (59 per cent of the sample) and "internal deterrents" (41 per cent of the sample). This grouping and a focus on the undereducated began to point to the complexity of the decisions made by the non-participants. Beder (1990a, 1990b) conducted the first major series of quantitative studies on undereducated adults. In Iowa, using telephone interviews among a relatively small number of non-participating and undereducated adults, he identified four clusters of factors for non-participation: i) low perception of need; ii) perceived difficulty; iii) dislike of school; and iv) situational barriers. This approach was highly revealing, since so many of the previous research studies had assumed that situational barriers and psychological deficiencies accounted for the "lack of motivation" among the undereducated.

In the mainstream research on non-participation, one can note adults' concern for lack of programme quality (e.g. Scanlan & Darkenwald 1984), a lack of relevance in courses offered (e.g. Darkenwald & Valentine 1985; Martindale & Drake 1989), and questions about the relevance of certain education or training programmes to professional practice (e.g. Blais, Duquette & Painchaud 1989; Beder 1991). However, Beder's (1991) conclusion was that the issue of non-participation among the undereducated was much more fundamental to the acceptance of schooling itself: "Negative attitudes toward adult education" existed among the undereducated and "these negative attitudes seem to pertain to school itself—and to the things associated with it" (p. 95). This perception has been confirmed by Baldwin (1991) in a nation-wide and quantitative survey conducted in the United States; by Fingeret (1985) in a qualitative research study carried out in North Carolina; by Thomas (1990) in her work in British Columbia; and by Quigley (1989 1993b) in his qualitative investigations conducted in Pennsylvania.

Quigley (1997) has found that undereducated non-participating adults often contextualize the normative construct "education", but rather than infer a set of "positive" connotations, as do the formally well-educated, many undereducated adults understand "education" to be but one concept—the most desirable concept—of a three-part continuum of access and acceptability: i) "education as a dream"; ii) "learning as necessity"; and iii) "schooling as unacceptable". Using in-depth interviews, subjects were asked about "education" for their children, themselves, or many of their relatives and friends. On this, they were highly positive. However, when asked if they would attend an adult basic education programme in a local centre, they invariably answered that they "did not want to return to school". Responses ranged from deep suspicion of the design of adult programmes (ideological/cultural resisters), to resigned acceptance—one would never attend due to circumstances or personal fears (personal/emotive resisters), to a sense of school irrelevance among the older adults (older resisters). These findings over recent years suggest that much more work is needed which involves the voice and disposition of non-participating adults.

The most recent research on the non-participation of undereducated adults in formal and non-formal programmes continues to suggest a barriers framework similar to that applied in mainstream adult education (e.g. Cross 1982). This framework is depicted in Figure 5.1.

Figure 5.1. Influences on the decisions of undereducated adults to participate or not in adult education programmes

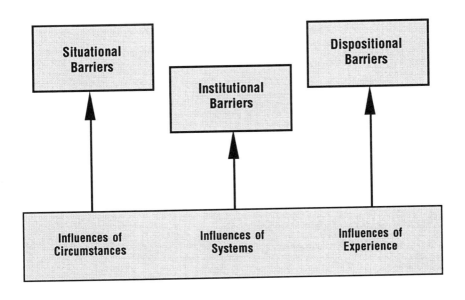

In his state-wide research in Iowa as well as in a review of relevant studies, Beder (1989: 81) confirmed that the factors affecting the non-participation decision can be clustered into what he termed two "constellations of influences": one is structural, the other attitudinal. Hayes (1987 1988), also found "two major constellations of reasons for non-participation".

Depicted as a framework of influences, Figure 5.1 indicates how the circumstances of life, the problems which may arise from institutions of education, and the dispositions developed by adults through time can create barriers of situation, institutions, and disposition (Quigley 1997). All three need much more consideration in future research but, for reasons suggested above, disposition might be the most meaningful area for theory development and, ultimately, for both policy and practice. The questions posed by situational barriers, including questions about the economy, culture, family structures, and technology, all open the door for policy analysis and research on the non-participation of undereducated adults. Such research has begun in both developing countries (e.g. Wagner 1992) and the industrialized countries (Hautecoeur 1994a). Behind the barriers created by institutions are issues concerning the cost of education, programme availability, technology issues, ineffective marketing, and the like (Darkenwald & Larson 1980)—all of which have serious institutional and programming implications for non-participation research. Finally, the area of dispositions—which Cross (1982) pointed out is "probably underestimated in adult survey data" (p. 106)— is the most enigmatic for research, but one which is proving to be vital if the field is to create more relevant and acceptable learning activities for undereducated adults. As Fingeret put it: "If we do not learn to work with them, many illiterate adults will continue to refuse to work with us" (1983: 144).

In the 21st century and the post-modern age, if the field is to gain a better understanding of the phenomenon of non-participation, it must investigate the non-participants themselves. "A heterogeneous system in which minorities are recognized, in which they can claim their rightful place, relative independence, and a new legitimate right to self-determination within a multicultural setting" (Hautecoeur 1994b: 339) cannot be realized if those who are passively or actively resisting adult education are not empowered to direct their own education and lives. As Wikelund, Reder, and Hart-Landsberg (1992) observed: "Individuals' *perceived* opportunity structures must be identified and understood before useful options for increasing literacy development can be created" (p. 23). This suggests that further non-participation research, both of a qualitative and a quantitative nature, should pay much closer attention to the social meaning of past and present structures and the influence on the lives and perceptions of non-participating adults.

5.4   Non-Participation and "Engagement" in Six Industrialized Countries

The research on the undereducated has repeatedly indicated that those with less than upper secondary education say they value an "education" for themselves, their children, and their friends (Fingeret 1985; Beder 1991; Quigley 1997). The construct is an absolute good. However, just as the absolute good contained in the construct, "justice" often degenerates to the less-than-desirable reality of the "court system" for many in today's industrialized societies, so does the dream of an "education" often seem to translate into something less than desirable, or less than fully accessible, for many of the undereducated in these countries. As discussed previously, many poorly educated adults say they desire an "education", but at the same time many express real reluctance about returning to "school".

Table 5.1 presents the levels of non-participation and participation of undereducated adults aged 25 to 65 years in formal and non-formal adult education and training activities in six industrialized countries. The data are derived from the International Adult Literacy Survey undertaken in 1994 (OECD & Statistics Canada 1995).

Table 5.1.   Participation and non-participation of adults (25-65[1]) with less than upper secondary education[2]

	Participated in adult education and training (percent)	
Country	Yes	No
Sweden	34.7	65.3
Netherlands	24.0	76.0
Canada	19.0	81.0
United States	13.2	86.8
Poland	6.2	93.8
All countries	**13.5**	**86.5**

Total N = 5,146.

1. *Population ages 25-64 for Switzerland (French and German-speaking) and Poland.*
2. *Population with ISCED 02 or less.*

Further country-by-country analysis would be needed to analyze each country's non-participation figure. It can be seen, however, that the non-participation rates of undereducated adults vary from 65.3 per cent in Sweden to a full 93.8 per cent in Poland. It can be speculated that a stable history of pro-active social policies for the undereducated has diminished barriers in Sweden.

Recent political and social changes in Poland may have had an opposite effect in that country. What is clear from the research literature reviewed previously in this chapter is that the differences in the non-participation rates are due not merely to differences in national education policies but, more particularly, to multiple forces and factors that pose or reduce various barriers to participation.

One of the consistent limitations of the research on undereducated adults, including the study referenced here, is that the focus is typically on educational activities undertaken in formal and non-formal settings—with "formal" defined as "the hierarchically structured education system which extends from primary school to graduate programmes at university" (Jarvis 1990: 133); and "non-formal" as "educational activity which occurs outside of the established formal system and is organized to serve the identifiable *learning needs* of specific groups" (Jarvis 1990: 244). In both cases, formal and non-formal, the education and/or training activity is organized and created based on "identifiable needs" as perceived by entities other than the learner or groups of learners.

The survey from which the data used in this chapter were derived asked about courses, private lessons, correspondence courses, workshops, on-the-job training, apprenticeship training, and, only to a much lesser extent in number of categories and questions posed, educational venues such as arts, crafts, and recreation courses. The interviewers consistently referred to "education and training"—terms which may have a connotation of less-then-desirable "schooling" when heard by some of the undereducated. When the question was posed: "What were the reasons you did not take this training or education", the possibility of dispositional negativity—such as wanting to avoid school, perceived programme irrelevance, or personal fears and anxieties arising from difficulties with reading and writing, were evidently captured under the response category "other". Given these questions related to the language used, the data can shed some light on institutional and situational barriers, but little can be derived on the critical area of dispositional barriers.

Increasing participation in formal and non-formal adult education

Non-participation has been seen to be an outcome of the effects of situational, institutional, and dispositional barriers. It would seem that if increased participation in formal adult education activities, including basic education and literacy classes, is ever to approach the level continually called for by adult educators around the world (e.g. Gayfer 1987; Haggis 1991), then the "deschooling" of formal and non-formal adult education may be called for. The deschooling of programme structures, programming images, course contents, and teaching methods would involve diminishing barriers and disincentives by reducing the projection of adult basic education as school-oriented. Indeed, the very terms "literacy" and "basic education" have been called problematic for this purpose (e.g. Beder & Quigley 1990; Fingeret 1984). Secondly, it has been repeatedly suggested that education and training for undereducated adults need to be reflective of potential learners' expressed and felt needs. Twenty years ago, Mezirow, Darkenwald, and Knox decried the "lack of involvement" of US adults in adult education courses, suggesting that "adults vote with their feet" (1975: 28). More recently, Hautecoeur (1994b) observed that, "the usual handling of literacy questions is normative; it reflects the ideological standards of the school or organization that defines them—a social service, a business, a vocational training programme, a charitable organization, etc." (p. 9). To assume that non-participating adults are universally unaware of this ideology and generally unaware of the consequences of not participating is to ignore the evidence and reality of non-participation.

At the programme level, Fingeret and Jurmo (1989) have advocated the use of participatory methods in formal adult basic and literacy education. Others such as Horsman (1991) and Kazemak (1988) have argued for the collaborative involvement of women in formal adult education. Others such as Gowen (1992), Quigley (1997), and Ziegahn (1992) have researched the influences of culture and proposed greater sensitivity to cultural contexts for formal programmes.

By contrast, researchers, theorists, and practitioners have also argued for the increased development of "community literacy" as one of many non-formal venues for adult education. Examples of community action have recently been documented by UNESCO, where adults use action research methods to effect economic and cultural change in rural settings (Hautecoeur 1994b). In these settings there is a facilitation role for the adult educator: "the educator's primary responsibility is to listen and understand his or her partners" (p. 346). Unlike the "autonomous" formal model described by Street (1987), these grassroots learning activities argue that adult educators should "speak of people's interests and potential, not their deficiencies" (p. 346). Action research and participatory research initiatives have a long history in adult education (e.g. Deshler & Hagan 1989; Hall 1996; Quigley, in press).

In short, for policy-makers and adult educators alike, threading through the non-participation research and recent educational initiatives in formal and non-formal settings is a common theme of enfranchizing learners to be real participants in decision-making, moving away from "educational intervention aimed at making up for psycho-social shortcomings" (Hautecoeur 1994a: 10). It is in this deschooling and empowerment philosophy that much potential for change exists.

The potential of "engagement" in informal adult learning

For future research, it is apparent that sociological and anthropological frameworks are needed to explore the uncharted world of non-participation in formal and non-formal adult education. It is also apparent that qualitative research methods, such as ethnography, in-depth interviewing, and phenomenography, hold much promise. However, it is desirable to also move beyond formal and non-formal education—beyond the normative knowledge created, legitimized, and measured by those within educational establishments. Much can be learned about the remarkable self-directed learning strategies, the various self-initiated cognition systems, and the sophisticated social networks existing among many of the undereducated adults. Since undereducated adults have been found to value learning, not simply education, the promising avenue for research and policy is to focus on the principles of *lifelong learning,* as opposed to lifelong education.

The scant research in this uncharted area suggests that the learning of the undereducated flourishes through informal and incidental venues. Informal learning has been defined as: "the type of learning that occurs when a person acquires knowledge, skill or attitudes through interaction in an informal situation, even if that situation is a network situation. It is often self-directed learning (Jarvis 1990: 165). Incidental learning has been defined as a subcategory of informal learning and is "a byproduct of some other activity, such as task accomplishment, interpersonal interaction [...] trial-and-error experimentation, or even formal leaning" (Marsick & Watkins 1990). The potential for this type of learning was touched upon by Fingeret (1983), who studied the "rich" social network of undereducated self-directed learners in the poorer communities of New York. Award-winning research by the Center for Literacy Studies (1992) found that the undereducated in both Tennessee and California had developed highly sophisticated ways to survive and flourish in a print society. Uhland (1995) found that cognitive processes among those with little or no reading ability can be more complex than those who have come to rely on print.

What is the potential of defining and exploring "engagement" in the venues of informal and incidental adult education among the undereducated? Table 5.2 shows that those very adults who had low participation levels in adult education and training (Table 5.1) nevertheless continued to "learn", but through less formal venues.

Table 5.2.   Engagement in informal and incidental learning about current events in six industrialized countries [1]

"I would like to know how you usually get information about current events, public affairs, and the government. How much information do you get from ..."

	Frequency distributions (percentages)			
Activity or education level	A lot	Some	Very little	None
Newspapers? N = 10,301				
• Lower secondary school or less	31.1	32.9	13.9	22.2
• Completed upper secondary school	44.9	37.9	11.5	5.8
• Non-university tertiary education	48.3	39.3	7.9	4.6
• University education	61.4	30.4	6.2	2.1
• All levels	46.9	35.4	10.1	7.6
Magazines? N = 10,279				
• Lower secondary school or less	6.5	23.9	24.2	45.4
• Completed upper secondary school	12.6	38.4	26.9	22.1
• Non-university tertiary education	18.2	46.7	24.0	11.1
• University education	23.4	42.8	26.2	7.6
• All levels	15.0	38.1	25.8	21.1
Radio? N = 10,289				
• Lower secondary school or less	35.5	34.0	12.4	18.1
• Completed upper secondary school	57.2	43.1	11.8	9.6
• Non-university tertiary education	36.1	19.0	8.5	3.8
• University education	46.5	36.2	10.9	6.3
• All levels	46.2	34.1	11.0	9.1
Television? N = 10,295				
• Lower secondary school or less	63.5	21.8	6.8	7.9
• Completed upper secondary school	70.2	25.3	6.7	2.7
• Non-university tertiary education	35.4	16.9	4.8	2.6
• University education	58.1	29.7	9.6	2.7
• All levels	58.6	23.8	6.9	3.5
Family members or friends? N = 10,294				
• Lower secondary school or less	19.3	39.9	18.8	22.1
• Completed upper secondary school	37.5	82.7	30.8	17.6
• Non-university tertiary education	31.0	57.4	26.5	7.2
• University education	17.5	50.2	25.8	6.6
• All levels	26.5	59.7	26.0	13.7

1.   *Population 25-65 years except in Poland and Switzerland (French and German-speaking), where the population refers to those aged 25-64.*

Those with lower secondary school or less appear to fall into a major cluster of the "engaged" with almost a third, 32 per cent, utilizing the newspaper "a lot", as compared to an average of 47 per cent for all educational levels. Further, 32 per cent reported "some" engagement compared to the average of 35 per cent. A smaller but significant cluster appears where 22 per cent said they did not use the newspaper, reporting "none", compared to an average of 8 per cent for all levels. The latter "non-engaged" group is quite possibly affected by low literacy rates, since people at all other educational levels report a much higher frequency of newspaper usage (see also Chapter 4). This leads to the not-so-surprising observation that, as the amount of reading required increases, the engagement of the undereducated decreases. Indicative of this, magazines are less utilized by the undereducated than newspapers, with only 7 per cent who had used magazines "a lot", compared with the average of 15 per cent. In fact, nearly half of the undereducated interviewed, 45 per cent, do not use magazines at all, compared with an average of 21 per cent for all levels.

By contrast, engagement for learning rises in situations where the printed word is less important as a medium, as when radio and television are involved. Comparatively more people used the radio to learn about current events than the newspaper. The undereducated actually exceeded the average when asked about use of the television to learn about current events. Those using the radio "a lot" comprise 36 per cent, compared with an average of 46 per cent. A full 63 per cent of the undereducated used the television, compared to an average for all levels of 59 per cent. Finally, it is apparent that the undereducated are reliant on family members and friends to learn about current events. Whereas 26 per cent was the average for all levels in this category, the undereducated show a rate of engagement similar to that of people with a university education.

As noted, as the requisite use of the printed word goes down, engagement in informal and incidental learning tends to go up, but there nevertheless remains a non-engaged cluster of those who do not use the newspaper, magazines, radio, or television to learn about current events. This smaller group relies on family members and friends, in excess of the average, at 22 compared with 13 per cent. However, their dependence is actually not far in excess of those with a high school or upper secondary education. Of those at this level, 18 per cent rely on family members and friends—only about 5 per cent more than the undereducated. Thus, a large proportion of the undereducated in the IALS sample learned about current events through incidental learning, but there remains a group which does not do so. Does this mean that they learn about topics other than current events through such systems? If so, what sorts of learning occur? Do the non-engaged learn about other topics but avoid current events? How do the two clusters seek, organize, process, and apply learning through these venues? What is the potential for learning and education through interactive systems in television and radio? Would normative and directive "schooling" reduce engagement, as seems to be the case with participation, if interactive systems were employed in oral media?

Since television is used the most extensively by the undereducated for current events, it is useful to examine this medium in more detail. Table 5.3 presents estimates of the number of hours the undereducated actually view television compared with other educational groups.

Table 5.3. **Comparison of engagement in television and video viewing in six industrialized countries (population 25-65 [1], percentages)**

Education level	"How much time do you usually spend each day watching television or videos?"				
	Not on a daily basis	1 hour or less per day	1 to 2 hours per day	More thans 2 hours but less than 5	5 or more hours per day
• Lower secondary school or less	3.9	14.2	30.2	37.6	14.1
• Completed upper secondary school	4.3	21.2	32.4	32.6	9.5
• Non-university tertiary education	7.8	23.0	33.1	28.5	7.6
• University education	5.0	34.6	36.3	21.8	2.4
• All levels	4.9	22.9	32.9	30.7	8.7

Total N = 12,442

1.   *Population 25-65 years except Poland and Switzerland (French and German-speaking), where the population refers to those aged 25-64.*

As can be seen, a small group of the undereducated hardly watch television at all. A reported 3.9 per cent do not watch on a daily basis, compared with an average for the whole population of 4.9 per cent. About 14 per cent are below the norm when reporting on one hour or fewer per day, compared with 23 per cent for all educational levels. As might be expected, television is not a medium for reaching or engaging the undereducated on a universal level. However, past this group of less than 20 per cent, television becomes a very promising medium. It is seen that they are close to the average when asked about 1-2 hours of viewing per day, and it is seen that television is again significant at 2-5 hours (30 per cent compared with the average of 33 per cent; and 38 per cent compared with the average of 31 per cent). If the two categories, 1-2 hours and 2-5 hours, are combined, then they comprise almost 68 per cent of the entire population. Finally, there is a small group of adults who exceed the average time spent in the 5 hours or more per day category—possibly due to underemployment. Here, 14 per cent watch 5 or more hours per day, almost double the average.

The implications of how undereducated adults choose to learn are many for policy and practice. It is clear that in their chosen use of informal and incidental learning modes, totally print-based systems are problematic. However, this is but one major factor. It is apparent from the research literature discussed previously that the undereducated have ambiguous feelings about school-oriented institutions and their programmes. This attitude is examined in Table 5.4, which shows how little the undereducated utilize public libraries, but how many nevertheless read books.

Table 5.4.   Educational contrast of engagement in reading books versus usage of public libraries (population 25-65 [1], percentages)

How often do you ...	Daily	Weekly	Monthly	Several per year	Never
Use a public library? N = 14,708					
• Lower secondary school or less	n.a.	3.6	7.3	12.3	76.5
• Completed upper secondary school	0.5	7.3	11.7	31.3	49.3
• Non-university tertiary education	n.a.	7.5	19.0	35.0	38.0
• University education	2.1	11.8	22.3	41.7	22.1
• All education levels	0.8	7.5	14.1	29.8	47.8
Read Books? N = 14,683					
• Lower secondary school or less	15.8	14.5	15.0	20.1	34.7
• Completed upper secondary school	30.4	16.8	15.9	21.2	15.8
• Non-university tertiary education	40.5	19.7	14.0	18.9	6.9
• University education	41.5	22.0	12.3	17.4	6.9
• All education levels	31.0	17.8	14.6	19.8	16.8

1   *Population 25-65 years except Poland and Switzerland (French and German-speaking), where the population refers to those aged 25-64.*

n.a.:   Sample size too small to yield reliable estimate.

Table 5.4 shows that over 76 per cent of the sample *never* use libraries; yet, they do read books and do not avoid print beyond obtaining information on current events. Only 35 per cent said they never read a book. The undereducated are close to the average for all levels of those who report that they read books several times a year. They are also very close with respect to reading books monthly. The undereducated fall slightly in weekly engagement rates (14.5 compared with 17.8 per cent) and drop to half of the average when asked about daily engagement (15.8 compared with 31 per cent).

In summary, the undereducated do read books—over 50 per cent do so weekly, monthly, and several times a year. However, most obtain their books without help from the public libraries—just as most evidently learn without the help of formal adult education institutions.

5.5   Conclusion

Despite the best efforts of adult educators and the various initiatives of policy-makers through the 20th century, the undereducated continue to comprise a major proportion of the adult populations in industrialized societies. Modernity has promised much but resolved little for this group. The undereducated are not only distanced by the institutional and situational barriers which have grown up around normative knowledge and the education industry, but they also make a conscious choice to distance themselves from schooling. This was seen in terms of dispositional barriers and the impacts of culture and socio-economic structuration in society.

For policy, it seems that normative knowledge through formal and non-formal adult education will only become more accessible to the undereducated if the barriers posed by institutions and socio-economic and cultural factors are better understood and more seriously confronted. A number of promising examples were presented in this area. Understanding their learning needs, listening to their voices, and enfranchizing non-participating adults are critical if real change is to occur in the future. This chapter has also suggested that more than education occurs in the lives of the undereducated; learning goes on in many ways, and some of these have typically been ignored or undervalued by formal education institutions. Apart from the learning that takes place in organized and structured settings for adult education, it was seen that many among the undereducated adults engage in extensive informal and incidental learning activities. Engagement in these self-directed forms of knowledge acquisition and transfer might well supplement, even challenge, the sharp duality that is assumed to exist between the participants on the one hand and non-participants on the other. If the issue were less how many participate in education and training versus how many do not; if we could ask how society learns, how it teaches its members; if we could ask those who cannot and often will not join the normative knowledge paradigm how they learn in a print-oriented society, then we would be in a better position to value and learn from the contributions made by all members and sectors of society.

References

Anderson, D., and Niemi, J. 1970. *Adult Education and the Disadvantaged Adult*. New York: Syracuse University and ERIC Clearinghouse.

Apple, M. 1991. *The Politics of the Textbook*. New York: Routledge.

Arnove, R., and Graff, H. 1987. *National Literacy Campaigns*. New York: Plenum Press.

Baldwin, J. 1991. "Why did they drop out? Reasons GED candidates give for leaving school". In: *GED Profiles: Adults in Transition* (dedicated issue) 4.

Beder, H. 1989. "Purposes and philosophies". In: S.B. Merriam and P.M. Cunningham (eds.), *Handbook of Adult and Continuing Education*. San Francisco: Jossey-Bass. 37-50.

Beder, H. 1990a. "Reasons for non-participation in adult basic education". In: *Adult Education Quarterly* 40: 217-218.

Beder, H. 1990b. "Reaching ABE students: Lessons from the Iowa studies". In: *Adult Literacy and Basic Education* 14: 1-18.

Beder, H. 1991. *Adult Literacy: Issues for Policy and Practice*. Malabar/ Florida: Krieger Publishing Company.

Beder, H. 1994. "The current status of adult literacy education in the United States". In: *PAACE Journal of Lifelong Learning* 3: 14-25.

Beder, H., and Quigley, B.A. 1990. "Beyond the classroom". In: *Adult Learning* 1 (5): 19-21.

Benseman, J. 1989. *The View from the Other Side of the Educational Door: Adult Education from the Perspective of People with Low Levels of Schooling*. (ERIC document reproduction service no. ED 305 433) Wellington: New Zealand Department of Education.

Bingham, M.B., and White, C. 1994. "Appalachian communities: Working to survive". In: J.-P. Hautecoeur (ed.). *Alpha 94: Literacy and Cultural Development Strategies in Rural Areas*. Hamburg: UNESCO Institute for Education.

Blaise, J., Duquette, A., and Painchaud, G. 1989. "Deterrents to women's participation in work-related educational activities". In: *Adult Education Quarterly* 39: 229-234.

Bohnenn, E. 1987. "Practice in the Netherlands". In: M. Gayfer (ed.). *Literacy in Industrialized Countries: A Focus on Practice*. Toronto: International Council for Adult Education.

Boraks, N., and Richardson, J. 1981. *Teaching the Adult Beginning Reader: Designing Research Based Reading Instructional Strategies*. (ERIC document reproduction service no. ED 216 329) Paper presented at the annual meeting of the College Reading Association.

Boraks, N., and Schumacher, S. 1981. *Ethnographic Research on Word Recognition Strategies of Adult Beginning Readers: Technical Report*. (ERIC document reproduction service no. ED 219 552) Richmond: School of Education, Virginia Commonwealth University.

Boshier, R. 1973. "Educational participation and dropout: A theoretical model". In: *Adult Education* 23: 255-282.

Boshier, R. 1977. "Motivational orientation re-visited: Life-space motives and the education participation scale". In: *Adult Education* 27 (2): 89-115.

Bourdieu, P. 1971. "Systems of education and systems of thought: New directions for the sociology of education". In: M.F.D. Young (ed.). *Knowledge and Control*. London: Collier-Macmillan.

Bourdieu, P., and Passeron, J.C. 1977. *Reproduction in Education, Society and Culture*. Beverly Hills, California: Sage.

Bowles, S., and Gintis, H. 1977. *Schooling in Capitalist America*. New York: Basic Books.

Bowren, F.F. 1981. "Teaching the learning disabled adult to read". In: *Adult Literacy and Basic Education* 5 (Fall): 179-184.

Brookfield, S. 1986. *Understanding and Facilitating Adult Learning*. San Francisco: Jossey-Bass.

Cain, S., and Whalen, B. 1979. *Adult Basic and Secondary Educational Programme Statistics: Fiscal Year 1976*. Washington D.C.: National Center for Education Statistics, Department of Health, Education and Welfare.

Carrasco, J.G. 1994. "A cultural empowerment process in rural areas". In: J.-P. Hautecoeur (ed.). *Alpha 94: Literacy and Cultural Development Strategies in Rural Areas*. Hamburg: UNESCO Institute for Education.

Carron, G., and Bordia, A. (eds.) 1985. *Issues in Planning and Implementing National Literacy Programmes*. Paris: UNESCO, International Institute for Educational Planning.

Center for Literacy Studies (University of Tennessee, Knoxville). 1992. *Life at the Margins: Profiles of Adults with Low-Literacy Skills*. (Contract no. H3.5365.0) Washington, DC: Office of Technology Assessment.

Cervero, R., and Fitzpatrick, T. 1990. "The enduring effects of family role and schooling on participation in adult education". In: *American Journal of Education* 99 (1): 77-94.

Clark, R. 1990. *Successful Illiterate Adults*. (Unpublished doctoral dissertation) Vancouver: Department of Administrative, Adult and Higher Education, University of British Columbia.

Cook, W. 1977. *Adult Literacy Education in the United States*. Newark, Delaware: International Reading Association.

Courtney, S. 1989. "Defining adult and continuing education". In: S.B. Merriam and P.M. Cunningham (eds.). *Handbook of Adult and Continuing Education*. San Francisco: Jossey-Bass.

Cross, K.P. 1982. *Adults as Learners*. San Francisco: Jossey-Bass.

Csikszentmihalyi, M. 1990. "Literacy and intrinsic motivation". In: *Daedalus* 119 (2): 115-140.

Daneman, M. 1991. "Individual differences in reading skill". In: R. Barr, M.L. Kamil, P. Mosenthal, and P.D. Pearson (eds.) *Handbook of Reading Research* (Vol. 2). New York: Longman.

Danis, C. 1988. "Relationship between learning strategies/meta-strategies and experiential learning styles of self-taught adults". In: *Proceedings of the Adult Education Research Conference*. Calgary, Alberta: CAAE.

Darkenwald, G.G. 1986. *Adult Literacy Education: A Review of the Research and Priorities for Future Inquiry*. (Unpublished paper) Literacy Assistance Center.

Darkenwald, G.G., and Larson, G.A. (eds.) 1980. "Reaching hard-to-reach adults". In: *New Directions for Continuing Education* 8. San Francisco: Jossey-Bass.

Darkenwald, G.G., and Valentine, T. 1985. "Factor structure of deterrents to participation". In: *Adult Education Quarterly* 39: 177-193.

Deshler, D., and Hagan, N. 1989. "Adult education research: Issues and directions". In: S.B. Merriam and P.M. Cunningham (eds.). *Handbook of Adult and Continuing Education*. San Francisco: Jossey-Bass.

Dionne, H., and Horth, R. 1994. "Challenges of development in rural Quebec and literacy". In: J.-P. Hautecoeur (ed.) *Alpha 94: Literacy and Cultural Development Strategies in Rural Areas*. Hamburg: UNESCO Institute for Education.

Eberle, A., and Robinson, S. 1980. *The Adult Literate Speaks Out: Personal Perspectives on Learning to Read and Write*. (ERIC document reproduction services no. ED 195 771) Washington, DC: National Institute for Community Development.

Fine, M. 1982. *Examining Inequity: View from Urban Schools*. (Unpublished manuscript) Philadelphia, PA: University of Pennsylvania.

Fingeret, H.A. 1983. "Social network: A new perspective on independence and illiterate adults". In: *Adult Education Quarterly* 33: 133-145.

Fingeret, H.A. 1984. *Adult Literacy Education: Current and Future Directions*. (Contract no. NIE-C-400-81-0035) Ohio: The Ohio State University, National Center for Research in Vocational Education.

Fingeret, H.A. 1985. *North Carolina ABE Instructional Programme Evaluation*. Raleigh: Department of Adult and Community College Education.

Fingeret, H.A. 1991. "Literacy in the USA: The present issues". In: *The Future of Literacy and the Literacy of the Future*. Hamburg: UNESCO Institute for Education.

Fingeret, H.A., and Danin, S. 1991. *They Really Put a Hurtin' on my Brain. Learning in Literacy Volunteers of New York City*. Durham: Literacy South.

Fingeret, H.A., and Jurmo, P. (eds) 1989. "Participatory literacy education". In: *New Directions for Continuing Education*. San Francisco: Jossey-Bass.

Floud, J., and Halsey, A.H. 1958. "The sociology of education". In: *Current Sociology* 8 (3).

Fogwill, L. 1994. "Literacy: A critical element in the survival of aboriginal languages". In: J.-P. Hautecoeur (ed.). *Alpha 94: Literacy and Cultural Development Strategies in Rural Areas*. Hamburg: UNESCO Institute for Education.

Gayfer, M. (ed.) 1987. *Literacy in the industrialized countries: A focus on practice* (International literacy seminar). Toronto: International Council for Adult Education.

Giddens, A. 1984. *The Constitution of Society*. Berkeley, CA: University of California Press.

Giroux, H.A. 1983. "Theories of reproduction and resistance in the new sociology of education: A critical analysis". In: *Harvard Educational Review* 53 (3): 257-293.

Gowen, S.G. 1992. *The Politics of Workplace Literacy: A Case Study*. New York: Teachers College Press.

Grattan, C. 1955. *In Quest of Knowledge: A Historical Perspective on Adult Education.* New York: Association Press.

Green, T.F. 1980. *Predicting the Behavior of the Educational System.* Syracuse/ NY: Syracuse University Press.

Griffin, C. 1987. *Adult Education as Social Policy.* New York: Croom Helm.

Haggis, S.M. 1991. Education for all: Purpose and context. *World Conference on Education for All.* Monograph 1. Paris: UNESCO.

Hall, B.L. 1996. "Participatory research". In: A.C. Tuijnman (ed.), *International Encyclopedia of Adult Education and Training.* (2nd ed.) Oxford: Pergamon Press.

Hallenbeck, W. 1964. "Role of adult education in society". In: G. Jensen, A.A. Liveright, and W. Hallenbeck (eds.). *Adult Education: Outlines of an Emerging Field of University Study.* Washington D.C.: Adult Education Association of the USA. 5-25.

Hautecoeur, J.-P. (ed.) 1994a. *Alpha 94: Literacy and Cultural Development Strategies in Rural Areas.* Hamburg: UNESCO Institute for Education.

Hayes, E. 1987. *Low-literate Adult Basic Education Students' Perception of Deterrents to Participation.* (Unpublished doctoral dissertation). New Brunswick/ NJ: Rutgers University.

Hayes, E. 1988. "A typology of low-literate adults based on perceptions of deterrents to participation in adult basic education". In: *Adult Education Quarterly* 39: 1-10.

Heisel, M., and Larson, G. 1984. Literacy and social milieu: Reading behavior of the black elderly. *Adult Education Quarterly* 34: 63-70.

Horsman, J. 1989. "From the learners' voice: Women's experience of il/literacy. In: M.C. Taylor and J.A. Draper (eds.). *Adult Literacy Perspectives.* Toronto: Culture Concepts. 365-374

Horsman, J. 1991. *Something in my Mind Besides the Everyday: Women and Literacy.* Toronto: Women's Press.

International Development Research Centre. 1979. *The World of Literacy: Policy, Research, and Action.* Ottawa: IDRC.

Irish, G. 1980. "Reaching the least educated adult". In: G.G. Darkenwald and G.A. Larson (eds.). *Reaching Hard-to-Reach Adults* (New Directions for Continuing Education. Vol. 8). San Francisco: Jossey-Bass.

Jarvis, P. 1983. *Adult and Continuing Education: Theory and Practice.* London: Croom-Helm.

Jarvis, P. 1990. *International Dictionary of Adult Continuing Education.* New York: Routledge.

Johnstone, J., and Rivera, R. 1965. *Volunteers for Learning.* Chicago: Aldine Publishing.

Kazemak, F.E. 1988. "Necessary changes: Professional Involvement in Adult Literacy Programmes". In: *Harvard Educational Review* 58 (4): 464-487.

Kirsch, I.S., Jungeblut, A. Jenkins, L., and Kolstad, A. 1993. *Adult Literacy in America: A First Look at the Results of the National Adult Literacy Survey.* Washington, DC: National Center for Education Statistics, Department of Education.

Manning, A. 1983. *Prosperous Illiterates.* (Unpublished doctoral dissertation) Syracuse, New York.: Syracuse University, Deptment of Education.

Marsick, V.J., and Watkins, K. 1990. *Informal and Incidental Learning in the Workplace.* London: Routledge.

Martindale, C.J., and Drake, J.B. 1989. "Factor structure of deterrents to participation in off-duty adult education programmes". In: *Adult Education Quarterly* 39: 63-75.

Merriam, S.B., and Caffarella, R.S. 1991. *Learning in Adulthood.* San Francisco: Jossey-Bass.

Mezirow, J., Darkenwald, G.G., and Knox, A.B. 1975. *Last Gamble on Education.* Washington DC: Adult Education Association of the USA.

Miller, H.L. 1967. *Participation of Adults in Education: A Force-field Analysis.* Boston: Center for the Study of Liberal Education for Adults.

Mills, C.W. 1940. "Situated actions and vocabularies of motive". In: *American Sociological Journal 5*, 904-913.

O'Brien, S.N. 1979. "Educational theory and ABE". In: *Adult Literacy and Basic Education* 3: 35-38.

OECD and Statistics Canada 1995. *Literacy, Economy and Society: Results of the First International Adult Literacy Survey.* Paris and Ottawa: Organisation for Economic Co-operation and Development and Statistics Canada.

Quigley, B.A. 1987. "Learning to work with them: Analyzing non-participation in adult basic education through resistance theory". In: *Adult Literacy and Basic Education* 11 (2): 63-70.

Quigley, B.A. 1989. "Literacy as social policy: Issues for America in the 21st century". In: *Thresholds in Education* 15 (4): 11-15.

Quigley, B.A. 1990. "Hidden logic: Resistance and reproduction in adult literacy and basic education". In: *Adult Education Quarterly* 40 (2): 103-115.

Quigley, B.A. 1993a. *Retaining Reluctant Learners in Adult Literacy Programmes.* Philadelphia, PA: Institute for the Study of Adult Literacy, State College, Pennsylvania State University.

Quigley, B.A. 1997. *Rethinking Literacy Education.* San Francisco: Jossey-Bass.

Quigley, B.A., and Kuhne, G.W. (in press). *Creating Practical Knowledge: Problem-posing and Problem-solving through Action Research.* San Francisco: Jossey-Bass.

Reissman, F. 1962. *The Culturally Deprived Child.* New York: Harper and Row.

Rubenson, K. 1977. Participation in recurrent education: A research review. Paper presented at the meeting of National Delegates on Developments in Recurrent Education, OECD, Paris.

Rubenson, K. 1989. "The sociology of adult education". In: S.B. Merriam and P.M. Cunningham (eds.) *Handbook of Adult and Continuing Education.* San Francisco: Jossey-Bass.

Rubenson, K., and Hoghielm, R. 1978. *The Teaching Process and Study Dropouts in Adult Education.* Stockholm: Stockholm Institute of Education.

Scanlan, C.L., and Darkenwald, G.G. 1984. "Identifying deterrents to participation in continuing education". In: *Adult Education Quarterly* 34: 155-166.

Schroeder, W.L. 1970. "Adult education defined and described". In: R.M. Smith, G.F. Aker, and J.R. Kidd (eds.). *Handbook of Adult Education.* New York: Macmillan.

Scribner, S., and Cole, M. 1978. "Literacy without schooling: Testing for intellectual effects". In: *Harvard Educational Review* 48 (4): 448-461.

Street, B.V. 1987. "Literacy and social change". In: D.A. Wagner (ed.). *The Future of Literacy in a Changing World* (Vol. 1). Oxford: Pergamon Press.

Stuckey, J. 1991. *The Violence of Literacy*. Portsmouth, NH: Boynton and Cook Publishers.

Taylor, M.C., and Draper, J.A. (eds.) 1989. *Adult Literacy Perspectives*. Toronto: Culture Concepts.

Thomas, A.M. 1983. *Adult illiteracy in Canada: A challenge.* (Occasional paper 42) Ottawa: Canadian Commission for UNESCO.

Thomas, A.M. 1990. *The Reluctant Learner. A Research Report on Non-participation and Dropout in Literacy Programmes in British Columbia*. Victoria: Government of British Columbia.

Uhland, R.L. 1995. *Learning Strategy Behaviors Demonstrated by Low-literate Adults Engaged in Self-directed Learning.* (Unpublished doctoral dissertation) Philadelphia, PA: State College, Pennsylvania State University.

Valentine, T., and Darkenwald, G.G. 1990. "Deterrents to participation in adult education: Profiles of potential learners". In: *Adult Education Quarterly* 41 (1): 29-42.

Van Tilburg, E., and Dubois, J. 1989, April. "Literacy students' perceptions of successful participation in adult education: A cross-cultural approach through expectancy valence". In: *Proceedings of the 30th Annual Adult Education Research Conference*. Madison: University of Wisconsin. 308-313.

Verner, C. 1973. "Illiteracy and poverty". In: *BTSD Review* 9 (2): 9-15.

Wagner, D.A. 1992. "World literacy: Research and policy in the EFA decade". In: D.A. Wagner and L.D. Puchner (eds.), *The Annals of the American Academy of Political and Social Science*. Beverly Hills: Sage. 12-26.

Wikelund, K.R., Reder, S., and Hart-Landsberg, S. 1992. *A Multi-site Study of Adult Literacy Training Programmes* (Technical Report no. 92-1). Portland/ OR: National Center on Adult Literacy.

Willis, P. 1977. *Learning to Labour: Why Working Class Kids Take Working Class Jobs*. New York: Columbia University Press.

Yates, B. 1996. "Striving for tino rangatiratanga". In: J. Benseman, B. Findsen and M. Scott (eds.), *The Fourth Sector: Adult and Community Education in Aotearoa*. New Zealand: The Dunmore Press.

Ziegahn, L. 1992. "Learning, literacy, and participation: Sorting out priorities". In: *Adult Education Quarterly* 43 (1), 30-49.

Chapter 6

New Trajectories of Learning Across the Lifespan

Max van der Kamp and Jo Scheeren

6.1 Introduction

The aim of this chapter is to give insight into the distribution of learning activities across the lifespan, within a broad international perspective. Mainly based on the dataset collected for the International Adult Literacy Survey (IALS), an analysis will be made of educational participation in relation to relevant categories of age and their coherence with other life activities, such as study and work. Although the core task to be accomplished by the IALS was the assessment of the literacy proficiency of adult populations, information about participation and non-participation in adult education was also collected as part of the survey.[1]

The information on adult education and training collected by means of the IALS background questionnaire was not exactly identical in all cases and in all of the participating countries. For example, there are fewer variables for Sweden, because certain questions were either not asked or were asked in a different way. There are also differences in age breakdowns, because most countries collected data only for the population 16-65 years. Older adults aged 65 to 74 years were included in the sampling frames in only three countries: Canada, the Netherlands, and Sweden. Nevertheless, the dataset makes it possible to obtain a global insight into the learning activities across the lifespan of the contemporary citizen in modern, industrialized societies.

The chapter will be divided into sections according to different lifespan phases. But first an overview will be given of modern lifespan theories. Then the overall distribution of participation in adult education and training across the lifespan will be analyzed. The chapter will conclude with implications for educational policy and practice.

---

[1] *See OECD and Statistics Canada (1995), Murray & Kirsch (1997), and the Appendices in this volume for a description of the survey and its objectives, the dataset, and the samples investigated in the different countries.*

6.2   Lifespan Theories and Modern Society

Although there is no single pathway from conception to death, there appears to be a widespread desire to standardize human life in lifespan models and stages. The stage model has traditionally been the dominant model, from the earliest times and in many different cultural contexts (Schuller 1992). Aristotle proposed a three-stage model, Bede a four-stage model, and Shakespeare most famously a seven-stage one in "As you like it". Well-known metaphors to order the lifespan are the ladder (leading man to heaven ...) and the staircase. Less well-known is the so-called "Arab model of development". This model (Heymans 1992) depicts a young palm tree in the desert, which has been covered with a stone. It will receive water only if the sprout can lift the stone and throw it off, because in this case it is likely that the investment will eventually bear fruit. The implication for educators may be that it can be worthwhile to put young individuals under some pressure by setting high standards and expectations and selecting at a young age.

The representation of different ages as symbolic figures placed on an ascending and subsequently descending staircase has been popular since the Middle Ages. An example can be seen in Figure 6.1. On this 19th-century children's print, life begins with infants in bed, at the top a married couple of fifty parades in fine clothes, and life ends in bed again at a high age. All stages of life are propped up by God and his angels, while the devil tries to destroy the divine work. The atmosphere, the clothing, and the moral lesson are typical for the period.

Figure 6.1.   The staircase of ages, Pellerin 19th century (source: Provoost 1986)

Besides the popular interest in lifespan development, there is also the scientific interest stemming from psychology, physiology, and education. The attention of developmental psychologists in particular was for a long time focused on children, but extended in several directions during the 1970s and 1980s (Thomas 1990). By the early 1990s, the field embraced the entire lifespan from conception to death. However, despite the accumulation of a vast body of writing on the theme of lifespan development, there still is a dearth of empirical evidence for the various theories of lifespan development. Even consensus on the precise meaning of the term "lifespan development" is still lacking.

This critical note has to be kept in mind when examining models of lifespan development, such as the one proposed by Fales (1989). Fales provides the following description of the various phases of the lifespan. For each, some of the key problems and challenges which individuals in modern Western societies face are indicated:

1. Separating from family (late teens to early twenties). Tasks include becoming self-supporting, forming attachment with peers, separating emotionally from parents, and forming an identity.

2. Provisional adulthood (early to late twenties). Tasks include selection of a mate and intimacy, forming a family, deciding on life-style, forming an occupational identity, and mastery of what one is "supposed" to be in life.

3. Thirties transition (late twenties and early thirties). Tasks include evaluating and exploring alternatives to choices in phase 2, and establishing an adult relationship with parents.

4. Thirties stabilization (early to late thirties). Tasks include succeeding at phase 3 choices, solidifying a sense of self, increasing the attachment to the family and procreation, and giving up mentors.

5. Forties (mid-life) transition (late thirties and early forties). Tasks include re-evaluating the "dream" of the first half of life, restructuring the time perspective, establishing a sense of meaning, establishing generativity, and expanding emotional repertoire.

6. Restabilization (middle forties to middle fifties). Tasks include succeeding at phase 5 choices, developing self-acceptance, maintaining growth and flexibility emotionally and intellectually, and grand-parenthood.

7. Preparation for retirement (late fifties to middle sixties). Tasks include developing adult relationships with children, preparing for the end of an occupational role, and developing alternative sources of self-esteem.

8.   Young old period (middle sixties to late seventies). Tasks include exploring uses of leisure, consolidating a sense of self as continuous, maintaining health, income, social relations, and emotional attachments, re-evaluating meaning, and the development of spirituality.

9.   Old-old period (late seventies to death). Tasks include establishing self-acceptance, a life review, maintaining emotional attachments, adjusting to declines in health, relationships, and mental functions, facing death, and providing for intergenerational continuity.

Age is a ubiquitous concept in developmental psychology. It is used either as the main or as a subsidiary criterion in anchoring virtually all accounts of change in the lifespan. Such a categorization of the developmental processes of people in accordance with age might be useful in certain ways. For example, it can provide a reference framework in relation to which individuals can put into perspective the expectations of others, thus helping them in accommodating social and cultural demands in their daily activities. However, the problems and dangers of using age as a general criterion for identifying the developmental tasks people are likely to face during certain periods in life are well worth noting, "since age itself is not a cause of change or an explanation of behaviour" (Sugerman 1986: 51). A major problem is that lifespan phases are to an extent culture-specific and often male-biased. The pattern of expectations in an advanced industrialized country in Europe may well be different from those existing in poor developing countries. Many of the pre-scientific and even the scientific models of the lifespan mentioned above reflect a static view of development and a certain amount of ageism, where old age is seen as a process of physical and mental decay.

It is within this balanced perspective of age that one might examine the distribution of educational opportunities across the lifespan. The IALS data offer an opportunity to explore empirically the relationship of different phases in modern life with learning needs, as expressed by indicators of educational participation. Is it possible to detect quantitative and qualitative differences in educational participation across the lifespan?

6.3   Adult Education Participation Across the Lifespan: A Global View

Although longitudinal data are ideally required, large-scale cross-sectional data of the type gathered for the IALS might also be useful to gain an insight into people's educational needs across the lifespan. Fales' lifespan model will be used as a heuristic framework for an analysis of the distribution of learning needs and educational opportunities over the lifespan. Fales' framework will have to be somewhat simplified, however, because the available data do not allow for a fine disaggregation by age in accordance with the nine phases identified.

Figure 6.2 shows the rate of participation in organized and structured adult education activities during the 12 months preceding the interview, by age groups from 16 to 75 years, in six OECD countries. The definitions of adult education and training adopted for the project called for the exclusion of full-time young students (see Appendix A of this volume). Hence respondents younger than 25 years who were enroled in formal education programmes at the time of the interview were excluded from the analysis.

In general, Figure 6.2 shows a decline in the participation rate as age increases. Only Sweden—and also, albeit to a smaller extent, the United States—show a relatively stable pattern of intensive learning until a relatively high age (55). This pattern may be considered characteristic for the "learning society". Poland also has a fairly stable pattern, but the rate of participation is low compared with the other countries. In all countries, a sharp decrease can be noted after age 55. In the group aged 66-75 years, only 10 to 15 per cent participate in structured learning activities.

Figure 6.2.   Rate of adult education participation by age, 1994

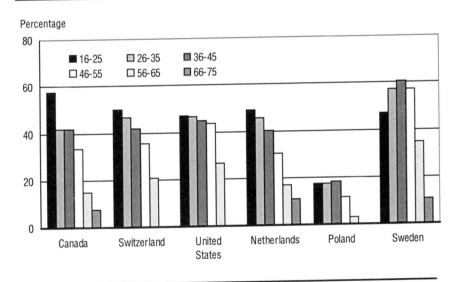

A more nuanced picture emerges from an analysis of the intensity or duration of the adult learning effort by age. Figure 6.3 shows the number of hours adults participated in organized adult education or training during the 12 months preceding the interview. Unfortunately, the Swedish dataset contains no information in this respect. In terms of total time allocated to adult learning, the investment is the highest for the youngest age group, 16-25 years. Because of the long duration of courses in Canada and the Netherlands, the education effort in these countries surpasses that of the other countries during this phase. After this first period, there is a sharp and then a relatively gradual decline in the level of investment and effort devoted to adult education and training across the lifespan. Thus, it appears that, during the life phases subsequent to the conclusion of formal, initial education, the most intensive adult learning efforts are made early on, during the phases "separating from family" (late teens to early twenties) and "provisional adulthood" (early to late twenties), when developmental tasks include becoming self-supporting and forming an occupational identity. The least intensive learning efforts are in the phases "preparation for retirement" (late fifties to middle sixties) and the "young old period" (middle sixties to late seventies), when the occupational role ends for most citizens. Although the IALS did not systematically collect data for the population in the "old old period" (late seventies to death), the rate and intensity of participation in organized and structured educational activities is assumed to be the lowest during this period in life. None of the other phases identified in Fales' lifespan model shows particularly high or low educational demand. In the next sections we will focus on this demand and the patterns of adult education participation for different age groups.

Figure 6.3.   Participation in adult education and training in hours by age, 1994

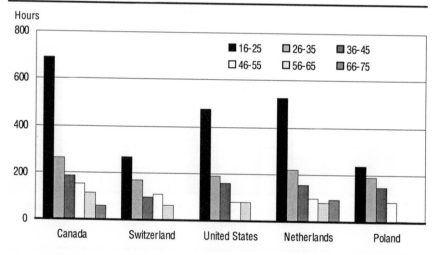

6.4   Participation in Initial, Formal Education

Even though the emphasis in this chapter is on the participation of adults in organized education and training, it is important to study this in relation to the investment in youth education. The lifespan model applied in this chapter invites us to examine the patterns of participation in initial, formal education in some of the IALS countries. This is done below, drawing on the education indicators developed by the OECD (1995 and 1996a).

Adult education builds on and benefits from a high-quality platform of foundation learning early on in life. Net enrolment rates offer a measure of access to foundation learning for young people. According to Table 6.1, in almost all of the countries studied in this chapter, more than 60 per cent of the population aged 5-29 years is enroled in education on a full-time equivalent basis. Variation between countries is for a large part due to the uneven weight of tertiary-level enrolments, which vary from 17 and 15 per cent in Canada and the United States to 7 and 5 per cent in Switzerland and Poland.

Table 6.1.   Number of students enroled per 100 persons in the population aged 5 to 29, 1994 (based on head counts)

	Early childhood education	Primary and lower secondary	Upper secondary education	Tertiary education	All levels of education combined
Canada	2.9	35.1	11.9	17.2	67.2
Switzerland	5.5	33.3	11.7	6.6	57.4
United States	3.7	37.0	10.7	15.4	66.8
Netherlands	3.5	37.1	14.2	10.1	64.9
Poland	5.1	35.8	15.9	5.1	61.9
Sweden	6.1	34.5	16.1	8.4	65.2

Source: OECD (1996a), p. 111.

The overall level of participation in formal education and training has risen in all countries since the mid-1970s, in some cases dramatically so. But participation rates do not reveal much about the quality and intensity of learning. At the secondary level, inadequate educational structures and inappropriate practices have hampered effective responses to the diverse learning needs, aptitudes, interests, and backgrounds represented by the student body, and resulting school failures have in turn led to student failures, partly because of weakened motivation and reduced readiness to learn. One consequence is that 15 to 20 per cent of young persons in many OECD countries leave school without a worthwhile qualification (OECD 1996b: 16).

Heightened fears of social exclusion, for example, that are encountered by many long-term unemployed youth who lack adequate foundation skills, have increased the incentives for younger people to stay longer in school after their compulsory schooling (OECD 1996a, p 21). In the IALS countries, almost all 5 to 14 year-olds are enroled in education. Participation for the age group 15-29 years varies from 41 per cent in the Netherlands to 32.7 per cent in Switzerland (Table 6.2).

Table 6.2.   Rate of enrolment in public and private educational institutions, 1994 (based on head counts)

	Students aged 5-14 as a percentage of the population aged 5-14	Students aged 15-29 as a percentage of the population aged 15-29
Canada	97.8	40.4
Switzerland	97.4	32.7
United States	97.7	37.6
Netherlands	99.1	41.0
Poland	91.5	37.9
Sweden	95.3	37.8

Source: OECD (1996a), p. 112.

The distinction made in Table 6.2 between the two age groups 5-14 and 15-29 must be considered a crude one. There is much variation in the net rate of enrolment by single years of age for the group 15-29. Once the stage of compulsory schooling is over, which is around the age of 16 or 17 in most countries, the participation rates decline sharply in all countries. But there are some significant differences among the countries studied. Table 6.3 shows that, at the age of 20, the proportion of students is nearly 60 per cent in Canada and the Netherlands. This contrasts with rates below 35 per cent in the comparison countries.

Table 6.3.   Net enrolment rates for population aged 15-24 in public and private institutions, 1994 (based on head counts)

	15	16	17	18	19	20	21	22	23	24
Canada	96.3	94.2	88.1	72.2	60.6	59.6	39.8	33.2	23.5	20.4
Switzerland	96.7	87.3	83.3	76.2	56.3	33.1	23.5	20.8	18.8	16.1
United States	97.1	95.4	85.9	61.2	45.4	34.9	33.6	28	22.3	19.2
Netherlands	98.9	97.5	90.6	79.8	67.3	57.1	45.6	36.2	28.9	22.2
Poland	—	—	—	—	—	21.9	20.1	17.1	14.9	10.6
Sweden	96.6	96.2	94.8	82.7	34.3	28.3	27.8	28	25.5	22.3

Source: OECD (1996a), p. 122.

In Switzerland and especially in Poland, the decrease in the rate of participation in formal, initial education for the age group 20-24 years is substantial. The data in Table 6.4 indicate that this decline is due to a large extent to a comparatively modest level of enrolment in tertiary education in these countries. For the group aged 22-25, about 23 per cent of Canadians and 21 per cent of Americans are enroled in tertiary education. These figures drop to 18 per cent in the Netherlands and 15 per cent in Sweden. It can be seen that Poland has the lowest enrolment rate.

Table 6.4. Rate of enrolment in tertiary education, 1994 (based on head counts)

	Ages 18-21	Ages 22-25
Canada	40.3	22.8
Switzerland	7.6	14.2
United States	34.9	20.9
Netherlands	22.1	18.4
Poland	14.6	10.8
Sweden	12.3	15.3

Source: OECD (1996a), pp. 127-128.

As participation increases in a diverse range of academic and professional education and training, especially at the tertiary level, and the application of information and communication technologies widens, the pathways followed by individual students become more varied and transitions—particularly from school and initial tertiary education to work—become more critical (OECD 1996b). Training opportunities at these levels are not available to all and, more significantly, are heavily tilted in favour of the already better educated and trained. The OECD recommends both to broaden access opportunities and to develop more flexible, visible, and interconnected pathways, based on the principle of learning while working and working while learning.

Summarizing, it can be concluded that in all countries there is a huge investment in "front-end" education. During the primary and secondary stages, the foundations are developed for continuing education and training in a framework of lifelong learning. After the ages of 16 and 17, the rates of educational participation begin to differ among the countries, because of variations in the compulsory-school leaving age and divergent patterns of participation in tertiary education. A minority of people in their early twenties remain on the trajectory of initial, formal education. From the age of 20, increasing numbers enter the labour-market; sometimes they combine work with continuing education and training.

6.5   Learning During the Twenties and Thirties

When in their twenties and thirties, many European and North American citizens went through a complex transition period, involving a move from education to work, coping with first job experiences and the start-up of a career, finding a partner, and commencing family life. What can be the significance of adult education in this period?

Data on participation in initial, formal education were already shown in Tables 6.3 and 6.4. At the age of 16, nearly 100 per cent are still in school, but after that age many are making the transition from school to working life. At the age of 20, only Canada and the Netherlands enrol more than 50 per cent in educational programmes. The IALS dataset can be used to shed light on the extent of participation in adult education and training during the first three lifespan phases proposed by Fales (1989): "separating from family"; "provisional adulthood", and "thirties transition". In Table 6.5, participation rates are presented for the employed population between 16-25 and 26-35 years.

Table 6.5.   Rate of participation in adult education and training, employed population, ages 16-35, 1994 (percentages)

	Ages 16-25	Ages 26-35
Canada	60.5	44.3
Switzerland	52.2	49.6
United States	51.6	49.8
Netherlands	49.9	49,9
Poland	22.4	22.0
Sweden	52.9	61.4

Table 6.5 reveals that the rate of participation in adult education and training of the young work force is very high, especially in Canada. The participation rate of the employed population in general is higher than the average participation rate of the whole population. This is the case even in Poland, where participation is relatively low compared to the other countries. The conclusion might be that the transition from initial education to working life is a gradual process for many young people, and that the updating and broadening of knowledge and skills are part of this process. Entering the labour-market is often combined with spells of specific on-the-job training, and even participation in more general adult education is a common behaviour during the first years of working life. There are little differences in the participation rates of the 16-25 and 26-35 year-olds in Switzerland, Netherlands, Poland, and the United States. In Canada, however, there is a significant decrease in the participation rate with increasing age, while in Sweden the trend is the opposite, with nearly two in three workers between the ages of 26-35 participating in structured educational activities.

Table 6.6 shows the adult education participation rates of the unemployed populations aged 16-25 and 26-35. It will be seen that the participation rates are generally much lower than those of their working peers. Being unemployed evidently reduces adult education and training probabilities. While unemployed youth in many cases have access to active labour-market schemes, this apparently does not fully compensate for the lack of access to employer-sponsored training opportunities and learning pathways offered in the workplace. The unemployed aged 26-35 are more frequently involved in adult education activities than the younger unemployed group. Sweden, the Netherlands, and Canada have the highest rates of adult education participation for the unemployed. Poland has a very low rate in this respect.

Table 6.6.   Rate of participation in adult education and training, unemployed population, ages 16-35, 1994 (percentages)

	Ages 16-25	Ages 26-35
Canada	44.2	42.8
Switzerland	33.8	34.1
United States	28.8	38.7
Netherlands	37.4	48.7
Poland	12.9	8.3
Sweden	40.4	48.7

Table 6.7 shows the adult education participation rates of the 26-35 age group separately for men and women. In the majority of the countries investigated, more men than women participate. The exception is the United States, where a somewhat higher proportion of young women take part. The largest gap between male and female participation rates is in Switzerland. Because home workers are still more often female than male, it is of interest to examine whether their participation rates confirm the general trend. The data in Table 6.8 show that the participation rates of young home workers are much lower than those of the general population—even lower than those of the unemployed. In Sweden, one in three home workers participates in adult education or training; in Poland, only one in twenty. These figures point to substantial cross-national differences in the cultural and socioeconomic circumstances faced by the populations outside the labour force.

Table 6.7.   Rate of participation in adult education and training, men and women, ages 26-35, 1994 (percentages)

	Men	Women
Canada	46.6	37.3
Switzerland	52.8	40.0
United States	45.7	47.2
Netherlands	49.7	42.0
Poland	18.7	16.1
Sweden	59.3	54.7

Table 6.8.   Rate of participation in adult education and training by home workers, 1994 (percentages)

	Ages 26-35
Canada	28.5
Switzerland	19.6
United States	23.6
Netherlands	26.4
Poland	4.6
Sweden	35.5

6.6   Learning in Mid-life

The period designated with the label, "learning during mid-life" (ages 36-45) is of interest because of mid-career job experiences and the characteristics of family life, both of which present new developmental and learning tasks. Most men and also many women at this age have been in the labour-market for an extended period; many have held several jobs, often with different employers. Table 6.9 shows the rates of participation in adult education for three groups: the employed labour force, the unemployed, and home workers.

Table 6.9.   Rates of participation in adult education by the employed labour force, unemployed and home workers, ages 36-45, 1994 (percentages)

	Employed	Unemployed	Home workers
Canada	43.3	36.7	44.2
Switzerland	45.1	47.5	26.1
United States	51.1	18.8	10.9
Netherlands	44.8	48.0	26.0
Poland	22.2	7.9	2.6
Sweden	62.9	45.8	34.6

The participation rates for the employed population in the age group 36-45 are still high compared with those of the younger age group, 16-35 (see Table 6.5). Only in Switzerland and the Netherlands is a decline noticeable. In Sweden, 63 per cent of the employed population in this age group participated in adult education and training in 1994.

There are large differences between the countries in the adult education participation rates of the unemployed population. The participation rates of the unemployed aged 36-45 surpass those of their working peers in Switzerland and the Netherlands. As in Sweden, where the participation rate is also high, in both countries adult education and training are considered as policy instruments in the fight against unemployment. The differences between the participation rates of the employed labour force and the unemployed in this age group are the largest for the United States and Poland.

The rates of participation by home workers also show remarkable differences between the comparison countries. In Canada and Switzerland, there is an increase in the participation rate from those aged 26-35 (Table 6.8) to the group 36-45, perhaps because women seeking to re-enter the labour-market at this age turn to adult education and training programmes. It is difficult to explain the sharp decline in the United States, where the participation rate of home workers drops from 24 per cent in the group aged 26-35 to 11 per cent in the group aged 36-45.

6.7   Learning Activities of Older Workers

The employability, skill level, and learning behaviour of older workers are paramount issues in all Western societies because of their ageing demographic structures. The mean age of the population in the countries under study will be higher in 2005 than in 1990. Table 6.10 indicates that most countries will experience an increase in the old-age dependency ratio (the population aged 65 and over as a percentage of the population aged 15-64).

Table 6.10.   Old-age dependency ratios 1990 and 2005

	1990	2005
Canada	16.0	18.1
Switzerland	22.0	24.0
Germany	21.6	27.2
United States	18.4	18.5
Netherlands	18.6	20.8
Sweden	28.4	26.4

Source: OECD (1994), p. 24.

Because of a decline in the number of young persons entering the work force in many OECD countries, there will be a gradual ageing of the labour force over the next decades. By 2005, one in three workers is likely to be over the age of 45 (OECD 1994). Because fewer workers will have to support a larger population in retirement, older workers will have to contribute more to the productivity of organizations, and they may even have to stay active for a longer period. The rapid pace of technological change and innovation in West European and North American societies, continuing globalization, and the lowering of many barriers to trade and investment are expected to accentuate the depreciation in the productivity and value of the skills possessed in particular by the poorly educated and older workers. For these groups, more retraining will be required in order to keep productivity levels up and prevent a decline in earnings potential. The increase in the importance of adult education and training for the older work force is also evident in East European countries, where the transition to a free-market economy calls for new skills and entrepreneurial attitudes. Coping with this transition is difficult, especially for older employees (van der Kamp 1991).

The IALS dataset offers an opportunity to examine the current patterns of educational participation of workers in six countries. Figure 6.4 shows the distribution of rates of participation in adult education and training for the employed population and different age groups.

Figure 6.4.   Adult education participation of the employed population by age, 1994

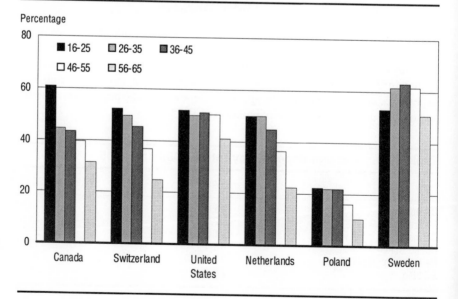

Compared with younger workers, a minor decrease in the participation rate is noticeable for the age group 46-55 years. In contrast, for workers over age 55, there is a steep decline in the rate of participation in training activities, especially in Switzerland, the Netherlands, and Poland. In all of the countries, workers between the ages of 46 and 65 years show higher rates of participation than adults of the same age without work. This is true especially for the age group 56-65 years. Differences in participation are even more pronounced if older workers are compared with the unemployed aged 46-65. After the age of 55, unemployed adults in general are barely involved in educational activities, with Sweden as an important exception, where 30 per cent of the unemployed adults between 56 and 65 participate in organized learning activities. In Canada, Switzerland, the Netherlands, and Poland, the participation rates of the older unemployed population are below 10 per cent. These findings may reflect, albeit only to a certain extent, inter-country differences in the use of adult education and training as instruments of active labour-market policy.

In the total sample of adults in the IALS dataset, there is a strong relationship between the level of initial education and adult education participation. Also, for older workers there is a high correlation between the level of initial formal educational attainment and engagement in adult education activities. Table 6.11 shows, for each of the countries studied, that there is a substantial difference in the participation rates of older workers with and without a post-secondary education (ISCED level 5 and higher), with the better-educated older workers demonstrating much higher rates. With the exception of Poland, over 50 per cent of the employed in the age group 46-55 with a post-secondary education participated in courses during the year preceding the interview. There is a marked under-representation of older workers with little initial education (ISCED levels 0/1 and 2). Only in Sweden do workers aged 46-55 with low levels of formal educational qualifications show relatively high rates of participation in learning activities.

Table 6.11. **Older workers' participation in adult education by initial educational attainment, 1994 (ages 46-55, ISCED levels, percentages)**

	ISCED levels 1					
	0/1	2	3	5	6	7
Canada	11.2	26.4	35.3	50.6	43.0	94.1
Switzerland	0.0	11.4	41.8	52.2	-	50.3
United States	26.0	18.4	38.4	70.0	71.3	71.8
Netherlands	30.3	26.1	32.7	-	55.7	34.9
Poland	3.3	14.8	19.8	33.4	30.4	18.8
Sweden	41.2	50.1	65.6	73.7	75.2	-

1. *ISCED 0/1 refers to six years or completed primary schooling or less; ISCED 2 refers to lower secondary schooling; ISCED 3 refers to upper secondary education; ISCED 4 is not currently in use; ISCED 5 refers to post-secondary education of a non-university type; ISCED 6 refers to undergraduate university-level education; and ISCED 7 refers to postgraduate university-level education.*

A similarly strong relationship exists between personal income and participation in learning activities. Older workers with high incomes participate more in adult education and training activities than older workers with low incomes. There is no statistically certain relationship between full-time and part-time work, on the one hand, and the rate of participation in organized learning activities, on the other.

It can be hypothesized that younger workers participate more frequently for job or career-related purposes than older workers, while the latter more frequently take part for reasons of personal development and the pursuit of enjoyment in leisure. The IALS dataset does not offer unequivocal support for this hypothesis. Table 6.12 shows that the large majority of older workers in the age groups 46-55 and 56-65 who take part in adult education activities consider that they do so for job-related purposes.

Table 6.12. **Older workers' rate of participation in adult education for job-related purposes, 1994 (percentages)**

	Ages 46-55	Ages 56-65
Canada	82.8	92.9
Switzerland	68.9	80.6
United States	89.5	92.8
Netherlands	67.6	63.9
Poland	86.9	80.9

It is striking that workers aged 56-65 are still to such a large extent motivated by job-related purposes and not by personal interest or other reasons for participation. Older workers who are active in education and training activities seem to be somewhat less job-oriented in the Netherlands compared with the other countries, but even in this country over 60 per cent of all participants are motivated by job-related reasons. This finding may reflect the favourable early retirement arrangements for low-skilled older workers that existed in the Netherlands during the 1970s and 1980s. The Dutch labour-force participation rate of older workers is indeed lower that those of the other countries under study.

Those older workers who said they participated because of job-related purposes were asked to what extent they could make use in the workplace of the knowledge and skills they acquired. Table 6.13 shows the results. Compared with the populations in the other countries, older workers in Poland who took part in education and training for job-related reasons often considered that the knowledge and skills they had acquired were not of great use to them in their work. Canada shows a different result; here, many older workers judged their education or training to have been useful for their work.

Table 6.13.   Older workers' judgment of the usefulness for their work of knowledge and skills acquired through job-related courses, 1994 (percentages)

	Ages 46-55 "to a great extent"	Ages 56-65 "to a great extent"
Canada	82.8	84.4
Switzerland	58.2	63.1
United States	62.6	58.6
Netherlands	65.2	71.7
Poland	30.8	34.4

Many older workers who took part in learning activities for job-related purposes were supported financially by their employer. In the countries involved, this was the case for between 50 and 75 per cent of the older workers who took part in courses. Nevertheless, between 25 and 43 per cent of the older workers had to finance at least a part of the costs of the training themselves. Most older workers took education or training on their own initiative. But many older employees were told or encouraged by their employers to take part in courses. In Canada and the United States, workers aged 45-55 participated as often on their own initiative as on the suggestion of their employers. For workers aged 56-65, however, participation was most often on the suggestion of employers. This may in part explain the older workers' very high rates of participation for job-related purposes. In Switzerland and the Netherlands, older workers aged 45-65 had to take the initiative themselves more often than they enroled with the support of their employers. In Poland, however, participation by older workers was most often initiated by the employer. Perhaps this is one of the reasons for the lower level of satisfaction with the usefulness of the training reported by Polish workers.

It is of interest to study the relationships between occupational groups and participation in adult education and training by older workers. In all countries, the older workers employed as managers, professionals, and technicians more frequently took part in adult education activities than workers in other occupational categories. In the United States and Sweden, the participation rate of professionals, managers, and technicians is on the order of 80 per cent. Also, clerks have a high participation rate. Older workers in the financial and personal services sectors have a higher rate of educational activity than persons of similar age in other sectors of the labour-market. The financial and personal services sectors are not only more adult-education friendly than other sectors, they also have the highest rates of employment and productivity growth, and they are characterized by rising skill demands due to technological innovation and changes in workplace organization.

In conclusion, in all countries, there is a decline in the participation rate of older persons (ages 46-65) compared with the rates of young people (26-35) and those in a mid-career stage (36-45). Although employers often support training, older workers participate in adult education in the first instance on their own initiative.

6.8   Learning in Old Age

In some of the IALS countries, data were collected for a representative group of people over 65-years-old. In Canada, no upper age limit was set for the inclusion of people in the sampling frame; in Sweden and the Netherlands, the sampling frame included older adults in the age bracket 66-75. The latter age group can thus be studied in an international perspective for three countries. The results of such a comparative analysis can contribute to the international debate on educational activities for the elderly.

Education for older adults appears to be a relatively new issue in the industrialized countries, mainly because of ageing populations and the increase in the share of non-work time in the lifespan. The elderly are an increasingly important consumer group in adult education. Many senior citizens are affluent and healthy and have an active interest and capacity for continued learning. To satisfy the demand expressed by this clientele, new modes of provision have been developed in many OECD countries, ranging from pre-retirement training courses to study circles, memory training, health education, special basic education programmes, evening classes, and "universities for the third age". This variety of provision is reflected in a fragmented financing system, an ad-hoc structure, and incompatible cultures originating in the worlds of work, formal education, and care for the elderly. Table 6.14 shows the adult education participation rates of two older age groups.

Table 6.14. Older adults' (56-75) rate of participation in adult education and training, 1994 (percentages)

	Ages 56-65	Ages 66-75
Canada	9.0	6.9
Switzerland	16.9	n.a.
United States	10.7	n.a.
Netherlands	13.3	9.7
Poland	1.1	n.a.
Sweden	15.9	10.2

The data in Table 6.14 reveal that Sweden has the highest rate of adult education participation also among the older age groups, with the Netherlands in a close second position. In Poland, in contrast, older adults participate in educational activities only to a very limited extent. The overall rate of participation of people over 56 is low in all countries, despite the augmented demand for learning expressed by the elderly. Specific data analyses show that the participants among older adults can be characterized as the initially better educated, with above median incomes and good literacy skills, who participate actively also in other spheres of social, cultural, and political life (van der Kamp & Scheeren 1996). In-depth interviews with elderly respondents conducted by van der Kamp & Scheeren (1996) reveal that many poorly educated older adults in the Netherlands have a marked negative attitude towards education. In many cases, the respondents recalled that they did not enjoy or succeed in school. The implied challenge for adult educators is to make education more attractive for older adults. But this is not enough. Because readiness for lifelong learning is developed in initial education, every effort must be made to prevent school failure and early school leaving.

6.9   Predicting Adult Education Participation Across the Lifespan

The results of a multivariate analysis of data are presented below. The purpose of the analysis was to estimate the relative weights of major predictor variables in determining educational participation across the lifespan. Because the dependent variable, adult education participation, is dichotomous, whereas independent variables such as age and initial educational attainment are continuous, a logistic regression method was used (Kerlinger & Pedzahur 1973).

Table 6.15 presents the results obtained for four variables in predicting adult education participation: initial educational attainment, labour-force status, gender, and age. The models specified for Canada, the Netherlands, and Sweden are estimated on the basis of the population 16-75; the others refer to the population 16-65. The "per cent correct" values offer an indication of the goodness of fit of the model, with higher values indicating better fit and predictability and lower values poorer fit and predictability. The index is a measure of the proportion between predicted and observed outcomes in adult education participation, given the variables included in the model. Even though the patterns of predictability are not similar in every case, the results of a pooled overall regression analysis across all countries are also presented.

Table 6.15.   Estimates obtained in a logistic regression model predicting adult education participation

	Initial educational attainment	Labour force status (employed)	Gender (0=male; 1=female)	Age	Per cent correct
Canada	.183*	.131*	.024	-.225*	73.6
Switzerland	.125*	.101*	.000	-.097*	61.8
United States	.277*	.163*	.039*	-.084	69.2
Netherlands	.129*	.088*	.025	-.145*	65.6
Poland	.265*	.164*	.000	-.105*	85.3
Sweden	.130*	.214*	.036	-.088*	67.8
All countries	.200*	.155*	.045*	-.115*	68.8

*   = *statistically significant at <0.01; percent correct).*

It is important to note that the "per cent correct" values are satisfactory. This means that the most important predictor variables have been specified in the model. The overall analysis based on the pooled dataset for all countries combined reveals that initial educational attainment is the best predictor of adult education participation. Further, labour-force status is also significantly related to participation in adult education and training. Age is another contributing factor: when people are older, they participate less. Compared with the weight of these three variables, the role of gender is insignificant.

The overall pattern is roughly similar in all countries, but there are a few differences worth noting. Initial educational attainment, for example, has the highest influence on adult education participation in the United States and Poland. Employment status is the most important determinant of adult education participation in Sweden; its weight is even higher than that of initial educational attainment. Age is the main predictor of adult education participation in Canada.

Table 6.16 shows the results obtained in a logistic regression analysis that predicts participation separately for six age groups. The analysis is based on the pooled dataset that includes all countries and age groups covered in the survey. While this approach has the disadvantage of masking interesting between-country differences, it was employed because the number of cases included in the data analysis would otherwise have been too small to yield reliable estimates. Because there is no variation in age within each separate regression, the influences of initial educational attainment, labour-force status, and gender on adult education participation can be compared for six age groups.

Again, the per cent correct values are high and satisfactory. The role of gender is limited, as was expected on the basis of previous results. A minor but significant effect of gender, with an advantage for women, operates only for the older age groups, 46-55 and 56-65. In these age groups, more women than men take part in educational activities. Labour-force status is a remarkably important predictor for the group aged 56-65. In many countries, this phase in the lifespan is associated with exits from the active labour force. Those who stay on in the work force at this age are more inclined—or are strongly encouraged by employers—to participate in adult education and training activities. Retirement from the labour force appears to coincide with a decrease in educational activity.

Table 6.16 offers overwhelming evidence in support of the so-called "accumulation hypothesis" in lifelong learning: the quality and amount of previous educational experience, both initial and post-initial, predict the quality and amount of learning experience gained in subsequent phases in life (Tuijnman 1989). Even for the population over 65, initial educational attainment remains the most powerful predictor of participation in adult education.

Table 6.16. Estimates obtained in logistic regression models predicting adult education participation for six age groups

Age groups	Initial educational attainment	Labour force status (employed)	Gender (female)	Per cent correct
16-25	.107*	.000	.000	55.6
26-35	.204*	.090*	.000	64.7
36-45	.231*	.103*	.000	65.6
46-55	.222*	.151*	.056*	69.2
56-65	.223*	.272*	.095*	82.5
66-75	.167*	.148*	.058	92.7

*   = *statistically significant at <0.01; percent correct*
1.   *Population includes students.*

6.10 Conclusions

A first point is that lifespan theories, for example, the one suggested by Fales (1989), and particularly the major changes across the various lifespan phases—and associated developmental tasks—that such theories purport to describe, cannot readily and empirically be translated into learning needs, educational demand, and participation behaviour. Lifespan theories are clearly in need of refinement with respect to the relation between age-bound developmental change and the function of education and learning more generally. In addition, more attention will have to be given to the role of social and cultural capital in predicting participation in adult education across the lifespan. Variables measuring aspects of personal interest, development, and leisure behaviour must be included in the models predicting engagement in adult education and learning. Further work using the IALS dataset might offer some new insights in this respect, but longitudinal cohort studies will have to be undertaken if theoretical and empirical advances are to be made and sustained in the long term.

In all countries investigated in this chapter, by far the largest portion of total human capital investment is allocated to the education of children and young adults. There are significant between-country differences in the portion of total investment that is allocated to adult education, for those over 20 who are no longer enroled in full-time programmes of formal education. Sweden is the front-runner; it can be considered an excellent example of a country reaching out towards the ideals of the "learning society". Poland is far behind the other countries in this respect. The correspondence between a country's ranking in terms of its measured literacy proficiency and its place based on rates of participation in adult education and training cannot be a coincidence (see also Chapter 7). Higher levels of literacy proficiency are associated with higher rates of participation in adult education. Literacy skills increase participation, and participation has a favourable influence on literacy skills (van der Kamp & Scheeren 1996).

In all countries, the level of participation of older adults is still comparatively low, despite the increase in learning needs and the growing diversity of suppliers specializing in educational provisions for the elderly. During all phases across the lifespan, labour-force participation is a major determinant of adult education and training. The training of older employees, however, appears to be relatively neglected in Poland and the Netherlands. The adult education participation rate of the unemployed is significantly below that of the employed population, but the unemployed take part more often than home workers and other people outside the labour force. The patterns of participation by home workers show surprising variation across lifespan phases, and they differ across the countries investigated. Some of this variation is specific to life phases, such as establishing a family and having children or re-entering the labour-market, and some of it may be due to cross-cultural differences in values of family and work. Gender plays only a limited role in adult education participation; it is only later in life that women participate more frequently than men. While this finding holds for the rate and frequency of educational participation, it is not necessarily true in terms of other variables, such as the reasons for participation, the choice of supplier, the medium of learning, and the qualitative experience of learning itself. The data indicate significant differences between men and women in the reasons for participation and the nature of the learning encounter, with women more often emphasizing personal interest and development and men more frequently mentioning job and career-related goals.

The results presented in this chapter offer strong evidence in support of the accumulation hypothesis in lifelong learning (Tuijnman 1989). In initial formal education, the foundation is laid for learning later in life. This means that the redistribution of opportunities to learn and participate in educational programmes in a lifespan perspective and in alternation with work and other significant activities can augment the skill inequalities that exist between well- and poorly educated citizens. The policy implication is that the key determining role of initial formal education, and issues such as access, quality, and effectiveness for all, cannot be neglected. It is also clear that current adult education provisions are insufficiently accessible and open to the poorly educated, especially older adults who have left the labour force. The development of more attractive and innovative pathways for lifelong learning that take account of the learning needs and desires of these priority groups poses a large and urgent challenge for policy-makers and educators.

References

Fales, A.W. 1989. "Lifespan Learning Development". In: C.J. Titmus (ed.). *Lifelong Education for Adults: An International Handbook*. Oxford: Pergamon Press.

Heymans, P.G. 1992. "Lifespan Learning: Developmental Tasks and their Management". In: A.C. Tuijnman and M. van der Kamp (eds.) *Learning Across the Lifespan: Theories, Research, Policies*. Oxford: Pergamon Press.

Kerlinger, F., and Pedzahur, E.J. 1973. *Multiple Regression in Behavior Research*. New York: Holt, Rinehart and Winston.

Murray, T.S., and Kirsch, I.S. (eds.). 1997. *International Adult Literacy Survey: Technical Report*. Washington, DC: National Center for Education Statistics, United States Department of Education.

OECD. 1994. *The OECD Jobs Study: Evidence and Explanations*. (Vol. I) Paris: Organisation for Economic Co-operation and Development.

OECD. 1995. *Education at a Glance: OECD Indicators*. (3d ed.) Paris: Centre for Educational Research and Innovation.

OECD. 1996a. *Education at a Glance: OECD Indicators*. (4th ed.) Paris: Centre for Educational Research and Innovation.

OECD. 1996b. *Lifelong Learning for All: Report of the meeting of the Education Committee at ministerial level, 16-17 January 1996.* Paris: Organisation for Economic Co-operation and Development.

OECD and Statistics Canada 1995. *Literacy, Economy and Society: Results of the First International Adult Literacy Survey.* Paris and Ottawa: Organisation for Economic Co-operation and Development and Statistics Canada.

Provoost, A. 1986. "Iconografie van de menselijke levensloop. Drie verkenningstochten". In: H.F.M. Peeters and F.J. Monks (eds.). *De menselijke levensloop in historisch perpectief.* Assen: Van Gorcum.

Schuller, T. 1992. "Age, Gender, and Learning in the Lifespan". In: A.C. Tuijnman and M. van der Kamp (eds), *Learning Across the Lifespan: Theories, Research, Policies.* Oxford: Pergamon Press.

Sugerman, L. 1986. *Lifespan Development: Concepts, Theories and Interventions.* London: Methuen.

Tuijnman, A.C. 1989. *Recurrent Education, Earnings, and Well-being.* (Acta Universitatis Stockholmiensis No. 24) Stockholm: Almqvist and Wiksell International.

Thomas, R.M. 1990. *Encyclopedia of Human Development and Education.* Oxford: Pergamon Press.

van der Kamp, M. 1991. "Not too old to learn—research on the learning activities of older adults". (Paper presented at the EARLI conference 1991, Turku, Finland, August 24-28) Groningen: University of Groningen, Department of Adult Education.

van der Kamp, M., and Scheeren, J. 1996. *Reken- en taalvaardigheden van oudere volwassenen.* Amsterdam: Max Goote Kenniscentrum.

Chapter 7

Literacy Proficiency and Adults' Readiness to Learn

David C. Neice and T. Scott Murray

7.1 Introduction

In a highly competitive and technically complex world in which advanced skills are paid a premium, the readiness of adults to continue learning—whether self-directed or through participation in adult education and training—has very serious consequences. Readiness for lifelong learning depends on the prior skill base held by individuals and developed through informal and formal learning. The purpose of this chapter is to assess the literacy skill base of adults in the seven countries that participated and released data in the first round of the International Adult Literacy Survey (IALS). A range of associations between literacy skills, demographic variables, labour force status, leisure and community activities, and experiences with adult education and training will be reviewed. From this composite picture, a sense of the readiness of adults to meet the adaptive skill requirements of the modern world will be derived. Differences among the participating countries, and their extension to similar societies, will be commented on.

7.2 Current Global Competitiveness Pressures

The period since the late 1980s has been one of strain and adjustment for many OECD countries. Leading economists and managers may quibble over the details but they concur broadly on at least one thing: that the disruptive changes presently at large in the advanced economies are not of the traditional business cycle type, but are instead deeper and more fundamental changes in the forces and factors of production (Handy 1990; Reich 1992; Drucker 1993; Romer 1993; Lipsey 1995; Rifkin 1995).

The two most important new economic factors are, firstly, the global reach of information and computer communications systems, which permit large transnational corporations to organize their activities on a global basis, and secondly, the priority now assigned to knowledge-based production, particularly work that leads to innovation and to proprietary intellectual property rights through patents and copyright. These changes are characterized in many different ways by various authors: as the shift to a knowledge economy; as the third industrial revolution; as the computer and information revolution; as the birth of a post-capitalist or post-modern economy and society; and as the shift from an economy of "atoms" to an economy of "bits".

Accompanying this shift has been a general commitment by policy-makers to deregulate and relax existing trade barriers. These modifications result from successive trade agreements, such as the Uruguay Round, the North American Free Trade Agreement, and, in Europe, the Maastricht Treaty. The near-instantaneous global reach of communications networks, along with the ability of investors to move capital swiftly to locations with a suitably skilled and low-cost work force, virtually anywhere, as well as the freer flow of goods and services, have ensured that the world has rapidly become a much more intensely competitive place. The new conditions have broad implications for the social order, the roles and responsibilities of governments, the effectiveness of educational institutions, and most pointedly, the prospects for specific economies to make a successful transition to the new age, and for their labour forces to adapt to new skill requirements.

Out of this broad set of forces and considerations, the foundation role of literacy skills has emerged as a key element in the debate. Literacy was taken for granted, by and large, in the industrial era, in part because school systems had been finely tuned over time to meet industrial needs. Education streaming, by design or by accident, had the net effect of supplying the industrial economy with sufficient numbers of the highly literate, who were headed for the professions and offices, and the moderately literate, usually headed for the shop floor. Below all this there was an unstated assumption, which held for several decades, that some basic level of literacy was being inculcated into everyone. This minimum was accomplished through universal public schooling and was an essential part of the exercise and rights of citizenship. In the industrial society, literacy was seen to be something taught to children and youth and primarily the responsibility of schools and educators. Schooling had succeeded, or so it was thought, to make everyone read and write sufficiently well to satisfy the requirements of work and daily life.

Somewhere around the mid-1980s, the literacy sufficiency assumption began to be called into question. Educational testing of young people began to show some disturbing trends toward skill bifurcation of the youth population (see Kirsch & Jungeblut 1986). Parents, at least in North America, were expressing concern about the range and level of skills their children were acquiring at school. Educators and researchers were raising alarms about the readiness of children to learn, and about the possible effects that enveloping media, such as television, were having on youth (Healy 1990). At the same time, micro-computers were proliferating at work, and many adults of all ages were faced with unique training circumstances and new skill requirements (OECD 1992). All this arrived on the public policy horizon, just as it was realized that many adults, when directly tested on their literacy skill levels, were often found to be surprisingly deficient, with only marginal functioning in their ability to use prose, document, and quantitative literacy materials.

Thus, in the midst of all this change and questioning, it was realized that literacy is not forever, that it is a skill that depends on adult practice and use. Some behaviours and practices seem to encourage its growth and development, while others reduce its potential. It was also discovered that literacy is not just for children and youth, it is also an adult skill and a continuing adult responsibility. This insight came just at about the time when recessions and technological displacement were churning people, in many cases middle-aged and middle-class people, through various labour-market transitions. It thus became evident that the adaptiveness of adults for further learning rested on their mastery of basic skills, and that adult literacy skills held the top priority amongst those foundation skills.

The shift towards an information economy has brought along a reconsideration of the meaning of literacy and what it entails. In turn, this has led to a renewed emphasis on the active promotion of adult education and training in a framework for lifelong learning (OECD 1996). The main purpose of this chapter is, therefore, to investigate the readiness of adults to continue learning in both formal and informal settings, based on the performance data available from the IALS. How do the seven countries compare in terms of the distribution of adult literacy skills? How amenable are these countries to the development of a lifelong learning culture based on the existing skill base?

7.3 Requirements for Readiness to Learn

From a skills perspective, there are a series of interlinked skills that can be said to underpin the potential for adults to achieve successful transitions within a knowledge-based economy. Many of these skills have been identified in various research traditions and are labelled as basic skills, foundation skills, or core competencies (Jones 1995; Tuijnman et al. 1996). The most central of these are functional literacy skills. These skills involve much more than the ability to read a simple sentence. They require adults actually to be able to work with and use various kinds of printed material commonly encountered at home, at work, and in their communities. Examples are newspaper articles, application forms and schedules, consumer warranties, and bank slips, as well as working with simple graphs and tables that require elementary numeracy skills.

Communicative competencies represent a second set of skills enabling successful adaptation and transition. These comprise oral communication skills and the ability to work successfully in groups and other organizational settings. A third category involves analytical and problem-solving skills, including the ability to deal with the unfamiliar—a key element in adaptation. A further essential skill is the ability to work with various information technologies.

There will be a wide spread in the skill mix available to individuals at any given moment in their life-course. In the aggregate, this also applies to any society. For instance, literacy skills may be strongest in one's youth, and then in some people may begin to decline. Communicative competencies may improve in middle age, whereas problem-solving skills may be strong or weak, depending on the opportunities afforded people to test and exercise their capacities. Digital literacy skills also will vary depending on age, education, income, and inclination.

These skills, taken together, form the basis for the readiness of adults to continue learning. If there were a way to measure them, with the same rigour now available for literacy skills, then those with high average scores across the skills would form the training- and learning-ready, whereas those with weak average scores would form the at-risk population. It will be some years before it will become feasible to measure the wider set of essential skills described previously. For the moment, therefore, the results from the more restricted set of skills measured as part of the IALS are the best available. Thus, for the purposes of this chapter, the performance of individuals on the IALS skill test will be treated as a proxy measure or indicator of "readiness and availability for lifelong learning" and of "potential for successful adaptation" to the conditions available in the knowledge-based economy and society (see also Neice 1996).

7.4   The Measurement of Literacy Proficiency

The goal of the IALS was to establish comparative benchmark measures on the literacy skills of adults in the participating countries (OECD & Statistics Canada 1995). The study represents a landmark in the direct measurement of human capital stock. The countries which chose to be included in the first round represent certain patterns of skill attainment which may be found in other, similar societies. Sweden is quite likely typical of the Nordic countries and the Netherlands an example of the Low Countries. Switzerland may set an example for advanced multilingual societies, and Poland for Eastern Europe, while Canada and the United States provide results for two major trading partners in North America.

The IALS was built on a series of literacy skill surveys carried out in the 1980s and early 1990s in the United States (Kirsch & Jungeblut 1986; Kirsch et al. 1993), Canada (Montigny et al. 1991), and Australia (Wickert 1989). They were fostered by the theoretical work on the factors underlying difficulty in reading contributed by Kirsch and Mosenthal (1990).

The meaning of literacy as applied in the survey

The IALS framework is concerned primarily with the measurement of a range of adult literacy skills, as determined through tested proficiency levels, using stimulus materials drawn from real world applications, found in specific contexts within OECD countries (OECD & Statistics Canada 1995; Murray & Kirsch 1997).

Common sense would suggest that literacy is treated as a cultural given for all the adults in OECD societies. While there are a small number of adults who are unable to read at all, they are often considered anomalies. In the IALS framework, in contrast, literacy is not merely about whether people can read simple sentences such as "the cat came back". Instead, it is first of all about what adults can actually do when faced with certain types of reading test materials. Their test results depend on their formal schooling, formal and informal adult learning, and their applications of reading practices and behaviours at work and in daily life. The approach is based on a powerful theory of reading, one which links reading difficulty to attributes of the text for the tasks which the reader must perform, and these stimuli in turn reflect the use made of literacy in daily life.

The survey aimed at establishing proficiency levels, using a sophisticated testing and scaling methodology developed and refined at the Educational Testing Service in Princeton, New Jersey. The applied scaling methodology employs item response theory modelling as a means of estimating both item difficulty and individual proficiency. The method does not result in the setting of a criterion level for literacy, nor does it establish a cut-off that differentiates "literates" from "illiterates". Instead, it portrays literacy as a skill continuum, where everyone is assumed to be literate to some degree. The question then shifts to the level at which adults perform.

The test materials used with adults are based on real world applications. They ask the adults being tested to work with materials found in everyday life. For instance, the materials employ a label from a medicine bottle, simple invoices and receipts, materials that provide directions to assemble things, transportation maps, prose articles from newspapers and magazines, and items that require simple numeracy skills, such as number addition or multiplication.

Few of the items used in the assessment are very difficult, objectively speaking, but the items differ significantly from casual or pleasure reading in that they all involve locating and working with specific bits of information in order to provide a correct answer to a question. One would hope, for instance, that a person reading a medicine bottle label would be able to determine the correct dosage for a child. But when tested, a surprisingly large number of adults get the answer wrong.

In keeping with its defining role as a test of adult literacy skills, the survey deals both with text and print decoding skills, as well as with decision skills. To be placed at a particular level, respondents have to consistently get tasks correct at that level, and the threshold for performance consistency was set at 80 percent. This approach does not take issue with the fact that most adults can in fact read, but it does take issue with the assumption that nearly all adults can read well enough to consistently obtain the correct answers on test items of varying difficulty. The ability to read printed materials carefully and critically while looking for key pieces of information is a highly-prized work-place skill.

Three Literacy Dimensions and Five Levels of Proficiency

The assessment results were reported using three scaling dimensions of literacy rather than a single measure. These dimensions are:

- *Prose literacy*—the knowledge and skills needed to understand and use information derived from printed texts, including editorials, news stories, poems, and fiction;

- *Document literacy*—the knowledge and skills required to find and use information contained in text formats, such as job applications, payroll forms, transportation schedules, maps, tables, and graphs;

- *Quantitative literacy*—the knowledge and skills required to apply arithmetic operations to numbers embedded in printed materials, such as balancing a cheque book, calculating a tip, or completing an order form.

The results for the three tested literacy dimensions were all scaled on a zero to five hundred range. Within this range, five empirically determined levels of proficiency were established. The five levels reflect qualitative shifts in the skills and strategies required to succeed on various tasks placed along the scale, ranging from simple to complex. For purposes of clarity, Figure 7.1 shows the applied scale range and fixes the numerical scale values which define each of the five levels. These values are the same across all three scales. Whereas the distinction between Level 4 and Level 5 makes sense on both conceptual and empirical grounds, these two levels are combined in the analyses that follow, because fewer than five per cent of the adult population in some countries were discovered to perform at the highest level, hence statistically reliable estimates of performance at the highest level could not be produced for all of the countries.

Figure 7.1.   Literacy scale range and skill level metric points

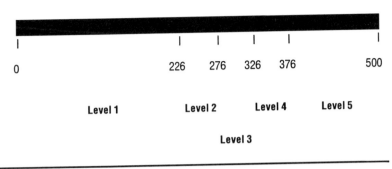

Figure 7.2 provides a summary of the scale score ranges and sample tasks for each of the three domains of prose, document, and quantitative literacy. The five levels, while successive, are not normative. It is not being said, for instance, that Level 2 is inadequate, or that Level 4 is preferred. Of course, if a society prizes literacy skills, then high scores, by the greatest numbers of people, might be socially valued. However, as a tool for the measurement of adult skills and proficiency, the test does not make any normative judgments.

The data show that many people with low educational attainment perform at Levels 1 and 2 on the three scales. It can be inferred that it might be better for a society if all of its members would perform at a high level of proficiency. People performing at a low level have not failed the IALS test; they have only demonstrated a lower level of proficiency when normed against others in their society. However, despite these caveats, there is a general sense among analysts that the empirical break between Level 2 and Level 3 is the most significant. Large differences in measures like labour-force status and earnings from work tend to show up most clearly at this cut point on the scale. Therefore, literacy proficiency Levels 1 and 2, for purposes of this analysis, should probably be viewed as insufficient to ensure effective social and economic integration. Level 3 represents the point of skill development and proficiency where real social inclusion and an escape from the marginalizing effects of poor reading skills is more assured. The same can be said of "readiness" for lifelong learning and adult education.

Figure 7.2.   Scale score ranges and task samples

Level	Score	Prose	Document	Quantitative
1	0–225	Use the instructions on the bottle to identify the maximum duration recommended for taking aspirin.	Identify the percentage of Greek teachers who are women by looking at a simple pictorial graph.	Fll in the figure on the last line of an order form, "Total with Handling", by adding the ticket price of $50 to a handling charge of $2.
2	226–275	Identify a short piece of information about the characteristics of a garden plant, from a written article.	Identify the year in which the fewest Dutch people were injured by fireworks, when presented with two simple graphs.	Work out how many degrees warmer today's forecast high temperature is in Bangkok than in Seoul, using a table accompanying a weather chart.
3	276–325	State which of a set of four movie reviews was the least favorable.	Identify the time of the last bus on a Saturday night, using a bus schedule.	Work out how much more energy Canada produces than it consumes, by comparing figures on two bar charts.
4	326–375	Answer a brief question on how to conduct a job interview, requiring the reader to read a pamphlet on recruitment interviews and integrate two pieces of information into a single statement.	Summarize how the percentages of oil used for different purposes changed over a specified period, by comparing two pie charts.	Calculate how much money you will have if you invest $100 at a rate of 6 per cent for 10 years, using a compound interest table.
5	376–500	Use an announcement from a personnel department to answer a question that uses different phrasing from that used in the text.	Identify the average advertised price for the best-rated basic clock radio in a consumer survey, requiring the assimilation of several pieces of information.	Use information on a table of nutritional analysis to calculate the percentage of calories in a Big Mac® that comes from total fat.

International comparisons

Even though the IALS was designed to be an international study with a comparative dimension, the purpose was not to turn the results into a literacy skill "olympics". The scale score results for different countries reflect a myriad of internal historical and structural factors, and bear the traces of decades of policy decisions in diverse fields, such as education, lifelong learning, employment, social affairs, and migration. Because of this complexity, it might be misleading to make simple comparisons across the countries. Attention needs to be given to the fact that each society studied is unique in circumstance and context.

The results presented in this chapter are available for all three scales, prose, document, and quantitative. However, for the sake of brevity, the document scale has been selected for the portrayal of most of the results. This scale is often particularly revealing, because it uses as test materials various forms, maps, schedules, and graphs and tables, and these often include prose-based introductions. These tasks are close to the kinds of semi-structured and non-narrative reading material which adults encounter daily.

7.5   General Findings and Discussion

While the analysis of overall country comparisons might appeal to some readers, for the purposes of this chapter it is necessary to isolate the factors that bear on the skill readiness of adult populations for lifelong learning and formal adult education. Below, the emphasis will be on the following factors: adult literacy proficiency, educational attainment, migration, age, gender, and labour-force status.

Overall distribution of adult literacy

Table 7.1 presents the main findings of the study for all three scales. A striking result is that Sweden, the one country in this group with a historic commitment to the principles of lifelong learning, outperforms all the other countries on all the scales. By way of example, Sweden has close to 75 per cent of its adult population functioning at Levels 3 and the combined Level 4/5 across the three scales. No other country is even close, particularly when one looks at the highest performance level, where over one-third of the adult Swedes are found, and at the lowest level, where less than seven per cent are found.

Table 7.1.a   Proportion of population (16-65) in each country at each literacy level, prose scale (percentages)

	Level 1	Level 2	Level 3	Level 4/5
Canada	16.6	25.6	35.1	22.7
Germany	14.4	34.2	38.0	13.4
Netherlands	10.5	30.1	44.1	15.3
Poland	42.6	34.5	19.8	3.1
Sweden	7.5	20.3	39.7	32.4
Switzerland (French)	17.6	33.7	38.6	10.0
Switzerland (German)	19.3	35.7	36.1	8.9
United States	20.7	25.9	32.4	21.1

Table 7.1.b   Proportion of population (16-65) in each country at each literacy level, document scale (percentages)

	Level 1	Level 2	Level 3	Level 4/5
Canada	18.2	24.7	32.1	25.1
Germany	9.0	32.7	39.5	18.9
Netherlands	10.1	25.7	44.2	20.0
Poland	45.4	30.7	18.0	5.8
Sweden	6.2	18.9	39.4	35.5
Switzerland (French)	16.2	28.8	38.9	16.0
Switzerland (German)	18.1	29.1	36.6	16.1
United States	23.7	25.9	31.4	19.0

Table 7.1.c   Proportion of population in each country for each literacy level, quantitative scale (percentages)

	Level 1	Level 2	Level 3	Level 4/5
Canada	16.9	26.1	34.8	22.2
Germany	6.7	26.6	43.2	23.5
Netherlands	10.3	25.5	44.3	19.9
Poland	39.1	30.1	23.9	6.8
Sweden	6.6	18.6	39.0	35.8
Switzerland (French)	12.9	24.5	42.2	20.4
Switzerland (German)	14.2	26.2	40.7	19.0
United States	21.0	25.3	31.3	22.5

In marked contrast to the Swedish results are the patterns for Canada and the United States, a pair of countries that invest huge sums in formal education and training (OECD 1996). In these two countries, across the three scales, between 55 and 58 per cent of the adult population function at proficiency levels 3 and 4/5. However, it must be noted that these two countries also display a more U-shaped distribution across the levels than do the others. Compared to Germany or the Netherlands, for example, more North Americans score at the top levels. But in the United States, there is a clear bifurcation between the proportion scoring at the highest level of literacy proficiency and those at the bottom, where about 20 per cent of adults are found. This pattern in the distribution of skill seems to reflect certain structural differences between European and North American countries, and draws out a sharp contrast between those who have obtained at least some education at the tertiary level and those who for one reason or another did not complete a course of foundation learning in secondary schools.

In Germany, the Netherlands, and the two French and German-speaking regions of Switzerland, there is a predominance of adults scoring at Level 3, even when compared to the two countries in North America. This phenomenon is most marked on the quantitative scale, where over 40 per cent of adults in the European countries score at Level 3.

Poland appears as a special case in the study. On the one hand, the country obviously represents important aspects of Eastern European experience. On the other hand, its results are much less favourable compared with the other OECD societies, and there is reason to believe that the results surprised even Polish observers. Nonetheless, the test materials were carefully developed to permit the removal of linguistic and cultural factors, so the results for Poland show that, relative to the other countries examined, there appear to be serious skill deficiencies. Almost in reverse of the Swedish results, close to 75 per cent of the Polish adults perform at the bottom two levels of literacy proficiency.

Overall, these aggregate trends speak volumes to the question of the comparative readiness of the adult populations in these countries for further education and training. For example:

- Sweden, and other societies like it, obviously have high readiness quotients, albeit with some people still lacking the requisite foundation skills;
- In Canada and the United States, the population seems more bifurcated between those with sufficient basic skills to foster further learning and a large group at the bottom who lack these foundations;
- In countries with a Level 3 bulge, there is a more likely chance of success with investment in adult education and training if these involve intermediate rather than highly advanced literacy skills;
- In any country with Poland's basic skill profile, the potential readiness for lifelong learning and formal adult education is quite weak, and policy-makers would do well to emphasize measures designed to improve the remastery of foundation skills.

In all the countries investigated, analysts have confirmed the existence of a noticeable empirical break between Level 2 and Level 3 performance. As previously noted, proficiency Levels 1 and 2 are indicative of weak literacy performance and limited reading strategies. The skills and competencies needed to achieve effective life and career transitions; individual confidence about the opportunities afforded by lifelong learning; and the adaptive skills needed to fill demanding roles in advanced societies are not found at either Level 1 or 2, and only begin to solidify at Level 3.

Literacy and educational attainment

An interesting feature of the dataset is that it allows for the possibility to study literacy skills as a function of outcomes of formal education systems. Hence, one can investigate the defining common characteristics of adults who have a combination of weak levels of formal education and weak literacy skills. For the purposes of the analysis reported below, these adults are defined empirically as those who did not complete a full cycle of secondary education or its equivalent, and who fall into Levels 1 and 2 on the literacy skill continuum.

The overall results are startling, as shown in Table 7.2, even if the trends are the most pronounced in North America. Large numbers of those who did not graduate from upper secondary education function at Levels 1 and 2 on the document scale. It is useful to examine the results country by country.

Table 7.2.   Proportion of population (16-65) at each ISCED level* for each literacy level, document scale (percentages)

Country		Level 1	Level 2	Level 3	Level 4/5
Canada	Less than ISCED 02	73.6	15.4	9.7	1.3
	ISCED 02	23.2	40.2	26.3	10.3
	ISCED 03	10.5	28.4	36.9	24.1
	ISCED 05	4.2	17.6	39.1	39.1
	ISCED 06/07	3.3	10.1	38.5	59.1
Netherlands	Less than ISCED 02	36.0	38.7	19.2	6.2
	ISCED 02	11.2	36.9	43.1	8.8
	ISCED 03	2.9	18.2	52.4	26.5
	ISCED 05 **	n.a.	n.a.	n.a.	n.a.
	ISCED 06/07	1.3	13.8	50.0	34.9
Poland	Less than ISCED 02	74.6	18.8	5.2	1.4
	ISCED 02	46.9	33.9	15.2	4.0
	ISCED 03	27.8	38.3	27.2	6.8
	ISCED 05	16.4	35.5	36.1	12.1
	ISCED 06/07	15.6	29.6	32.8	22.0
Sweden	Less than ISCED 02	22.5	38.1	33.2	6.2
	ISCED 02	6.8	16.9	45.5	30.8
	ISCED 03	3.9	19.1	42.1	34.9
	ISCED 05	1.1	11.1	37.8	50.1
	ISCED 06/07	0.7	8.1	29.8	61.4

Table 7.2   Proportion of population (16-65) at each ISCED level* for each literacy level, document scale (percentages) (Concluded)

Country		Level 1	Level 2	Level 3	Level 4/5
Switzerland	Less than ISCED 02	41.9	39.7	16.4	2.0
(French-speaking)	ISCED 02	31.1	46.9	19.9	2.1
	ISCED 03	9.0	31.1	45.1	14.4
	ISCED 05	2.0	19.5	47.9	30.6
	ISCED 06/07	4.9	7.1	47.9	40.1
Switzerland	Less than ISCED 02	72.6	16.7	10.6	0.0
(German-speaking)	ISCED 02	31.6	40.2	17.9	10.3
	ISCED 03	9.7	30.9	42.9	16.5
	ISCED 05	5.1	24.9	49.1	20.9
	ISCED 06/07	6.8	15.7	39.1	38.4
United States	Less than ISCED 02	74.0	18.8	6.3	1.0
	ISCED 02	45.2	27.9	21.1	5.9
	ISCED 03	21.2	33.7	32.5	12.6
	ISCED 05	11.7	25.0	39.4	24.0
	ISCED 06/07	6.7	13.3	38.9	41.1

*   *ISCED 02 refers to completed lower secondary education; ISCED 03 refers to completed upper secondary education; ISCED 05 refers to non-university tertiary education; and ISCED 06/07 refers to completed university education, at both undergraduate and postgraduate level.*
**   *The Netherlands does not report ISCED level 05.*

Probably the most dramatic outcome is for the United States, which will be referred to as the *Type 1* pattern. Almost three quarters (74%) of those with completed primary education or less scored at Level 1 on the document scale, and another 18 per cent fell into Level 2. Those with a lower secondary education fared only a little better, with 45 per cent at Level 1 on the document scale, and nearly 28 per cent at Level 2. Only when educational attainment hits completed upper secondary education do the proportions at Level 3 and Level 4/5 begin to look like the national distributions. This association between educational attainment and the distribution of literacy skills in the adult population is not exclusively a defining characteristic of the United States. Observers will readily note that the *Type 1* pattern, with a virtually similar distribution, is also found in Poland, and, with only a modest adjustment, in Canada too. While the national literacy scores for Poland, overall, are much lower than for Canada or the United States, the results are remarkably similar when controlling for formal educational attainment.

The defining characteristics of the *Type 1* pattern can be made clear in a comparison with the *Type 2* pattern, which exemplifies Germany, the Netherlands, and Sweden. In these countries, a significant proportion of those with primary schooling as the highest completed level score at Levels 1 and 2 on the document scale, but there are also many who perform on a higher than expected level. In the case of Sweden, for example, only 7 per cent of the less educated adults function at Level 1, and another 17 per cent perform at Level 2. In the *Type 2* pattern, completed upper secondary education also signifies substantial numbers of people functioning at Levels 3 and 4/5, as might be expected.

The results for the French- and German-speaking cantons in Switzerland are somewhat more ambiguous, but the Swiss-German results tend to be more like the *Type 1* pattern, whereas the Swiss-French results tend to conform more with the *Type 2* pattern.

However, the association between levels of educational attainment and literacy proficiency is more complex than suggested above, since even quite high levels of educational attainment—including university education—do not necessarily guarantee that someone will have a high tested proficiency. For instance, it might be expected that all those with a completed university education would function at Level 3 or better. Sweden is the only country among those investigated which approximates this skill profile, and, even in Germany, a combined total of 19 per cent of those with a tertiary qualification function at the two lowest levels of literacy skill.

There are, of course, factors that may explain part of the observed discrepancies, for example, ageing or low motivation to do well on the test. Leaving such cases aside, however, the absence of a perfect correlation between educational attainment and literacy skill is disturbing.

The two characteristic patterns, *Type 1*, where school non-completion at the secondary level predicts very weak literacy skills, and *Type 2*, where there is a somewhat better chance of adequate skilling despite the non-completion of secondary-level schooling, can inform the discussion about the readiness of adults to continue learning and how this varies across countries. In both cases, there is a substantial increase in literacy skills marked by the attainment of upper secondary education through formal schooling. In the *Type 1* pattern, adult education and training for those who did not complete secondary education might require an economic return to the mastery of foundation skills. For societies characterized by the *Type 2* pattern, however, there is some reason to believe that for many people the foundations are already in place, and inclusion in a culture of lifelong learning is more likely, despite the occurrence of secondary school non-completion in some cases.

If adult literacy skills are used as a criterion to evaluate the overall performance of national education systems, the messages sent by these data are clear. The skills and competencies required for effective life transitions from school to work, and increasingly from work to education and back, are critically dependent on the completion of upper secondary education, at a minimum. Thus, as is already the case in countries like Belgium and Japan, every effort should be made by OECD countries to ensure that all young people acquire a full cycle of secondary education, and school and student failure must be combated at all costs. Only within these parameters can it be assumed with any confidence that people have the requisite skills to participate in and contribute to a culture of lifelong learning. Countries with a *Type 1* pattern will need to devote serious attention to the emphasis they place on the development of foundation skills for lifelong learning. The comparison with *Type 2* countries suggests that the school systems of Canada and the United States do not consistently yield foundation results which are commensurate with the huge costs of investment.

Literacy and migration

Table 7.3 provides a glimpse of the impact of immigration on the distribution of literacy skill in the adult populations of the participating countries. However, it should be noted at the outset that the test was administered only in the official languages of the countries under review. Thus, for instance, Canada admitted about 250,000 immigrants annually during the 1980s and early 1990s, and over this period net immigration accumulated, so that the foreign-born population constituted a significant segment of the national population by the mid-1990s. For Canada, it may well be the case that many immigrants have high-level literacy skills in mother tongues other than English or French, yet this investigation is concerned only with skills in the national languages. These skills are seen as essential to full socioeconomic participation, and to successful transitions, including immigrant integration in the society.

Table 7.3.   Proportion of population who are immigrants or native born at each literacy level, document scale (percentages)

Country		Level 1	Level 2	Level 3	Level 4/5
Canada	Born in Canada	14.8	25.6	35.4	24.2
	Immigrant	31.1	21.3	19.3	28.3
Germany	Born in Germany	7.8	32.1	40.7	19.4
	Immigrant	23.2	40.1	24.8	11.9
Netherlands	Born in the Netherlands	8.9	25.4	45.2	20.5
	Immigrant	27.4	30.8	30.0	11.8
Sweden	Born in Sweden	4.3	18.0	40.3	37.3
	Immigrant	24.7	27.3	30.8	17.2
Switzerland (French-speaking)	Born in Switzerland	10.2	29.3	42.6	18.0
	Immigrant	31.5	28.1	29.4	11.0
Switzerland (German-speaking)	Born in Switzerland	8.7	31.3	41.9	18.1
	Immigrant	56.6	20.7	14.5	8.2
United States	Born in the United States	17.5	27.4	34.0	21.2
	Immigrant	54.2	19.7	19.1	6.9

The net effect of immigration into Canada on the distribution of literacy skills is to boost both the high end and the tail of the distribution. This result contrasts with the effect of immigration on the adult skill profile of the United States, where the large majority of the immigrants cluster at the lowest level of literacy proficiency (54 per cent). The pattern observed for the United States also holds for the Swiss German cantons. The results for the other four countries tend to indicate that immigration increases the numbers at Levels 1 and 2 and reduces the numbers at Levels 3 and 4/5, but to a far lesser extent than for the United States. The results thus show that many members of the immigrant populations of the advanced OECD countries are far less likely than the indigenous populations to be skill ready for the challenges of lifelong learning in the officially designated languages. In the case of the United States, the data point to an enormous basic skill deficit for immigrants in what is essentially an officially monolinguistic and monocultural civil society.

Literacy and age

Table 7.4 presents the distributions of adult literacy skill by age groups. Overall, the young (ages 16-25) do better than older adults. The performance levels of 26 to 35 year-olds show remarkable consistency, and in countries such as Germany, the Netherlands, and Sweden, they actually get stronger. Proficiency levels begin to decline for those aged 36-45, accelerating for the 46-55 year-olds, and further weakening for the 56-65 year-olds. An example of a smooth age-related skill distribution is demonstrated by the Netherlands.

Table 7.4.   Proportion of those within each age group at each literacy level, document scale (percentages)

Country	Age groups	Level 1	Level 2	Level 3	evel 4/5
Canada	16-25	10.4	22.3	36.4	31.0
	26-35	13.5	25.3	33.8	27.5
	36-45	13.8	22.0	36.8	27.4
	46-55	23.0	31.0	23.6	22.4
	56-65	43.8	23.7	23.8	8.7
Netherlands	16-25	6.1	16.8	51.1	26.0
	26-35	5.9	19.2	45.7	29.3
	36-45	9.2	24.2	49.5	17.1
	46-55	12.6	35.7	38.0	13.7
	56-65	22.6	40.5	30.1	6.8
Poland	16-25	32.2	33.1	26.2	8.5
	26-35	39.2	33.8	19.7	7.4
	36-45	42.6	33.6	18.1	5.7
	46-55	55.6	27.0	13.3	4.1
	56-65	70.1	20.9	7.6	1.4
Sweden	16-25	3.1	16.6	39.6	40.7
	26-35	3.9	10.4	38.1	47.6
	36-45	6.6	18.2	39.8	35.4
	46-55	6.8	19.7	43.1	30.3
	56-65	12.2	33.3	36.0	18.5
Switzerland	16-25	8.7	24.9	40.4	26.0
(French-speaking)	26-35	11.5	22.4	44.5	21.6
	36-45	19.2	32.9	34.2	13.7
	46-55	18.0	29.8	42.4	9.7
	56-65	27.5	38.1	29.8	4.6
Switzerland	16-25	7.1	25.7	41.0	26.3
(German-speaking)	26-35	17.4	20.7	38.8	23.1
	36-45	21.5	30.3	36.3	12.0
	46-55	21.0	33.8	35.0	10.2
	56-65	22.8	39.9	30.6	6.7
United States	16-25	24.7	30.9	28.4	16.1
	26-35	21.6	22.9	34.5	21.0
	36-45	23.5	19.7	31.4	25.4
	46-55	21.4	28.2	33.2	17.3
	56-65	29.3	32.9	26.0	11.7

There are, however, a few anomalies to this empirical pattern that deserve comment. In the United States, the optimum score profile is found for those aged 36 to 45. However, the noticeably weak performance of the youngest age group in the United States would appear to be indicative of failure in developing uniformly high performance. In Poland, skill deficiencies seem to soar in the age group 46 to 55, where over 55 per cent are at Level 1. The jump in proportions between age groups 46-55 and 56-65 performing at Level 1 is the most pronounced for Canada and Poland. In both countries, the near-retirement population has a serious skill deficit.

The relationship between age and literacy proficiency once again points to the challenge of building a civil culture supportive of lifelong learning. The apparent decline in skills emerges in some countries as early as in the bracket aged 36-45, and in all countries by ages 45-55. It is precisely at these life stages that important transitions are likely to occur.

Literacy and gender

The results in Table 7.5 do not reveal great differences between male and female performance on the document literacy scale. Parenthetically, it should be noted that in the overall results on the prose scale, women tend to do a little better than men, and the inverse is the case on the quantitative scale. Hence, the results on the document scale represent a point of balance. In Table 7.5, men outperform women in the Netherlands. A possible explanation for this, at least, is the early apprenticeship and skill training required of young people. On balance, however, Table 7.5 and the corresponding results for the prose and quantitative dimensions of literacy do not indicate that gender per se is a barrier to basic skill development.

Table 7.5.   Proportion of each sex at each literacy level, document scale (percentages)

Country	Gender	Level 1	Level 2	Level 3	Level 4/5
Canada	Male	17.0	25.7	31.8	25.0
	Female	19.3	23.8	32.3	24.7
Netherlands	Male	8.5	23.9	45.0	22.7
	Female	11.9	27.7	43.3	17.1
Poland	Male	43.7	31.1	18.7	6.4
	Female	47.0	30.4	17.4	5.2
Sweden	Male	5.0	16.8	39.6	38.6
	Female	7.3	21.0	39.3	32.4
Switzerland (French-speaking)	Male	14.0	27.0	40.3	18.7
	Female	18.5	30.6	37.5	13.4
Switzerland (German-speaking)	Male	15.2	26.7	39.7	18.4
	Female	21.1	31.4	33.6	13.9
United States	Male	25.2	24.9	30.4	19.5
	Female	22.4	26.7	32.3	18.5

Literacy and labour-force status

Table 7.6 compares the various labour-force categories in terms of their measured skill levels. In every country except the United States, where a sampling anomaly had occurred for the students in the youngest group, the students perform at higher skill levels than the other labour-force categories. Of the three active labour-force categories—student, employed, and unemployed—the unemployed are in every case more weakly skilled. The really surprising finding, however, is the exceptionally weak overall literacy skills of those who are outside of the active labour-force. In Canada and the United States, around 65 per cent of those who are not in the active labour-force perform at Levels 1 and 2 on the document scale. Even in Sweden, with otherwise outstanding overall skill performance, 47 per cent of those who are not a member of the active labour-force function at Level 1 and 2.

Table 7.6.   Proportion of each labour-force category at each literacy level, document scale (percentages)

Country		Level 1	Level 2	Level 3	Level 4/5
Canada	Employed	11.9	24.0	34.5	29.6
	Unemployed	30.4	29.4	23.1	17.1
	Student	8.1	26.0	31.9	33.9
	Other out of labour force	38.0	24.8	27.5	9.7
Netherlands	Employed	5.7	21.7	48.5	24.0
	Unemployed	16.5	26.0	46.8	10.7
	Student	4.7	14.4	47.1	33.8
	Other out of labour force	20.9	38.3	32.8	8.0
Poland	Employed	41.3	31.0	20.6	7.1
	Unemployed	46.9	33.5	16.1	3.5
	Student	22.7	34.7	31.5	11.1
	Other out of labour force	63.1	27.4	7.5	1.9
Sweden	Employed	4.8	16.7	40.6	37.9
	Unemployed	11.9	23.0	35.2	29.9
	Student	2.6	16.7	39.7	41.1
	Other out of labour force	15.4	31.8	33.4	19.5
Switzerland (French-speaking)	Employed	12.0	30.3	41.1	16.6
	Unemployed	15.3	27.9	36.3	20.5
	Student	2.0	19.7	49.7	28.5
	Other out of labour force	27.5	32.4	30.7	9.3
Switzerland (German-speaking)	Employed	14.1	30.6	38.4	16.9
	Unemployed	24.4	23.2	35.2	17.1
	Student	1.9	16.2	42.4	39.5
	Other out of labour force	21.7	35.4	35.3	7.6
United States	Employed	17.8	25.5	34.0	22.7
	Unemployed	35.7	26.5	24.6	13.1
	Student	23.8	25.7	33.7	16.8
	Other out of labour force	37.3	29.8	25.2	7.6

With respect to readiness for lifelong learning, there are many implications. It is often believed that those who are outside the labour-force act as a kind of labour reserve, offering supplementary or replacement skills if and when needed. The very poor showing of the inactive population in terms of tested ability casts doubt on this idea. The very weak tested skills of the unemployed and inactive populations suggest that an OECD country that needs a large influx of people into its active work force would be required to invest substantially in adult basic and remedial education. Advancement of the concept of lifelong learning seems to rest primarily in the hands of those who are already well skilled.

7.6   Workplace Training Readiness

Besides the demographic variables analyzed in the above, the study has collected indicators of reading practices and behaviours, as well as other measures of community and social participation. Some of these indicators refer to experience in the workplace, whereas others refer to experience in the home and community. These variables shed additional light on the readiness of adults to engage in a culture of lifelong learning.

Tables 7.7 and 7.8 summarize responses, valid for the employed population, to a series of questions concerning adults' experience with specific workplace reading and writing tasks. The reading of letters and memos dominates the list, although the reading of reports, articles, manuals, and reference books fall close behind. It is particularly revealing that a much higher proportion of adults report the regular use of reading materials for the top three categories of materials for Germany, Sweden, and the German-speaking cantons of Switzerland. One might refer to these societies as providing highly enriched environments for literacy use and development. This contrasts sharply with the low use of reading materials in Polish workplaces, across all the types of materials reported. For countries with highly enriched contexts, the enhanced weekly exposure ranges across all types of materials. For instance, 62 per cent of working Germans and 61 per cent of German-speaking Swiss workers deal with bills, invoices, spreadsheets, or budget tables every week, compared to only 48 per cent for Canada and the United States and 43 per cent for the Netherlands.

Table 7.7.   **Proportion of population in each country who reported engaging in each of several workplace reading tasks at least once a week (percentages)**

Country	Directions or instructions for medicines, recipes or other products	Bills, invoices spread-sheets or budget tables	Diagrams or schematics	Manuals or reference books, including catalogues	Reports, articles, magazines or journals magazines	Letters or memos
Canada	30.4	48.0	32.5	49.2	55.4	70.2
Germany	31.9	62.0	51.4	60.8	66.9	80.4
Netherlands	23.8	43.2	39.9	52.1	61.5	66.7
Poland	24.1	28.2	21.0	27.0	29.9	33.6
Sweden	N/A	57.6	63.2	71.9	66.6	78.5
Switzerland (French)	19.1	56.8	38.2	50.3	72.3	72.9
Switzerland (German)	17.0	61.2	31.8	56.1	70.4	81.0
United States	33.8	47.6	37.6	61.6	59.8	71.6

Similar patterns are noticeable for responses to those questions which indicate the respondent's contact with workplace writing tasks on a weekly basis. More working Germans, Swedes, and German-speaking Swiss report writing letters or memos on a weekly basis, while more Germans and German-speaking Swiss are responsible for writing bills, invoices, and budgets. However, Table 7.8 also indicates that it is amongst the working Swedes that one finds the largest proportion of people (55 per cent) who actually write reports and articles on a weekly basis. This may be an important factor contributing to the high literacy performance in Sweden.

Table 7.8.   **Proportion of population in each country who reported engaging in each of several workplace writing tasks at least once a week (percentages)**

Country	Letters or memos	Forms or things such as bills, invoices or budgets	Reports or articles	Estimates or technical specifications
Canada	53.8	47.2	39.4	26.6
Germany	72.4	57.8	48.3	27.0
Netherlands	53.4	26.4	36.1	30.8
Poland	29.6	28.8	17.7	8.3
Sweden	74.0	47.8	54.6	30.2
Switzerland (French)	60.8	47.0	46.1	24.4
Switzerland (German)	79.0	57.3	42.8	25.3
United States	58.7	51.8	44.2	29.2

It is known now, after a decade of literacy skill research, that the contexts that adults inhabit, at work, at home, and in the community, can exert an important influence on the range of their basic skills. As far as the workplace is concerned, there are literacy-rich and literacy-poor environments. The results in Tables 7.7 and 7.8 indicate that, across specific societies, the contexts for exposure to reading materials and the demands for writing vary, and that there are some literacy-enriched settings. More consistent skill use and skill demand are important features of these enriched settings. It is likely that the carry-over effects of basic skill use will further enable the populations of these societies to be ready for constructive engagement in a culture of lifelong learning.

Certain long-term trends in employment growth underscore the reinforcing nature of enriched environments for workplace reading. Figure 7.3 compares the employment growth and reading patterns for two of the countries investigated, Canada and Germany. The two graphs plot the percentage change in employment in specific labour-market sectors from 1979 to 1990 by the proportion of the adult population reporting to read several times a week at work.

Figure 7.3 shows that, in employment sectors that are declining, literacy skill demands are few, and in sectors with growth, in particular financial and personal services sectors, workplace literacy skill demands are much higher. This reinforces the importance of basic skills to the making of successful transitions. Job losses in the evolving knowledge-based economy are heaviest in the primary industrial and manufacturing sectors, precisely those sectors where many people will need extensive retraining, skill upgrading, and transition counselling. Yet the data show that these are the sectors where the workplace environments tend to be the least enriched, and where remedial or basic education will probably have to precede any commitment to further education and training.

Figure 7.3.   Employment growth and literacy patterns Canada

Percent change in employment, 1979-1990

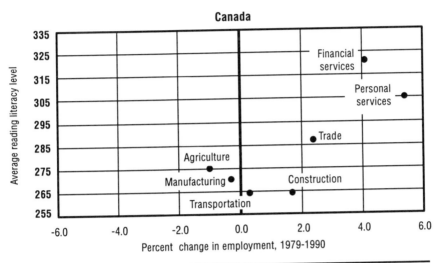

Table 7.9.   Proportion of each level who gave a particular self-assessment of their reading skills for their main job, document scale (percentages)

Country		Level 1	Level 2	Level 3	Level 4/5
Canada	Excellent	22.4	45.4	65.1	75.9
	Good	26.4	42.5	26.6	22.3
	Moderate	15.3	9.4	6.4	0.8
	Poor	15.9	0.7	0.5	0.0
	No opinion	19.9	2.1	1.5	1.0
Netherlands	Excellent	8.9	10.8	20.2	28.9
	Good	44.5	54.3	61.1	57.4
	Moderate	32.3	31.2	16.6	11.1
	Poor	6.5	0.8	0.7	0.0
	No opinion	7.8	3.0	1.3	2.6
Poland*	Excellent	11.2	20.2	29.9	39.1
	Good	68.0	68.1	65.2	57.0
	Moderate	18.4	11.5	4.6	3.3
	Poor	2.5	0.2	0.3	0.7
Switzerland	Excellent	19.0	36.2	60.8	71.0
(French-speaking)	Good	46.9	44.7	32.2	22.5
	Moderate	15.9	15.2	6.6	5.5
	Poor	13.1	1.6	0.4	0.0
	No opinion	5.1	2.5	0.0	1.1

Table 7.9.   Proportion of each level who gave a particular self-assessment of their reading skills for their main job, document scale (percentages) (Concluded)

Country		Level 1	Level 2	Level 3	Level 4/5
Switzerland	Excellent	36.3	64.4	76.1	81.4
(German-speaking)	Good	32.4	31.3	22.3	18.2
	Moderate	14.1	3.4	1.7	0.3
	Poor	15.2	0.2	0.0	0.0
	No opinion	2.0	0.6	0.0	0.0
United States	Excellent	23.1	53.9	66.2	77.2
	Good	40.2	37.7	29.1	22.1
	Moderate	16.0	7.0	3.6	0.3
	Poor	17.0	1.0	0.0	0.3
	No opinion	3.7	0.4	1.1	0.1

*   *The no opinion category was not an option in the Polish questionnaire.*

Tables 7.9 and 7.10 provide a close look at the self-assessments of working individuals in terms of their reading and writing skills for their main job. Because the pertinent questions were not asked in the Swedish questionnaire, the data for this country are not available. Any detailed analysis of self-reported literacy skill tends to cast some doubts on the adequacy of self-assessment indicators, since people tend to inflate their notions of their skills and abilities when this is compared to their actually tested performance (Neice & Adsett 1992; Murray 1997). This phenomenon can be verified with reference to Tables 7.9 and 7.10. For instance, in Canada, 22 per cent of those at Level 1 on the document scale self-rated their reading skills for their main job as excellent, and 45 per cent of the Level 2 respondents thought their workplace reading skills were excellent. In these cases, the objective skill test performance is by far the better indicator.

However, there can be no doubt that those who both test poorly (Levels 1 and 2) and also indicate that their self-assessed skills are only moderate or weak are unlikely candidates for mainstay adult education programmes. Table 7.9 shows that, for the poorly skilled (Level 1), a combined total of 38 per cent in the Netherlands, followed by 33 per cent in the United States, self-assess their main job reading skills as moderate to poor. This suggests that large numbers of people in most of the countries studied may delude themselves about their own skill base. Level 1 skill performance must be considered inadequate as a basis for adult education, other than remedial or basic skills training.

A perhaps even more surprising result revealed in Table 7.10 is the recognition by the working respondents that their self-assessed writing skills for their main job are weaker than their reading skills. For those at Level 1 on the document scale, there is a reduced tendency to self-assess their skills as excellent or good, and a more realistic appraisal that they are moderate or weak. In the case of the Netherlands, nearly 54 per cent of Level 1 performers rate their writing self-assessment as moderate to poor. This is followed by about 40 per cent of Canadian and United States adults who self-rate their workplace writing skills as moderate or poor. However, in Poland, where overall tested performance levels are very weak, only 3 per cent of the working Poles who tested at Level 1 self-assessed their main job writing skills as weak, and 75 per cent rated their writing skills as good to excellent.

Table 7.10.   **Proportion of each level who gave a particular self-assessment of their writing skills for their main job, document scale (percentages)**

Country		Level 1	Level 2	Level 3	Level 4/5
Canada	Excellent	19.7	36.8	56.3	60.1
	Good	26.6	41.3	32.1	34.9
	Moderate	15.9	15.2	7.0	3.6
	Poor	24.3	1.0	2.8	0.2
	No opinion	13.6	5.6	1.9	1.3
Netherlands	Excellent	3.7	8.3	14.0	22.7
	Good	36.1	44.4	58.3	57.0
	Moderate	43.6	36.9	23.9	16.8
	Poor	9.7	6.9	2.3	0.5
	No opinion	6.8	3.6	1.4	3.1
Poland*	Excellent	8.4	17.1	23.8	28.6
	Good	66.6	68.8	67.3	66.9
	Moderate	22.3	13.6	8.6	3.7
	Poor	2.7	0.6	0.3	0.7
Switzerland (French-speaking)	Excellent	13.4	24.8	46.2	50.8
	Good	28.5	38.2	34.8	38.4
	Moderate	24.0	27.3	14.7	9.2
	Poor	27.7	8.2	4.3	1.6
	No opinion	6.4	1.6	0.0	0.0
Switzerland (German-speaking)	Excellent	34.0	50.9	64.0	72.7
	Good	22.9	36.7	31.0	24.7
	Moderate	18.7	10.1	3.9	2.6
	Poor	18.6	1.9	0.6	0.0
	No opinion	5.8	0.4	0.5	0.0
United States	Excellent	17.2	40.4	51.8	62.9
	Good	38.6	45.7	38.6	31.4
	Moderate	19.6	11.2	6.7	5.2
	Poor	21.1	1.8	1.3	0.3
	No opinion	3.6	0.8	1.6	0.2

*   *The no opinion category was not an option in the Polish questionnaire.*

There is some reason to think that self-assessed writing skills are a more stringent tool for determining the readiness of adults for further training in the societies studied. The large proportions of adults with weak tested skills who self-rate their skills as above average is a serious limitation to a full appreciation by adults in these societies of the real-world skill base needed to benefit from training and learning experiences beyond formal education. This gap in perception between tested performance and the realities of a changing world in which skill demands keep climbing is further revealed in Tables 7.11 and 7.12. These tables provide the results from questions that asked respondents to assess the extent to which their reading and writing skills might limit their job opportunities.

Table 7.11.   Proportion of respondents in each literacy level who reported whether their reading skills limited their job opportunities, document scale (percentages)

Country		Level 1	Level 2	Level 3	Level 4/5
Canada	Greatly limiting	13.3	4.1	1.2	0.1
	Somewhat limiting	27.2	12.3	6.5	1.1
	Not at all limiting	59.5	83.6	92.3	98.8
Netherlands	Greatly limiting	7.4	1.0	1.5	1.2
	Somewhat limiting	11.4	9.1	7.4	4.9
	Not at all limiting	81.2	89.9	91.1	94.0
Poland	Greatly limiting	2.0	1.0	0.3	0.0
	Somewhat limiting	11.4	7.5	2.1	2.8
	Not at all limiting	86.6	91.5	97.6	97.2
Switzerland (French)	Greatly limiting	8.0	0.8	1.8	2.6
	Somewhat limiting	16.2	16.5	11.3	2.6
	Not at all limiting	75.7	82.7	86.9	94.8
Switzerland (German)	Greatly limiting	8.8	0.9	1.5	0.0
	Somewhat limiting	8.9	5.5	2.2	0.0
	Not at all limiting	82.2	93.6	96.3	100.0
United States	Greatly limiting	15.5	1.3	0.2	1.0
	Somewhat limiting	18.6	9.6	4.6	2.5
	Not at all limiting	65.9	89.2	95.2	96.5

Of course, as Table 7.11 shows, there is broad recognition by those most highly skilled at Level 4/5 that they are not limited in their job opportunities by their reading skills. But the patterns for those with tested ability at Levels 1 and 2 are disturbing. In the United States, 66 per cent of those testing at Level 1 see no limitations for their job opportunities arising from their weak reading skills. This figure rises to 75 per cent of French-speaking Swiss, 81 and 82 per cent of Dutch and German-speaking Swiss, and nearly 87 per cent of working Polish. For Level 2 performers, the percentages are even more startling, peaking at over 90 per cent in some countries for those who actually perform at Level 2 but do not see this as a hindrance. Indeed, this rosy outlook is only moderated somewhat when people were asked if their writing skills might limit their future employment prospects. As can be seen from Table 7.12, large numbers of those with tested literacy performance at Levels 1 and 2 reluctantly admit that their writing skills might limit their job opportunities in the future.

Table 7.12.   Proportion of respondents in each literacy level who reported whether their writing skills limited their job opportunities, document scale (percentages)

Country		Level 1	Level 2	Level 3	Level 4/5
Canada	Greatly limiting	16.9	2.5	2.5	0.2
	Somewhat limiting	18.4	15.4	7.2	3.1
	Not at all limiting	64.7	82.0	90.2	96.6
Netherlands	Greatly limiting	7.1	3.1	2.3	1.2
	Somewhat limiting	12.8	10.0	6.7	4.5
	Not at all limiting	80.0	86.9	91.0	94.3
Poland	Greatly limiting	1.3	1.4	0.2	0.0
	Somewhat limiting	11.9	6.6	3.9	2.3
	Not at all limiting	86.9	92.0	95.8	97.7
Switzerland	Greatly limiting	13.8	2.2	3.5	2.0
(French-speaking)	Somewhat limiting	22.0	26.1	13.9	9.6
	Not at all limiting	64.2	71.7	82.6	88.4
Switzerland	Greatly limiting	7.9	1.3	2.2	0.0
(German-speaking)	Somewhat limiting	15.5	7.4	3.7	2.2
	Not at all limiting	76.6	91.3	94.1	97.8
United States	Greatly limiting	18.0	1.9	0.6	0.9
	Somewhat limiting	17.9	9.0	4.4	4.6
	Not at all limiting	64.1	89.1	94.9	94.5

It is difficult to square these attitudes toward present and future employment prospects with objective conditions. In most of the advanced OECD economies, the recognition that employment opportunities depend on high-level performance and skill upgrading is widespread. In addition, many people have had either direct or secondary experience with the consequences of workplace restructuring, displacement, and unemployment. The facts about people's self-reports embedded in Tables 7.11 and 7.12 suggest that those who are most in need—i.e. those who are weakly skilled and most vulnerable to the effects of displacement—are also those who are the least perceptive about their objective conditions. For advocates of lifelong learning and education, these data highlight the public policy challenge.

Other behavioral indicators of literacy uses and practices also point to the barriers impeding the achievement of an inclusive culture of lifelong learning. Table 7.13 indicates that reading newspapers (at least once weekly) is a widely shared and adopted behaviour across all the countries investigated, even for those at the lowest levels of literacy performance. However, when more discriminating indicators of reading behaviours, such as reading books (at least once a week) and visiting libraries (at least once a month) are examined, they show that the incidence of this kind of learning-related literacy activity varies quite widely for different skill levels. For many countries, close to 60 per cent at Levels 4/5 read a book every week. For Level 1 performers, reported book use is little more than half of that. In some countries, close to 40 per cent of the Level 4/5 respondents use a library once a month. In the case of Level 1 performers, the rate is typically less than half of that. In some cases, the proportional differences are quite large. Over 35 per cent of Germans at the highest skill levels use libraries monthly, compared to only 8 per cent at the lowest skill level. It is useful to remember that these are adult patterns and behaviours, and therefore they are more deeply seated and enduring than if they were the behaviours of children or youth.

Another important set of behaviours affecting basic skills and adult time allocation involves the use of television. Table 7.14 summarizes data on the consumption of television, and distributes the results across the document literacy performance levels. For several countries, notably Canada, the United States, Germany, and the Netherlands, about 15 to 18 per cent of the adult population, performing at Level 1, watch more than five hours of television per day. For the same countries, another 30 to 50 per cent of the Level 1 performers watch between two and five hours a day. In contrast, in all the countries except Poland, more than 20 per cent of those with Level 4/5 literacy skills watched less than an hour of television a day, and many reported not watching it on a daily basis at all.

Table 7.13. **Proportion of respondents within a level who reported engaging in each of several literacy activities in their daily lives, document scale (percentages)**

Country		Read newspapers at least once a week	Read books at least once a week	Write letters at least once a week	Visit a library at least once a month
Canada	Level 1	71.8	36.4	10.8	15.9
	Level 2	89.8	44.7	19.1	21.3
	Level 3	91.5	57.1	18.1	27.0
	Level 4/5	93.1	60.6	21.4	33.7
Netherlands	Level 1	87.2	27.6	8.2	15.1
	Level 2	94.1	42.3	14.1	30.9
	Level 3	95.9	46.1	20.9	40.4
	Level 4/5	97.3	51.9	23.4	40.4
Poland	Level 1	84.8	26.8	7.0	13.1
	Level 2	93.9	42.7	14.2	21.4
	Level 3	96.9	52.8	23.0	28.2
	Level 4/5	96.4	61.0	30.2	38.7
Sweden	Level 1	92.7	33.4	6.8	19.6
	Level 2	98.4	47.7	12.5	27.3
	Level 3	98.9	50.6	11.6	32.5
	Level 4/5	99.2	59.3	17.1	40.0
Switzerland (French-speaking)	Level 1	95.9	43.2	12.6	12.8
	Level 2	96.4	49.0	22.2	14.0
	Level 3	96.4	59.5	32.6	19.2
	Level 4/5	96.8	62.5	31.3	27.9
Switzerland (German-speaking)	Level 1	91.1	37.0	14.9	4.9
	Level 2	96.8	51.4	24.8	11.5
	Level 3	97.8	56.1	25.0	18.5
	Level 4/5	97.6	68.4	29.5	25.0
United States	Level 1	71.2	36.0	12.7	15.5
	Level 2	88.7	47.6	19.6	20.0
	Level 3	93.7	57.5	22.6	28.7
	Level 4/5	94.2	57.9	23.4	32.5

Table 7.14.   Proportion of each level who reported various frequencies for watching television each day, document scale (percentages)

Country		Level 1	Level 2	Level 3	Level 4/5
Canada	Not on a daily basis	6.1	7.8	9.3	14.7
	1 hour or less per day	12.4	19.4	27.6	22.2
	1 to 2 hours per day	23.6	29.5	24.5	37.2
	More than 2 hours but less than 5	38.6	35.1	34.3	24.5
	5 or more hours per day	17.4	7.5	3.6	1.3
	Do not have a television	2.0	0.7	0.7	0.1
Netherlands	Not on a daily basis	3.2	3.3	5.3	7.2
	1 hour or less per day	5.1	12.5	16.3	21.6
	1 to 2 hours per day	22.0	31.1	36.9	35.7
	More than 2 hours but less than 5	52.3	43.4	36.9	32.9
	5 or more hours per day	16.7	7.9	3.6	1.3
	Do not have a television	0.8	1.8	1.0	1.1
Poland	Not on a daily basis	7.8	7.8	11.0	10.9
	1 hour or less per day	11.3	12.5	13.0	11.9
	1 to 2 hours per day	38.8	41.9	45.8	42.4
	More than 2 hours but less than 5	34.9	33.1	26.8	32.3
	5 or more hours per day	6.7	4.6	3.2	1.2
	Do not have a television	0.4	0.1	0.2	1.3
Switzerland (French-speaking)	Not on a daily basis	7.2	7.2	15.5	21.3
	1 hour or less per day	17.6	17.1	16.5	14.9
	1 to 2 hours per day	35.9	39.0	38.2	34.5
	More than 2 hours but less than 5	33.4	30.5	20.7	17.8
	5 or more hours per day	4.5	2.4	3.3	1.4
	Do not have a television	1.4	3.9	5.8	10.2
Switzerland (German-speaking)	Not on a daily basis	15.1	18.2	24.6	27.3
	1 hour or less per day	20.3	24.6	25.0	30.4
	1 to 2 hours per day	30.7	34.8	30.0	17.2
	More than 2 hours but less than 5	30.1	18.5	14.1	12.5
	5 or more hours per day	2.7	1.2	0.6	0.9
	Do not have a television	1.0	2.7	5.7	11.7
United States	Not on a daily basis	2.2	3.9	4.2	4.7
	1 hour or less per day	18.7	19.1	25.8	34.5
	1 to 2 hours per day	28.0	29.8	32.6	33.5
	More than 2 hours but less than 5	30.9	33.0	30.1	22.8
	5 or more hours per day	18.5	12.9	6.8	3.7
	Do not have a television	1.7	1.3	0.5	0.9

There is little doubt that high levels of watching television draw time and energy away from other activities, including reading and writing practices and behaviours. Rather than watching television programming, the fostering of a culture of lifelong learning depends more critically on a wider appreciation for print-related learning materials. The inverse correlation between tested adult literacy skills and television use points to yet another obstacle in the formation of supportive environments for adult education and training.

Table 7.15.   **Proportion of each level who reported participating in community or voluntary activities at least once a month for each scale (percentages)**

Country		Prose	Document	Quantitative
Canada	Level 1	10.6	9.0	7.0
	Level 2	15.9	19.7	18.2
	Level 3	24.1	30.5	27.8
	Level 4/5	39.6	28.0	34.7
Netherlands	Level 1	24.1	22.3	18.3
	Level 2	28.9	30.9	30.2
	Level 3	33.1	31.1	31.4
	Level 4/5	37.1	38.0	40.3
Poland	Level 1	6.9	6.7	5.6
	Level 2	10.3	10.9	10.8
	Level 3	11.1	9.7	10.9
	Level 4/5	7.4	12.4	11.5
Sweden	Level 1	34.1	28.3	30.3
	Level 2	42.1	43.5	40.7
	Level 3	46.7	46.9	47.6
	Level 4/5	54.3	52.9	53.4
Switzerland (French-speaking)	Level 1	10.3	9.4	3.8
	Level 2	21.0	20.6	18.5
	Level 3	22.2	22.3	22.8
	Level 4/5	24.2	23.5	24.8
Switzerland (German-speaking)	Level 1	11.6	9.8	6.1
	Level 2	21.9	19.7	20.6
	Level 3	25.9	25.3	24.7
	Level 4/5	36.8	36.1	32.5
United States	Level 1	18.5	20.1	17.2
	Level 2	29.9	27.3	27.6
	Level 3	37.7	42.2	40.1
	Level 4/5	44.4	42.8	44.6

Table 7.15 taps another indicator: community activity and involvement. It presents data on those who reported they had participated in community or voluntary activity at least once a month during the reference period. All three scales are itemized in Table 7.15, as a reminder to readers that data are available for all three scales, and also to show how basic patterns tend to hold across the three scales.

In all countries, higher skill levels predict greater community participation, but there are some other important points to notice. For Sweden, one can observe much higher reported levels of community participation across all scales and across all performance levels, ranging close to 55 per cent for the top literacy performers. Thus, for all the countries, increases in adult basic skills reinforce the tendency to help serve in one's community. In behavioural terms, those with higher skills put more energy into their communities through voluntary participation than people with a weaker skill base. However, the inverse is also true. The poorly skilled are a priority target for adult education; yet they also are least likely to be well integrated in their communities through voluntary community activity.

7.7   Conclusion

While this chapter has been primarily descriptive, it does point to the need for more extensive correlational analysis of literacy skills and literacy behaviours and practices. Still, when all the analysis is set aside, the challenges, already foreseen by many, for a successful transition by each country to a knowledge-based economy, will critically depend on the development of a pedagogical ethic and value commitment to a culture that supports lifelong learning for adults. The evidence gathered from the first round of the International Adult Literacy Survey suggests that, for many countries, this will require vigorous and highly directed policy attention. The obstacles to its achievement are formidable, at least from the perspective of basic skill performance and adult readiness. Of all the societies examined in the first round of the IALS, only Sweden stands out, with its long-standing and encompassing commitment to adult education. The exemplary Swedish results documented in this chapter, while no doubt stemming from several factors, must surely rest in part on an enlightened view of the value of adult learning.

References

Drucker, P.F. 1993. *Post-Capitalist Society*. New York: Harper Business Books.

Handy, C. 1990. *The Age of Unreason*. Boston: Harvard Business Press.

Healy, J.M. 1990. *Endangered Minds: Why Our Children Don't Think*. New York: Simon and Schuster.

Jones, S. 1995. *Background Documentation for the Canadian Basic Job Skills Test* (mimeo). Hull/Quebec: Human Resources Development Canada.

Kirsch, I.S., and Jungeblut, A. 1986. *Literacy: Profiles of America's Young Adults*. Princeton/ N. J.: Educational Testing Service.

Kirsch, I.S., and Mosenthal, P. 1990. "Exploring document literacy: Variables underlying the performance of young adults" In: *Reading Research Quarterly* 25: 5-30.

Kirsch, I.S., Jenkins, L., Jungeblut, A., and Kolstad, A. 1993. *Adult Literacy in America: A First Look at the Results of the National Adult Literacy Survey*. Washington, D.C.: National Center for Education Statistics, Department of Education.

Lipsey, R.G. 1995. *A Structuralist View of Technical Change and Economic Growth*. (Reprint no. 38) Ottawa: Canadian Institute for Advanced Research.

Montigny, G., Kelly, K., and Jones, S. 1991. *Adult Literacy in Canada: Results of a National Study*. Ottawa: Statistics Canada.

Murray, T.S. 1997. "Proxy Measurement of Adult Basic Skills: Lessons from Canada". In: A.C. Tuijnman, I.S. Kirsch, and D.A. Wagner (eds.). *Adult Basic Skills: Advances in Measurement and Policy Analysis*. Creskil/N.Y.: Hampton Press.

Murray, T.S., and Kirsch, I.S. (eds.) 1997. *International Adult Literacy Survey: Technical Report*. Washington D.C.: Department of Education and Government Printing Office.

Neice, D. 1996. *Information Technology and Citizen Participation* (mimeo). Ottawa: Department of Canadian Heritage.

Neice, D., and Adsett, M. 1992. "Direct versus proxy measures of adult functional literacy: A preliminary re-examination". In: OECD. *Adult Illiteracy and Economic Performance*. Paris: Organisation for Economic Co-operation and Development.

OECD 1992. *Adult Illiteracy and Economic Performance*. Paris: Organisation for Economic Co-operation and Development.

OECD 1996. *Lifelong Learning for All: Report of the meeting of the Education Committee at ministerial level, 16-17 January 1996*. Paris: Organisation for Economic Co-operation and Development.

OECD and Statistics Canada 1995. *Literacy, Economy and Society: Results of the First International Adult Literacy Survey*. Paris and Ottawa: Organisation for Economic Co-operation and Development and Statistics Canada.

Reich, R.B. 1992. *The Work of Nations: Preparing Ourselves for 21st Century Capitalism*. New York: Vintage Books.

Rifkin, J. 1995. *The End of Work: The Decline of the Global Labour-force and the Dawn of the Post-Market Era*. New York: Putnam Books.

Romer, P. 1993. "Ideas and Things", *In: The Economist* (September 11th).

Tuijnman, A.C., Kirsch, I.S., and Wagner, D.A. (eds.) 1997. *Adult Basic Skills: Advances in Measurement and Policy Analysis*. Creskil, New York: Hampton Press.

Wickert, R. 1989. *No Single Measure: A Survey of Australian Adult Literacy*. Canberra, ACT: Commonwealth Department of Employment, Education and Training.

Chapter 8

Gender Differences In Work-Related Training

Edwin Leuven

8.1 Introduction

Gender differences in the acquisition of human capital are of interest because they are likely to impede the personal and professional development of individuals and increase economic inequality between the sexes. Less training not only leads to lower earnings, it also decreases subsequent job opportunities and increases the risk of unemployment. This can subsequently be magnified if those who received training in the past are more likely to receive training in the future.

It is, therefore, important to know what mechanisms lie at the basis of the different training patterns of men and women. Various explanations have been put forward. The arguments advanced in the economic literature are usually derived from human capital theory. The most common argument points to the lower labour-force attachment of women, which may cause employers to invest less (see, for example, Royalty 1996). Others suggest that the lower training probabilities result from the fact that women hold jobs that require less training (see, for example, Oosterbeek 1996). Booth (1991), among others, points to discrimination as a possible source of gender differences in training. Finally, differences in preferences might be at the basis of the different training patterns of men and women.

Most studies of the incidence and determinants of participation in work-related training find that women receive less training than their male counterparts (OECD 1991; Bishop 1996). There is, however, increasing evidence that gender differences are specific to the type of training considered. In Chapter 3 in this volume, Houtkoop & Oosterbeek, using the same dataset, find equal participation rates for men and women when looking at all incidences of participation in adult education and training. Women are less likely to participate if only work-related adult education and training is taken into consideration. Miller (1994) finds that in Australia (1989 data) women undertake more external training but less on-the-job training than men. Greenhalgh and Stewart (1987) find similar results using 1975 data for the United Kingdom, as does Veum (1993) for the United States (1986-91 data).

Whereas the evidence on training incidence is somewhat mixed, there is a more consistent body of research suggesting that women receive less training in terms of duration. For the United Kingdom (1984 data), Green (1991) finds that men receive 40 hours more training than women *ceterus paribus*. Analysing US data, Altonji & Spletzer (1991) and Veum (1993) find that men receive both more weeks of training (longer duration) and more hours per week (higher intensity). Pischke (1996) finds similar results for Germany.

Finally, gender differences might predate the training decision if women hold jobs that require less training, for which there is some evidence (Duncan & Hoffman 1979; Oosterbeek 1996). One explanation that has been put forward is that employers might not select women for capital-intensive jobs if women are more likely to quit. Turnover is costly because of the underutilization of capital while searching for replacement and subsequent training (Barron, Black & Loewenstein 1993).

The studies cited above illustrate that, although not always explicitly recognized, worker-firm bargaining precedes the training decision. Different types of training will have different consequences for the distribution of costs and benefits between the employee and the firm. How costs and benefits are divided might also be dependent on labour-market institutions.[1]

The finding that women are more likely to undertake adult education and training externally suggests that they invest more in general training. This is a potential explanation for the finding that they receive less training than men. This chapter presents a descriptive analysis of gender differences in work-related adult education and training among the employed population. It will examine the hypothesis that women receive less training than men because they undertake more general training. The second goal of the analysis is to examine the extent to which women are rationed in their training opportunities compared with men. Finally, differences in training and rationing probabilities are attributed to different individual human-capital endowments and job characteristics of men and women.

The analysis is organized as follows. Section 8.2 briefly describes the data and definitions used in the analysis. Section 8.3 compares the training probabilities of men and women and investigates whether women are more likely to be rationed

---

[1]   *Leuven and Oosterbeek (1997) attempt to separate worker and employer preferences. They find evidence that, in Canada and the United States, employer preferences explain the lower participation rate of women, whereas worker preferences are relevant in the Netherlands and Switzerland (all 1994 data).*

in their training opportunities. Differences in training initiative, finance, and supply characteristics are also investigated. Section 8.4 then attempts to attribute the gender differences in training and rationing probabilities to gender differences in human-capital endowments and job characteristics. Section 8.5 presents a summary and conclusions.

8.2   The Dataset

Chapter 3 of this volume, and particularly the relevant Appendices, describe at length the dataset utilized for this study. The dataset, which is derived from the International Adult Literacy Survey (IALS), will therefore only briefly be commented on here.

The IALS was an initiative that collected comparative data about literacy performance and literacy practices of the adult populations of seven countries: Canada, Switzerland, Sweden, Germany, Poland, the Netherlands, and the United States. The background questionnaire employed for the survey included a set of questions about adult education and training practices. Only four countries are investigated here: Canada, the Netherlands, Switzerland, and the United States. The Polish data are excluded because of the low effective sample size, the German data because of an anomaly in the instrument translation, and the Swedish data because the training supplement was not entirely included in the background questionnaire. Houtkoop and Oosterbeek provide more details; they also give a brief description of the education and training delivery systems of the four countries studied.

The samples investigated in this chapter comprise only the employed population; the self-employed are excluded. Table 8.1 provides the means and standard deviations for the key variables employed in the data analysis.

Before proceeding with the data analysis, it is necessary to explain how the training variable is constructed, because measured participation rates are sensitive to the phrasing of the question and the reference period involved (OECD 1991; Loewenstein & Spletzer 1996). Three elements of information are combined to determine whether the respondents participated in work-related adult education or training. The first is whether a respondent reported that he or she had received any adult education and/or training during the 12 months prior to the interview. This group was then restricted further by selecting only those who had indicated that the education or training they had undertaken was for job and/or career-related reasons. Finally, those adults who reported to have been enrolled in courses leading to a formal educational qualification were excluded. This resulted in the group of respondents considered in the analysis to have received work-related training. Respondents also reported the number of weeks the training lasted, and how many days per week and hours per day. Using this information, the number of hours spent on training was calculated (divided by 40).

Table 8.1.   Descriptive statistics: Sample means and standard deviations

	Age 16-25	Age 26-35	Age 46-55	Age 55-65	Primary education or less	Lower secondary education	Upper secondary education	Tenure <1 year	Migrant	Urban resident	Temporary employment	Full-time employment
Canada												
Men	0.22 (0.41)	0.26 (0.44)	0.16 (0.37)	0.06 (0.24)	0.08 (0.26)	0.19 (0.40)	0.37 (0.48)	0.12 (0.33)	0.07 (0.26)	0.74 (0.44)	0.04 (0.20)	0.93 (0.26)
Women	0.21 (0.41)	0.29 (0.46)	0.17 (0.37)	0.05 (0.21)	0.04 (0.21)	0.14 (0.35)	0.47 (0.50)	0.14 (0.35)	0.08 (0.27)	0.76 (0.43)	0.08 (0.27)	0.76 (0.43)
Switzerland												
Men	0.08 (0.27)	0.33 (0.47)	0.22 (0.41)	0.12 (0.33)	0.03 (0.17)	0.06 (0.24)	0.34 (0.47)	0.07 (0.25)	0.18 (0.39)	0.73 (0.45)	0.04 (0.19)	0.97 (0.18)
Women	0.11 (0.32)	0.34 (0.47)	0.19 (0.40)	0.09 (0.29)	0.05 (0.22)	0.08 (0.26)	0.21 (0.41)	0.13 (0.34)	0.20 (0.40)	0.76 (0.43)	0.07 (0.25)	0.64 (0.48)
United States												
Men	0.11 (0.32)	0.27 (0.45)	0.19 (0.39)	0.11 (0.32)	0.10 (0.29)	0.08 (0.27)	0.45 (0.50)	0.12 (0.32)	0.21 (0.41)	0.20 (0.40)	0.04 (0.19)	0.94 (0.24)
Women	0.13 (0.33)	0.27 (0.45)	0.22 (0.42)	0.11 (0.31)	0.09 (0.28)	0.06 (0.24)	0.42 (0.49)	0.15 (0.35)	0.18 (0.38)	0.17 (0.38)	0.04 (0.20)	0.82 (0.38)
Netherlands												
Men	0.08 (0.27)	0.33 (0.47)	0.20 (0.40)	0.06 (0.24)	0.09 (0.28)	0.28 (0.45)	0.30 (0.46)	0.07 (0.25)	0.06 (0.23)	0.80 (0.40)	0.03 (0.18)	0.95 (0.21)
Women	0.13 (0.34)	0.36 (0.48)	0.19 (0.39)	0.03 (0.18)	0.04 (0.19)	0.29 (0.45)	0.32 (0.47)	0.09 (0.29)	0.05 (0.21)	0.82 (0.39)	0.07 (0.26)	0.53 (0.50)

8.3   Gender Differences in Training Characteristics

Training Participation and Duration

Table 8.2 shows that the overall training participation rate is between 2 and 7 per cent lower for women than for men (except in the United States). But inequality in training incidence is not only measured by participation rates. Training duration can differ dramatically between men and women, even if training probabilities are identical.

Table 8.2.   Participation, rationing and duration of job-related training

	Canada		Switzerland		United States		Netherlands	
	Men	Women	Men	Women	Men	Women	Men	Women
Training Participation rate	0.38	0.36	0.31	0.27	0.39	0.39	0.35	0.28
Training Duration (weeks)	1.02	0.60	0.79	0.45	0.81	0.57	1.04	0.89
Among trained	2.68	1.68	2.52	1.64	2.08	1.46	2.94	3.15

Overall differences in training duration between men and women are indicated in Table 8.2. The results show that, when training duration is measured in full-time weeks, a consistent picture emerges in all countries: the unconditional expected training duration is lower for women than for men. Men are expected to receive between four and five days training, whereas women are trained less by one to two days. Conditional training participation changes little; women receive training of a briefer duration than men, except in the Netherlands.

Rationing

Given the finding that women receive less training than men, it is natural to ask whether women have fewer opportunities to enrol in training than men. In other words: are women rationed? The respondents were asked whether there was any job or career-related training that they would have liked to receive but did not. Table 8.3 shows the percentages of men and women in each country who indicated having been rationed in their training opportunities. In Canada, Switzerland, and the United States, women are 4 per cent more likely to report that they are rationed than men, and 2 per cent more likely in the Netherlands.

Table 8.3.   Rationing characteristics by country for men and women

	Canada		Switzerland		United States		Netherlands	
	Men	Women	Men	Women	Men	Women	Men	Women
Rationing rate	0.30	0.34	0.29	0.33	0.24	0.28	0.21	0.23
• Trained	0.33	0.43	0.27	0.28	0.30	0.34	0.24	0.20
• Not trained	0.27	0.29	0.29	0.35	0.19	0.23	0.20	0.25
Intensity (weeks)	1.02	0.60	0.79	0.45	0.81	0.57	1.04	0.89
• Those not rationed	1.28	0.86	0.65	0.19	0.97	0.59	0.82	0.74
• Those rationed	0.90	0.47	0.85	0.57	0.75	0.57	1.10	0.94
• Trained and not rationed	2.51	1.51	2.65	1.94	2.14	1.59	3.23	3.16
• Trained and rationed	3.04	1.91	2.18	0.85	1.95	1.20	2.03	3.13
Why rationed?								
• Busy, lack of time	54.7	47.8	50.0	56.5	48.1	50.6	37.0	51.2
• Busy at work	26.2	21.7	26.5	26.1	25.3	21.7	22.0	11.6
• Inconvenient time	7.6	13.5	2.9	13.0	13.0	16.3	12.0	9.3
• Course not offered	8.1	15.0	4.4	4.3	4.5	9.6	10.0	4.7
• Family responsibilities	11.0	17.9	5.9	8.7	6.5	22.3	1.0	2.3
• Too expensive	22.1	29.0	11.8	6.5	22.1	28.9	11.0	18.6
• Not qualified	5.2	0.5	8.8	2.2	1.3	1.8	2.0	2.3
• Lack of employer support	9.3	4.3	10.3	6.5	12.3	9.6	6.0	7.0
• Other	8.1	6.8	11.8	19.6	3.2	6.0	12.0	2.3

A substantial number of trained workers indicate that they are in some way rationed. But are trained workers less likely to be rationed? Surprisingly, this is not always the case; trained workers are more likely to be rationed in North America, and in the Netherlands for the male population. Apart from the women in the Netherlands who received training, it remains true that women are more likely to be rationed than men irrespective of whether they are trained. There is, therefore, a strong indication that women, compared to men, face higher rationing probabilities.

Although this indicates that rationed workers are not necessarily less likely to be trained than their non-rationed counterparts, it is possible, however, that they receive less training in terms of duration. Table 8.3 shows that this is true for the two countries in North America but not for the European countries studied. Those trained workers who indicate that they have been rationed indeed receive less training, except in Canada. It is concluded, therefore, that rationing as measured in this study appears to correspond to lower training intensities, except for Canada.

Respondents could also indicate why they were unable to undertake the training in question. Table 8.3 lists the possible response categories. The majority report that they did not have enough time to undertake training (i.e. busy, lack of time, busy at work, inconvenient time). Here, there are no clear gender differences that are valid across countries. However, there are two discernible differences between men and women that are interesting to note. First, a substantially higher proportion of North American women than men indicates that they did not undertake training because of family responsibilities. Second, women are more likely to point to financial reasons for not taking training. There is also some indication that women are less likely to report that lack of employer support prevented them from engaging in training.

In summary, women are not only less likely to participate in job-related training but also more likely to experience training of a briefer duration than men. In addition, they are more likely to be rationed. For both men and women, rationing seems to be reflected more in lower training duration than in lower training probabilities. Finally, women are more likely to mention financial reasons or family responsibilities as a reason for being rationed.

Training Characteristics

Table 8.4 and 8.5 describe the training courses undertaken by the respondents. This means that each of the maximum three courses that could be listed is counted separately.

Table 8.4 lists which parties were responsible for the training initiative and who financed the training. The general pattern is as follows: compared to men, women are more likely to take the training initiative, whereas firms seem to be less likely to take the training initiative with their female workers. This seems to confirm the higher rationing probabilities for women. Finally, women are less likely to report legal or professional requirements as the reason for undertaking training. This is in line with Oosterbeek's (1996) finding that at least part of the gender difference in training is explained by differences in job characteristics.

Table 8.4.   Training initiative and finance by country for men and women, percentages

	Canada		Switzerland		United States		Netherlands	
	Men	Women	Men	Women	Men	Women	Men	Women
Initiative								
● Respondent	44.4	49.2	58.4	65.5	31.2	33.4	35.6	38.8
● Employer	67.2	67.7	61.5	56.7	72.4	70.0	58.9	56.8
● Legal/professional requirements	9.6	7.8	11.1	7.6	7.3	3.0	3.5	1.3
● Other[a]	11.2	14.0	6.5	5.8	4.1	4.1	10.3	11.0
Finance								
● Respondent	9.2	17.5	17.6	31.0	9.1	10.1	10.5	15.0
● Employer	82.1	80.9	76.3	65.5	87.2	81.6	86.7	83.7
● Government	19.8	15.2	13.7	17.0	5.5	6.9	5.0	3.1
● Other[b]	8.3	7.2	3.4	4.1	5.9	5.8	3.0	2.2

Notes:
a.   *Including colleagues, union/trade association, collective agreement, social services/labour center.*
b.   *Including union sponsorship and "no fees".*

Table 8.3 presented data showing that women are more likely to point to financial reasons for not undertaking training. Table 8.4 shows that women are also more likely to contribute financially to their training than men. Moreover, employers are less likely to financially support the training of women compared to that of men.

Can the lower training and higher rationing probabilities of women be explained by the fact that women are more likely to take part in general rather than specific training? Human capital theory predicts that employers are expected to be unwilling to contribute financially to general training. Table 8.4 showed that employers are apparently less willing to initiate and finance training for their female employees. Table 8.5 provides information about the training provider, the place where the training occurred, and the methods used. This information can be used to examine whether women enrol more in general rather than job-related courses.

Table 8.5.   Training characteristics, percentages, by country for men and women

	Canada		Switzerland		United States		Netherlands	
	Men	Women	Men	Women	Men	Women	Men	Women
Company	47.9	46.3	37.8	28.1	43.6	50.5	40.1	41.4
Commercial organization	21.6	20.8	5.3	9.4	22.7	19.3	25.1	19.8
Producer/supplier of equipment	9.4	6.2	7.6	6.4	12.0	5.4	6.8	3.1
Non-profit organization[a]	24.2	27.2	19.1	14.6	24.7	22.1	13.8	20.3
Other	3.3	6.2	38.9	48.5	6.3	7.5	14.5	16.3
Place								
Work	37.7	38.3	21.0	18.7	43.4	47.3	24.8	22.9
Training center	19.6	13.6	33.2	34.5	18.9	13.7	n.a.	n.a.
Conference center	18.9	16.7	16.8	8.8	18.9	14.3	n.a.	n.a.
University/business school	4.5	7.2	12.6	14.6	6.5	5.4	n.a.	n.a.
Formal education institution	11.8	15.2	5.3	6.4	7.3	11.1	n.a.	n.a.
Elsewhere[b]	7.5	8.8	11.1	17.0	4.9	7.7	75.2	77.1
Method								
On-the-job training	42.0	37.2	22.5	23.4	22.3	25.9	33.8	22.5
Class/seminar	83.9	85.8	88.5	82.5	86.2	82.9	79.7	76.2
Audio/video	45.0	41.8	21.4	19.3	23.1	17.6	44.6	38.3
Reading	68.0	68.7	49.2	41.5	31.2	24.8	75.9	70.5
Software	20.0	23.3	24.8	25.7	9.5	12.0	29.8	23.8
Other	2.8	3.5	5.3	5.8	2.4	1.7	4.3	5.7

Notes:
a.   *Including higher education institutions and further education colleges.*
b.   *Including community/sports centers and home.*

The most obvious provider of specific training is the employer. About two in five courses taken by both men and women in the Netherlands are provided by the firm. This compares to about one in two in Canada. Compared with Canada and the Netherlands, the differences between men and women are more pronounced in Switzerland and the United States. Women are, however, more likely to be trained by the firm in the United States and less likely in Switzerland.

The workplace is the most likely setting for the provision of specific training. Again, no systematic gender pattern appears. Differences are more striking between countries than between men and women. On-the-job training is most likely to be used to convey firm-specific competencies. In line with the above findings, men are not typically more likely to receive such on-the-job training. This is the case in Canada and the Netherlands, but not in Switzerland and the United States.

The findings obtained in this section can be summarized as follows. Women are less likely to report legal or professional requirements as the reason for undertaking training. Women are not only less likely to participate in job-related training than men, but also more likely to experience lower training intensities. In addition, they are more likely to be rationed. For both men and women, rationing seems to be reflected more in lower training intensities than in lower training probabilities. Women are more likely to list financial reasons for being rationed. At the same time, women are more likely to take the training initiative than men, and employers seem to be less likely to take the training initiative with their female workers. This latter finding coincides with the fact that women are also more likely to contribute financially to their training than men, whereas employers are less likely to financially support the training of women as compared to that of men. This cannot be explained by the fact that women undertake more general training than men.

So far, the higher rationing rate of women cannot be explained. Hence, discrimination cannot be dropped as a possible source of gender differences. The fact that women are more likely to be rationed and the finding that there are no clear gender differences in the training characteristics might reflect similar training preferences among men and women. There is some direct evidence in support of the job characteristics hypothesis. The different training and rationing rates of men and women might be due to differences in human capital endowments and job characteristics. How this translates into different training and participation rates is studied more closely in the next section.

8.4   The Role of Worker Characteristics

Appendix to Chapter 8

Methodology

The differences observed in training participation may be caused by differences in, for example, the human capital endowments of men and women, the jobs they hold, the industries they work in, and whether they have full-time jobs or temporary contracts. This section takes a closer look at whether gender differences in the rate of participation in work-related training as well as in the incidence of rationing can be explained by differences in the distribution of measured characteristics between men and women. A probit model explaining training and rationing is estimated for each subgroup. These estimates are then used to calculate the extent of discrimination. The methods applied for the data analysis are explained below with respect to training participation. However, the analysis of rationing proceeds in an identical way.

The net benefit of training y^* is assumed to be a linear function of human capital endowments and job characteristics X and an error term that captures unobserved characteristics.[2] The probability that an individual i is trained corresponds to the probability that the net benefits of training are positive:

$$(1) \qquad P(X_i ; \beta) = P(y_i^* > 0) = P(X_i \beta - \varepsilon_i > 0) = P(\varepsilon_i < X_i \beta)$$

This is essentially a reduced-form model of training choice, and the parameter coefficient can be interpreted as reflecting the influence of institutions and preferences. The estimated coefficients in the probit equation determine the probability that individuals receive training. It is assumed that there exists an allocation structure where there is no discrimination between men and women.

In order to analyze the influence on training probabilities of differences in the human capital endowments and job characteristics of men and women, the training probability is decomposed into two parts: 1) the difference in characteristics, and 2) the difference in the training parameters. Discrimination is said to occur if women and men with the same characteristics have an unequal chance of receiving training. This is essentially an index number problem, because the results are dependent on the non-discrimination base (β_0) that is employed for the analysis.

---

[2]   *The error term is assumed to follow a standard normal distribution.*

The difference in participation rates can be decomposed in the following way:

$$\bar{P}(X_M;\beta_M)-\bar{P}(X_F;\beta_F)=\left(\bar{P}(X_M;\beta_0)-\bar{P}(X_F;\beta_0)\right)+$$

(2)
$$\left[\left(\bar{P}(X_M;\beta_M)-\bar{P}(X_M;\beta_0)\right)+\left(\bar{P}(X_F;\beta_0)-\bar{P}(X_F;\beta_F)\right)\right]$$

The bar over P stands for the sample mean. The left-hand side of (2) is the difference in observed participation rates. The first term in brackets on the right-hand side of the equation reflects the effect of individual characteristics and the second term in square brackets that of the coefficients, that is, institutions and preferences (see, for example, Gomulka & Stern 1990). This second term is often interpreted as a measure of discrimination in a broad sense. The findings are presented taking both the results for men and women as the base. If the no-discrimination structure is that of men $(\beta_0=\beta_M)$, then the difference in training probabilities can be decomposed in the following way:

(3) $\quad \bar{P}(X_M;\beta_M)-\bar{P}(X_F;\beta_F)=\left(\bar{P}(X_M;\beta_M)-\bar{P}(X_F;\beta_M)\right)+\left(\bar{P}(X_F;\beta_M)-\bar{P}(X_F;\beta_F)\right)$

If the female participation equation is taken as the no-discrimination structure $(\beta_0=\beta_F)$, then the decomposition would be as follows:

(4) $\quad \bar{P}(X_M;\beta_M)-\bar{P}(X_F;\beta_F)=\left(\bar{P}(X_M;\beta_F)-\bar{P}(X_F;\beta_F)\right)+\left(\bar{P}(X_M;\beta_M)-\bar{P}(X_M;\beta_F)\right)$

In both (3) and (4), the first term on the right-hand side of the equation represents the impact of measured characteristics, whereas the second term reflects the degree of discrimination.

End of Appendix

Participation

The impact of individual characteristics on training participation is estimated in a probit model. The results, presented in Table 8.6, are briefly discussed below. Each coefficient shows the effect of a given explanatory variable on the probability of being trained evaluated at the sample mean.

Table 8.6.   Training participation and individual characteristics, by country and gender

Training	Canada Men Coef.	s.e.	Canada Women Coef.	s.e.	Switzerland Men Coef.	s.e.	Switzerland Women Coef.	s.e.	United States Men Coef.	s.e.	United States Women Coef.	s.e.	Netherlands Men Coef.	s.e.	Netherlands Women Coef.	s.e.
16-25	0.026	(0.07)	-0.123[2]	(0.05)	0.247[2]	(0.08)	0.081	(0.08)	-0.140[1]	(0.07)	-0.256[2]	(0.05)	0.034	(0.07)	0.022	(0.06)
26-35	-0.057	(0.05)	-0.058	(0.05)	0.119[2]	(0.06)	0.040	(0.06)	-0.086[1]	(0.05)	0.075	(0.05)	-0.007	(0.05)	0.023	(0.05)
46-55	-0.187[2]	(0.04)	-0.177[2]	(0.04)	0.070	(0.07)	0.104	(0.07)	-0.043	(0.05)	0.126[2]	(0.06)	-0.073	(0.05)	-0.089	(0.05)
56-65	-0.108	(0.06)	-0.006	(0.09)	0.030	(0.08)	0.009	(0.09)	-0.087	(0.07)	0.054	(0.08)	-0.177[2]	(0.07)	-0.012	(0.12)
Urban	-0.101[1]	(0.06)	-0.042	(0.06)	0.006	(0.05)	-0.050	(0.05)	0.062	(0.05)	-0.011	(0.05)	-0.022	(0.05)	-0.020	(0.05)
Migrant	-0.022	(0.05)	-0.046	(0.05)	-0.066	(0.05)	-0.091	(0.05)	-0.153[2]	(0.05)	-0.168[2]	(0.05)	0.103	(0.08)	0.084	(0.09)
ISCED 0/1	-0.104	(0.08)	0.045	(0.10)	-0.213[1]	(0.07)	-0.217[2]	(0.05)	0.005	(0.09)	-0.137	(0.10)	-0.136[2]	(0.06)	-0.164[1]	(0.07)
ISCED 2	-0.105[1]	(0.05)	-0.087	(0.06)	-0.176[2]	(0.06)	-0.204[2]	(0.05)	-0.024	(0.10)	-0.277[2]	(0.08)	-0.070	(0.05)	-0.026	(0.05)
ISCED 5/6//7	0.188[2]	(0.05)	0.029	(0.05)	0.084[1]	(0.05)	0.110[1]	(0.07)	0.266[2]	(0.05)	0.137[2]	(0.05)	0.064	(0.05)	0.093	(0.06)
Full-time	0.096	(0.09)	-0.001	(0.04)	0.098	(0.10)	-0.040	(0.05)	0.228[2]	(0.08)	0.116[2]	(0.05)	0.104	(0.08)	0.119[2]	(0.04)
Temporary	-0.013	(0.12)	-0.184[2]	(0.06)	-0.014	(0.11)	-0.027	(0.08)	-0.088	(0.13)	0.021	(0.11)	-0.008	(0.10)	0.059	(0.08)
Tenure <1 year	-0.221[2]	(0.04)	0.243[2]	(0.06)	-0.032	(0.07)	-0.051	(0.06)	0.107[1]	(0.07)	0.035	(0.06)	0.074	(0.08)	0.032	(0.07)
N observations	785		812		564		434		754		699		748		561	
c2(d.f.=25)	161.3		204.45		66.39		71.69		173.16		149.51		56.39		84.09	

Notes:
Coefficients (standard errors) refer to the effect of the explanatory variable on the training probability evaluated at the sample mean. The estimation included 8 industry and 7 occupational controls.
1. *Statistically significant at the .10 level.*
2. *Statistically significant at the .05 level.*

Human capital theory predicts that more training will be undertaken early in life because of the longer pay-off period. The age effects in Table 8.6 are relative to 36 to 45-year-olds. Mixed results are obtained. There is no significant age effect for Swiss and Dutch women. The probability of being trained is .12 lower for Canadian women aged 16 to 25 and .26 lower for young women in the United States, compared to middle-aged women. For the older female age groups (46 to 55-year-olds), the effects are positive in the United States (.13) and negative in Canada (-.18). The negative age effects for young women in North America can possibly be explained by their higher (expected) turnover. Young men in the United States are also less likely to be trained than middle-aged men, whereas young Swiss men face substantial higher training probabilities (.25). For the older male age groups, the effects are negative, except in Switzerland, but only statistically significant in Canada (46 to 55-year-olds) and the Netherlands (56 to 65-year-olds). The direction of the age effects for older men can be reconciled with human capital theory.

The effects found for education point in the expected direction: those who received less formal education initially are less likely to undertake work-related training. A few additional results are worth noting. The effect of education on training probabilities is very similar for men and women in the Netherlands and Switzerland but not in the North American countries. There is no significant effect of education on training participation for Canadian women, while there is a steep education effect for men. North American men seem to benefit more than women from higher education, in terms of training probabilities.

Migrants are less likely to be trained except in the Netherlands, although the effect is only significant in the United States, both statistically and in terms of magnitude: about 15 percent. Although only statistically significant in the United States, full-time employed men are more likely to participate in training than their part-time employed counterparts (this effect is .23 in the US and about .10 in the other countries). Female employees in Canada with a temporary contract are less likely to be trained. The effect of temporary employment is in general negative, small, and not statistically significant. Finally, for those who are with their employer for less than 1 year, results are very mixed. In Canada, the effect is large, about .20, and is opposite for men (positive) and women (negative). American men in their first tenure year are .10 more likely to be trained. This tenure effect is not statistically significant in the European countries in the sample.

Table 8.7 shows the predicted participation rates.[3] It can be seen that the choice of the structure that is not discriminatory generally influences the magnitude (for the female non-discrimination structure, the effects roughly

---

[3]   *Participation rates differ slightly in this table as compared to Table 8.2 because of missing observations in the explanatory variables that enter the probit equations.*

double), but not the direction of the effect. For Canada, Switzerland, and the United States, the effects of the characteristics, and coefficients point in the opposite direction. In the Netherlands, this is only the case if the no-discrimination structure is taken to be that of women. If a pooled equation is estimated for the Netherlands and taken as the no-discrimination structure, the results are similar to those obtained using the coefficients of men as the base. Given this, plus the lower labour-force participation and the higher incidence of part-time employment of Dutch women compared to women in the other countries, the male training participation structure is taken as the non-discriminatory one.

Table 8.7.   Predicted training rates for men and women (per cent)

| | Observed | | | No-discrimination structure | | | |
| | | | | Men | | Women | |
	Men	Women	Diff.	Char.	Coef.	Char.	Coef.
Canada	37.2	37.2	0.1	-5.8	5.8	-9.4	9.5
Switzerland	30.3	29.3	1.1	4.3	-3.3	7.2	-6.1
United States	38.6	38.0	0.6	-1.9	2.5	-5.2	5.8
Netherlands	36.4	29.0	7.4	2.8	4.7	-5.9	13.4

For Canada and the United States, the results point in the same direction. Due to their characteristics, men would receive less training than women, the effect being between 6 and 9 percentage points in Canada and 2 and 5 percentage points in the United States. This is, however, counterbalanced by the fact that the institutional arrangements and/or preferences of men are more beneficial to training than is the case for women.

In the Netherlands and Switzerland, different results are obtained. In these countries, men would receive more training as a result of their characteristics (3 to 4 percentage points). For Dutch men, this is enhanced by 5 percentage points as a result of preferences/institutions. For Swiss men, there is an opposite effect that lowers their training rates by 3 percentage points.

Although the effects found are not remarkably high in absolute levels, they are not negligible relative to the training rates of women (and men). If the discrimination effect is expressed relative to the female participation rates and taken to be the average (as an approximation) of the effect found for the male and female no-discrimination structures, the countries rank as follows. The discrimination effect is smallest in Switzerland, where it is minus 16 per cent, followed by 11 per cent in the United States, 20 per cent in Canada, and 31 per cent in the Netherlands.

Table 8.8.   Training rationing and individual characteristics, by country and gender

Training	Canada Men Coef.	s.e.	Canada Women Coef.	s.e.	Switzerland Men Coef.	s.e.	Switzerland Women Coef.	s.e.	United States Men Coef.	s.e.	United States Women Coef.	s.e.	Netherlands Men Coef.	s.e.	Netherlands Women Coef.	s.e.
16-25	0.199[2]	(0.08)	-0.129[2]	(0.05)	0.052	(0.07)	-0.128[1]	(0.06)	-0.089	(0.05)	0.026	(0.06)	0.044	(0.06)	-0.100[1]	(0.05)
26-35	0.188[2]	(0.05)	-0.066	(0.05)	0.087	(0.06)	-0.035	(0.06)	-0.033	(0.04)	0.086[1]	(0.05)	0.058	(0.04)	-0.092[2]	(0.04)
46-55	0.011	(0.05)	-0.310[2]	(0.03)	-0.053	(0.06)	-0.169[2]	(0.06)	-0.127[2]	(0.04)	0.054	(0.05)	-0.084[2]	(0.04)	-0.098[1]	(0.05)
56-65	-0.083	(0.07)	-0.071	(0.08)	-0.176[2]	(0.06)	-0.150[1]	(0.07)	-0.088	(0.05)	-0.124[1]	(0.05)	-0.097	(0.05)	-0.111	(0.07)
Urban	0.078	(0.05)	0.000	(0.05)	0.000	(0.05)	0.040	(0.05)	-0.045	(0.04)	-0.032	(0.04)	0.012	(0.04)	0.014	(0.05)
Migrant	0.039	(0.05)	0.123[2]	(0.05)	0.126[2]	(0.07)	0.040	(0.06)	0.002	(0.05)	-0.043	(0.05)	0.093	(0.07)	-0.046	(0.07)
ISCED 0/1	-0.112	(0.08)	-0.123	(0.08)	-0.207[2]	(0.06)	0.115	(0.11)	-0.099	(0.06)	-0.168[2]	(0.06)	-0.036	(0.05)	0.031	(0.09)
ISCED 2	-0.029	(0.06)	-0.220[2]	(0.04)	-0.159[2]	(0.06)	-0.060	(0.07)	-0.104	(0.06)	-0.159[1]	(0.07)	-0.031	(0.04)	-0.076	(0.05)
ISCED 5/6/7	0.095[2]	(0.05)	0.152[2]	(0.05)	-0.030	(0.05)	0.022	(0.07)	0.089[2]	(0.04)	0.148[2]	(0.04)	0.037	(0.04)	0.089	(0.06)
Full-time	0.235[2]	(0.05)	0.223[2]	(0.04)	0.077	(0.11)	0.037	(0.05)	-0.021	(0.09)	0.052	(0.04)	0.065	(0.06)	0.075[1]	(0.04)
Temporary	0.335[2]	(0.13)	0.277[2]	(0.09)	0.029	(0.11)	0.156	(0.11)	-0.114	(0.08)	-0.057	(0.08)	-0.088	(0.06)	0.067	(0.07)
Tenure <1 year	-0.032	(0.05)	0.084	(0.06)	0.141[1]	(0.09)	0.000	(0.07)	0.123[2]	(0.06)	0.141[2]	(0.06)	0.089	(0.07)	-0.043	(0.06)
Number of obs	785		815		549		439		754		695		748		558	
c2(d.f.=25)	127.74		212.39		57.66		28.96		71.41		62.52		42.67		50.56	

Notes:
Coefficients (standard errors) refer to the effect of the explanatory variable on the training probability evaluated at the sample mean. The estimation included 8 industry and 7 occupational controls.
1. *Statistically significant at the .10 level.*
2. *Statistically significant at the .05 level.*

Rationing

The impact of measured characteristics on training rationing is estimated in a probit model. The results are presented in Table 8.8.

As with the analysis of training participation, the coefficients show the effect of a given explanatory variable on the probability of being trained evaluated at the sample mean.

The first remarkable finding is that, with one exception, the coefficients that are statistically significant in both the participation and the rationing analysis have the same direction. This means that a higher (lower) training probability goes together with a higher (lower) rationing probability.[4] The exception is the effect of temporary employment for Canadian women. Their temporary employment status lowers their training probability by .18 and increases their rationing probability by .28.

The age pattern of rationing is as follows: older workers aged 46 to 65 are less likely to be rationed than middle-aged workers (36 to 45) irrespective of their gender. Young male workers (16-35) are more likely to be rationed, and young female workers less likely. Lower educated workers (up to lower secondary education) are less likely to be rationed. More highly educated workers are more likely to be rationed.

Migrant workers seem more likely to be rationed, although this effect is only statistically significant for Canadian women and Swiss men (and substantial: about 12 percentage points).

Full-time workers tend to face higher rationing rates, but this is statistically significant only in Canada, with an effect in the order of .22. Canadian workers in temporary employment have higher rationing probabilities. Workers in their first year of tenure are more likely to be constrained in their training opportunities, except European women and Canadian men. This effect is statistically significant for men in the United States and in Switzerland.

Table 8.9 presents a decomposition of rationing probabilities. The discussion will focus on the results where the no-discrimination structure is assumed to be that of men. As with the analysis of the participation rates, the choice of the structure that is not discriminatory generally influences the magnitude but not the direction of the effect. The exception is the Netherlands. The sizeable effects found in the Netherlands for the female no-discrimination structure are the consequence of large and imprecisely estimated industry and occupations effects in the female rationing equation.

---

[4]   *The underlying assumption is that the training and rationing probability are independent.*

Table 8.9.   Predicted rationing rates for men and women (percent)

| | | | | No-discrimination structure | | | |
| | Observed | | | Men | | Women | |
	Men	Women	Diff.	Char.	Coef.	Char.	Coef.
Canada	29.5	34.1	-4.6	3.5	-8.1	4.5	-9.1
Switzerland	29.7	30.9	-1.3	-3.7	2.4	-2.2	0.9
United States	24.4	26.6	-2.2	0.4	-2.6	1.0	-3.2
Netherlands	20.5	23.8	-3.3	0.6	-3.9	15.6	-18.9

Differences in the gross rationing rates between men and women are modest, being 1 to 5 percentage points higher for women. Differences due to characteristics are negligible in the Netherlands, and the United States, and about 3.5 percentage points in Canada and Switzerland. This effect, however, is negative in Switzerland: men would face higher rationing probabilities given their human capital endowment and job characteristics.

The discrimination effect benefits men in Canada, the Netherlands, and the United States, whereas it creates a higher rationing rate for men in Switzerland. This effect is relatively large in Canada (8 percentage points) and modest in the other countries (2 to 4 percentage points).

As mentioned before, the effects found are not always high in absolute levels, but they are not negligible relative to the rationing rates of women (and men). If the discrimination effect is expressed relative to the female rationing rates and taken to be the average of the effect found for the male and female no-discrimination structures, the countries rank the same as before. The discrimination effect is smallest in Switzerland, where it is 5 percent, followed by minus 11 per cent in the United States, minus 25 per cent in Canada, and minus 48 per cent in the Netherlands.

8.5   Summary and Conclusion

This chapter analyzed gender differences in work-related training in four countries. For Canada, the Netherlands, Switzerland, and the United States, the training participation of men and women was analyzed. The focus was on the lower training incidence among women and their higher probability of being rationed.

The findings obtained in this chapter can be summarized as follows. Women are less likely to report legal or professional requirements as the reason for undertaking training. They are not only less likely to participate in job-related training than men, but also more likely to experience lower training intensities. In addition, women are more likely to be rationed, by an average of 4 percentage points. Except in Switzerland, rationing seems to be reflected more in lower training intensities than in lower training probabilities, while women are more likely to list financial reasons for being rationed. At the same time, in all countries in the sample women are more likely to take the training initiative than men. Although the differences are small, employers seem to be less likely to take the training initiative with their female workers. This latter finding coincides with the fact that in all countries women are also more likely to contribute financially to their training than men, whereas employers are less likely to financially support the training of women as compared to that of men. This cannot be explained by the fact that women undertake more general training than men.

These gender differences are due either to differences in background characteristics, or to differences in preferences and/or institutional arrangements. If the latter explanation is examined using probit models to estimate the size of the discrimination effect, then the following results are found. Switzerland stands aside from the other countries; the discrimination effect works to the advantage of women. For training participation this effect was estimated to be about 16 per cent, and for rationing 5 percent. In the other three countries, discrimination lowered the training rates of women and increased their rationing rates. For training participation, this amounted to 11 per cent in the United States, 20 per cent in Canada, and 31 per cent in the Netherlands. For rationing, these numbers were respectively 11, 25 and 48 percent.

It is therefore found that although a substantial part of the differences in training participation and rationing rates of women compared to men can be explained by differences in human capital endowments and job characteristics, sizeable discrimination effects remain.

References

Altonji, J.G., and Spletzer, J.R. 1991. "Worker characteristics, Job Characteristics, and the Receipt of On-the-job Training". In: *Industrial and Labour Relations Review*. 45 (1): 58-79.

Barron, J.M., Black, D.A., and Loewenstein, M.A. 1993. "Gender differences in Training, Capital, and Wages" In: *Journal of Human Resources* 28 (2): 343-364.

Bishop, J. 1996. "What We Know about Employer-provided Training: A Review of the Literature". (CAHRS Discussion Paper no. 96-09) Ithaca: Cornell University.

Booth, A. 1991. "Job-related Formal Training: Who Receives it and what is it Worth?" In: *Oxford Bulletin of Economics and Statistics* 53: 281-294.

Duncan, G.J., and Hoffman, S. 1979. "On-the-job Training and Earnings Differences by Race and Sex". In: *Review of Economics and Statistics* 61: 594-603.

Gomulka, J., and Stern, N. 1990. "The Employment of Married Women in the United Kingdom 1970-83". In: *Economica* 57: 171-199.

Green, F. 1991. "Sex Discrimination in Job-related Training". In: *British Journal of Industrial Relations* 29 (2): 295-304.

Greenhalgh, C., and Stewart, M. 1987. "The Effects and Determinants of Training". In: *Oxford Bulletin of Economics and Statistics* 49 (2): 171-190.

Leuven, E., and Oosterbeek, H. 1997. "Demand and Supply of Work-related Training: Evidence from Four Countries". (Discussion Paper no. 97-013) Rotterdam: Tinbergen Institute.

Loewenstein, M., and Spletzer, J. 1996. "Formal and Informal Training: Evidence from the NLSY". (Paper presented at the Seminar: "New Empirical Research on Employer Training: Who Pays? Who Benefits?", November 1996) Ithaca: Institute of Labour Relations and Policy, Cornell University.

Miller, P.W. 1994. "Gender Discrimination in Training: An Australian Perspective". In: *British Journal of Industrial Relations* 32 (4): 539-564.

OECD 1991. *Employment Outlook*, Paris.

Oosterbeek, H. 1996. "A Decomposition of Training Probabilities". In: *Applied Economics* 28: 799-805.

Pischke, S. 1996. "Continuous Training in Germany" (paper presented at ILR-Cornell Institute for Labour-market Policies Conference, New Empirical Research on Employer Training: Who Pays? Who Benefits?, November 1996) Ithaca: Institute of Labour Relations and Policy, Cornell University.

Royalty, A.B. 1996. "The Effects of Job Turnover on the Training of Men and Women". In: *Industrial and Labour Relations Review* 49: 506-521.

Veum, J.R. 1993. "Training Among Young Adults: Who, What Kind and for How Long?". In: *Monthly Labour Review* (August): 27-32.

Chapter 9

Beyond the Walls of the Household: Gender and Adult Education Participation

Sofia Valdivielso Gomez

9.1 Introduction

Adult learning is a growing social phenomenon in each society. There is a large and increasing social demand for more opportunities to learn throughout the lifespan. The question is, however, whether the general aspirations and socioeconomic realities and needs of communities and societies lead to a similar involvement of women and men in organized learning. This question is addressed in this chapter. At first glance, the data presented in Chapters 2 and 3 would appear to suggest that there are no significant gender-related differences in the overall rate of participation in adult education. The more in-depth analysis of data presented in the previous chapter demonstrated that there are some important dissimilarities in the patterns of participation between men and women, dissimilarities which relate to different labour-market experiences and conditions, and the associated learning opportunities. This analysis is taken further in the present chapter, in which additional social and cultural variables are introduced. The interpretation of the findings is facilitated by an analysis of additional data on adult education participation collected in the Canary Islands.

9.2 At First Glance: Emerging Learning Societies Well Balanced on Gender

Time-series data collected by national statistical offices indicate that overall rates of participation in adult education tended to increase in many countries over the last decade (OECD 1996). The evidence shows that participation in organized adult learning is no longer a marginal issue. The previous chapters suggest that nearly half of the adult population in countries such as Sweden, the Netherlands and the United States were involved in organized learning activities during 1994. In the Netherlands, for example, the participation rate was about 15 percent in the mid-1970s. By the late 1980s it had reached 25 percent, and according to the results of the IALS survey, the participation rate was 38 percent in 1994 (Van der Kamp 1997). In Sweden the participation rate increased from 32 percent in 1974 to 53 percent in 1994 (Rubenson 1997).

The changes in the labour-markets, the technological innovations introduced in the work place, the essential skills expected from all citizens in increasingly information-intensive societies, and the new aspirations of women and men for more autonomy and active participation, are important factors behind the increase in the individual and social demand for adult education and continuing vocational training (European Commission 1996)

Table 9.1 presents the overall rates of adult education participation of women and men in organized adult learning in the six countries surveyed (OECD and Statistics Canada 1995). The results show that more than one in three adults aged 16-64 took part in five of the countries. The overall participation rate was 14 percent in Poland and 53 percent in Sweden. In the Canary Islands, which is a special European Region, the overall participation rate was 21.4 percent for all women and men who are less than 65 years of age (Valdivielso & Rodriguez 1996).

The evidence suggests that there are no important gender disparities in the overall participation rates. Where there are differences in the participation rates of men and women, they tend to be very small, with men taking part more often than women in all countries but Sweden. As in the latter country, in the Canaries women tend to participate slightly more frequently than men (21.9 percent versus 19.9 percent).

Table 9.1.   Overall rate of participation in adult education for men and women, 1994

	Canada n= 4,417	Switzerland (German) n= 1,263	Switzerland (French) n= 1,296	United States n= 2,668	Nether- lands n= 2,566	Sweden n= 2,123	Poland n= 2,668
Men	39.5	45.9	38.1	41.6	39.6	51.4	15.4
Women	37.9	44.2	29.7	40.5	35.8	55.4	12.6
Total	**38.6**	**45.0**	**33.9**	**41.0**	**37.7**	**53.3**	**14.0**

Since there appears to be no significant difference in the overall participation rates of men and women, it might be concluded that both groups participate equally in organized learning activities, and hence that there is no gender bias in the operation of adult education and training markets. However, the previous chapter has shown, albeit for job training and for the employed population only, that underneath this apparent equality lie important differences in gender-related patterns of participation. In the sections below the focus is on the social and cultural factors that may introduce gender-related differences for the general population and for general adult education rather than job-specific training only. The analysis will show that participation in adult education is a complex phenomenon, and that social and cultural factors can have different and at times contradictory effects.

Potential Participants

Those respondents who answered that they had not taken part in any organized learning activity during the year preceding the interview were asked if they nevertheless would have liked to do so. Tables 9.2 and 9.3 indicate that in Switzerland, Canada and the United States about one in four non-participants said that this was the case. For all countries the results indicate that there are no statistically significant differences between men and women in so far as job-related programmes are considered. However, there are significant differences between men and women in French-speaking Switzerland, the Netherlands and the United States with respect to the wish to take part in adult education programmes of a general nature.

Table 9.2.   Non-participants expressing a wish to take part in job-related adult education, 1994

	Canada n= 4,408	Switzerland (German) n= 1,255	Switzerland (French) n= 1,296	United States n= 2,642	Netherlands n= 2,566	Poland n= 2,667
Men	31.1	25.4	29.3	23.4	19.7	13.9
Women	28.9	23.2	27.7	24.2	18.2	11.5
Total	**30.0**	**24.3**	**28.5**	**23.8**	**19.0**	**12.7**

Note: gender differences are not statistically significant.

Table 9.3.   Non-participants expressing a wish to take part in general adult education, 1994

	Canada n=4,408	Switzerland (German) n= 1,255	Switzerland (French) n= 1,296	United States n= 2,642	Netherlands n= 2,566	Poland n= 2,667
Men	24.2[1]	28.9	26.6[1]	13.7[1]	17.7[1]	6.8
Women	37.7	35.3	33.1[1]	22.1[1]	24.3[1]	7.9
Total	**31.0**	**32.2**	**29.9[3]**	**18.2[1]**	**20.9[1]**	**7.3**

Note: gender differences are significant:
1. $= p < .001$.
2. $= p < .01$

Tables 9.2 and 9.3 show, moreover, that more men than women expressed a desire to take part in job-related courses whereas more women than men answered that the courses in which they would have liked to participate were related to their personal interests. If those who did participate are added to those who wished to but did not then it becomes clear that the desire to take part in adult education is present in over half the adult population in all the countries surveyed. The only exception is Poland, where a majority did not participate and did not want to.

This trend is also observed in the Canary Islands. More men than women (30.4 versus 18.3 percent) would have liked to participate in job-related courses whereas more women than men (30.7 versus 16.8 percent) expressed a wish to take part in courses related to personal development and interests. These differences are statistically significant.

9.3   Beyond Apparent Equality: Different Patterns of Participation

The overall picture, which shows only small differences between men and women, changes completely if the reasons for participation are considered. The participation patterns are clearly gender biased in relation to type of programme. As can be seen in Tables 9.4 and 9.5, the tendency in each country is for women to participate more frequently for personal reasons whereas men do it more often for job-related reasons.

Table 9.4.   Participants citing job-related interest as main reason for participation (percentages)

	Canada	Switzerland (German)	Switzerland (French)	United States	Netherlands	Sweden	Poland
Men	89.2	70.4	72.8	90.8	74.8	38.2*	78.9
Women	69.1	47.8	54.6	84.7	51.5	39.5*	71.7
Total	**79.2**	**58.9**	**64.4**	**87.6**	**64.3**	**38.9**	**75.6**

*   *Unreliable estimate; number of cases below 100.*

Table 9.5.   Participants citing personal interest as main reason for participation (percentages)

	Canada	Switzerland (German)	Switzerland (French)	United States	Netherlands	Sweden	Poland
Men	9.1	26.2	26.4	6.1	15.6	49.2	15.7*
Women	28.5	50.7	43.3	11.9	43.6	48.7	25.7*
Total	**18.7**	**38.6**	**34.2**	**9.1**	**28.1**	**48.9**	**20.2**

*   *Unreliable estimate; number of cases below 100.*

The current trend favoring job-related over general purpose adult education provision has probably contributed to these results. If so, the gender-related gap may well increase further in the future. As Rubenson (1995) reported in a paper presented at a meeting of the European Society of Researchers in Adult Education, "not only has there been a steady increase [in overall participation levels in Sweden], but also a change in the composition of adult education [...] The most importance change is the increase in the importance of employer-sponsored education". A similar trend is observed in Canada and the United States, where the non-work oriented dimension of adult education has lost out importance over the past two decades.

9.4   Beyond Apparent Equality: Different Learning Conditions

It is in the analysis of the learning conditions which are offered to men and women that one will find the most important gender-related differences. There is a clear gender bias in the financial support which participants obtain to facilitate their participation. As Table 9.6 shows, in every country the first source of funds is the individual or the family. After this the employer is the most important sponsor. However, in all countries except Sweden employers who finance or subsidize the learning activities of their workers tend to do so more often for men than for women. In the Netherlands, for instance, men are twice as much more likely to obtain financial support from their employers than women.

Table 9.6.   Participants' sources of financial support by gender (most often mentioned sources; percentages)

	Canada n= 2,848	Switzerland (German) n= 920	Switzerland (French) n= 670	United States n=1,910	Netherlands n= 1,454	Poland n= 484
Self or family						
Men	38.8	42.5	38.1	28.9	27.1	27.0
Women	43.8	61.4	56.6	33.8	55.2	35.5
Total	**41.2**	**52.1**	**46.6**	**31.5**	**39.7**	**30.9**
Employer						
Men	49.9	52.9	51.6	65.8	64.3	64.5
Women	40.3	32.2	38.8	56.0	35.0	53.7
Total	**45.2**	**42.4**	**45.7**	**60.7**	**51.2**	**59.5**
Government						
Men	16.4	12.9	14.0	9.5*	9.5	4.7*
Women	22.7	14.2	10.9	8.5*	9.4	6.3*
Total	**19.5**	**13.6**	**12.9**	**9.0***	**9.5**	**5.4***

*   *Unreliable estimate; number of cases below 100.*

Accordingly, more women than men have to pay for their participation in adult education and training. This is likely to be one of the factors which influences women's decision whether to take part or not. This bias may also be related to a finding mentioned previously, namely that women tend to participate more often for personal reasons than men.

In the Canary Islands an enlarged questionnaire was used for the survey. This included items on the amount of non-working and working time used for adult learning. The results show that women tend to devote a larger share of their free time to organized learning activities, whereas men have more possibilities to use their working time for such activities. In the Canary Islands, the proportion of men who said they participated in organized learning during working hours is three times that of women (20 versus 7 percent). This finding illustrates another dimension of hidden discrimination at work—an issue that will become even more prominent when the reasons for non-participation are analyzed.

Who takes the decision to participate?

In all countries the majority of the participants made the enrolment decision on their own initiative (see Table 9.7). However, an analysis of the data by gender shows that more women than men tend to make the decision on their own and, second, that more men than women participated on the suggestion of their employer. The fact that more women than men make the decision on their own is related to the level of support and type of programme, probably more so than to the freedom to decide.

Table 9.7   Who initiated the enrolment decision, by gender (most often mentioned alternatives; percentages of those participating)

	Canada n= 2,832	Switzerland (German) n= 970	Switzerland (French) n= 669	United States n=1,907	Netherlands n= 1,456	Poland n= 494
You did yourself						
Man	60	71	74	45	46	49
Women	69	80	71	50	62	54
Total	**62**	**76**	**73**	**48**	**53**	**51**
Friend or family						
Man	9	7	5	5	4	5
Women	10	5	6	4	9	4
Total	**9**	**6**	**6**	**5**	**6**	**5**
Employer						
Man	36	37	34	51	41	48
Women	34	26	27	46	22	49
Total	**35**	**32**	**31**	**48**	**33**	**48**

The question on whose initiative the enrolment decision was taken was introduced in order to examine whether the participants took courses at the request or under pressure of external actors. The intention was to provide an insight into the incidence of "workfare" programmes, whereby welfare recipients or unemployed people may be obliged to follow education or training, under what Courtney (1992) calls conditions of "compulsory adult education". The picture that emerges is far from simple. Women tend to make the decision to enrol on their own to a greater extent than men. But it is not entirely clear how this finding should be interpreted.

The fact that employers encourage men more often than women is linked to the gender biased distribution of financial support for adult education participation. Men obtain financial assistance from their employer more often than women, but men apparently also have to take part more frequently in courses provided or proposed by employers. Gender differences in the rate of participation in job-related adult education, where applicable, are probably due not to a lack of interest or motivation on the part of women, but rather to poorly adapted provision, a lack of facilities, and little financial support. This interpretation might also explain the comparatively low number of men who participate in non-work-related learning initiatives. And in both cases, the gendered nature of provisions and learning environments—which tend to be more men-oriented in job-related courses and more women-oriented in non-work-related programmes may also have an impact. Further studies will be needed to test these hypotheses on the impact of the hidden curriculum of the different types of provision and of their cultural contexts.

The survey instruments employed in the Canary Islands included a question in addition to the one that asked on whose initiative the enrolment decision was taken. This question asked the respondents how they had obtained the information about the course they had attended. Table 9.8 shows the results. The main source of information was by "word of mouth". More than one third of the participants stated that they obtained the information through informal channels, from talking to family, friends or neighbours. The majority of those who gave this answer were women. The employer was the next most frequent source of information, but this was directed mainly to male workers. Twice as many men than women responded that they obtained the information about the adult education programme from their employer. As the educational level increases, the use of informal sources of information decreases and the importance of the employer increases. Whilst only five percent of those with the lowest levels of formal education get the information from employers, this percentage rises to over 30 percent for university graduates (Valdivielso & Rodriguez 1996).

Table 9.8   Canarian participants' main source of information about the adult education course (percentages)

	Employer	Family	Friends or neigh- bours	News paper, radio or TV	Mail	Union or profes- sional organization	Non- profit organi- zation	Govern- ment agency	Other
Men	23.2	8.4	22.6	14.7	4.2	3.2	2.1	14.2	7.4
Women	10.6	6.9	31.0	15.7	6.9	1.4	6.5	10.6	10.2
Total	16.5	7.6	27.1	15.3	5.7	2.2	4.4	12.3	8.9
n=406	n= 67	n= 31	n=110	n= 62	n= 23	n= 9	n= 18	n= 50	n= 36

In the Canary Islands the majority of participants in adult basic education are women. During the school-year 1993/94, 70.123 adults (6 percent of the total adult population) were registered in adult basic education courses provided by the government. The proportion of women who were participating in these courses was 65 per cent, compared with 35 percent for men (Gobierno de Canarias 1995). The more basic the level of the course, the more women were over-represented among the participants. For instance, 4.342 adults took part in Level 1 programmes, which include the literacy courses. More than 90 percent of them were women. When they were asked where they had gotten the information about the course they generally responded that it came from their neighbours, friends, or family. It is important to recognize that many poorly educated adults use informal channels to obtain the information they need. The consequence of failing to do so can be that these people will not participate. The difficulties many poorly educated adults encounter in accessing the formal information channels of government, employers, and the media is an additional factor in social and economic exclusion.

The rate of drop-outs from adult education programmes in the Canary Islands was higher among women than men (19.4 versus 12.1 percent). The most important reason for dropping out, both for men and women was lack of time. More women than men declared that the courses they had participated in had been of no use to them. This feeling that scarce free time is being wasted can be one of the reasons why women drop out more frequently than men. The curriculum could be another explanation. The adult education courses that are provided in the Canary Islands are generally designed by people who work at the top of the social and political structure. At this level of the social hierarchy, the workers are generally male. They impose their own understanding of reality by considering culture as "neutral". Many of the women who decided to participate in an adult basic education course and who usually belonged to the lower educational levels, had to learn contents designed by men, topics dealingwith alien to their own cultural contexts. This is another example of hidden discrimination operating through the curriculum women have to master if they want to obtain the certificate that will allow them to find a job or feel empowered.

Providers

The data in Table 9.8 indicate that, in no country is a single provider covering more than 30 percent of the total provision for adult education and training. This is an indication of the sheer diversity of what was referred to as the "training market in the previous chapter. Employers are important providers, every where followed by commercial and private organizations, universities, and colleges. The supply of adult education and training organized by employers tends to reach slightly more men than women. The average rate of participation in employer-sponsored provision is 28 percent for men and 24 percent for women.

A mirror image emerges when data for the commercial organizations is studied. In this case more women than men participated in adult education courses, the average, being 18 percent for men and 21 percent for women. This kind of organization is often private and for profit, which means that the people who take part in a course organized by them have to pay for their participation. Women are thus paying more often than men. Women also tend to receive less subsidies from employers and allocate more of their own free time, whereas men have more opportunities to learn during their working time and do so with fewer direct financial costs. The United States is an exception to this trend, with women participating more frequently than men in courses provided by employers (31 versus 28 percent), whereas men more often join courses provided by commercial organizations than women (20 versus 15 percent).

Table 9.9.   Participants classified by provider categories and gender (percentages*)

	Canada	Switzerland (German)	Switzerland (French)	United States	Netherlands	Poland
University level institution						
Men	16.5	12.5	20.1	25.8	12.4	6.2
Women	10.8	8.6	14.7	27.8	11.4	11.7
Total	**13.7**	**10.7**	**17.7**	**26.8**	**12.0**	**8.8**
Further education college						
Men	17.7			4.7	12.1	19.3
Women	14.1			6.7	18.4	13.9
Total	**15.9**			**5.8**	**14.9**	**16.8**
Commercial organization						
Men	15.2	17.1	13.8	19.9	23.1	17.7
Women	14.5	27.0	23.5	15.3	20.2	23.0
Total	**19.4**	**22.0**	**18.2**	**17.5**	**21.8**	**20.1**
Producer of tools or equipment						
Men	8.7	9.2	8.8	8.9	5.2	6.9
Women	5.0					
Total	**6.9**	**7.7**	**7.1**	**7.2**	**3.3**	**4.6**
Non-profit organization						
Men	8.6	14.3	18.3	12.1	2.0	8.3
Women	14.6	17.4	13.4	7.5	8.8	10.1
Total	**11.6**	**15.8**	**16.1**	**9.7**	**5.0**	**9.1**

Table 9.9.   Participants classified by provider categories and gender (percentages*) (Concluded)

	Canada	Switzerland (German)	Switzerland (French)	United States	Netherlands	Poland
Employer						
Men	29.8	30.7	30.4	28.5	26.1	22.5
Women	28.8	19.8	25.7	30.9	19.1	20.7
Total	**29.3**	**25.7**	**28.3**	**29.8**	**23.0**	**21.7**
Other provider						
Men	7.4	68.0	62.2	8.6	20.2	28.8
Women	17.8	77.0	71.7	12.4	22.4	22.3
Total	**12.5**	**72.7**	**66.5**	**10.6**	**21.2**	**25.8**

*   *Based on the total of responses, not on cases.*

Both in Canada and the United States, university-level institutions are a more important provider category than they are in the European countries. In these two countries the university sector is also a more important provider than commercial organizations. In general more men than women participated in courses provided by the universities, except in Poland and the United States. For Canadian women the commercial organizations are more important than universities. In the United States, university institutions are a more important provider than commercial organizations both for men and women.

The amount of time on average devoted to participation can be considered as high. As Table 9.10 shows, this varies from 169 hours per year in Poland to 317 hours in Canada. The gender differences are relatively small except in the United States, where the number of hours allocated by men is 25 percent higher than that by women. It is nevertheless an important indicator of differential learning conditions for men and women, since it refers directly to the intensity of the learning activity.

Table 9.10.   Average duration of the learning activity by gender (number of hours per year)

	Canada	Switzerland (German)	Switzerland (French)	United States	Netherlands	Poland
Men	306	234	310	191	256	161
Women	328	256	297	154	236	178
Total	**317**	**245**	**304**	**172**	**247**	**169**

These differences in average time devoted to participation in organized adult learning can be analyzed in relation to other variables such as sources of financial support and provider categories. Learning programmes offered by employers tend to be of a briefer duration than those supplied by academic institutions or private organizations. Men more often received financial support from their employer than women, and the curriculum of courses provided by employers tends moreover to have a male-culture orientation. These differences in support structures and the orientation of content are reflected not only in the different participation rates of men and women but also in the time they devote to organized learning.

Reasons not to participate: Job-related courses

The most frequently cited reason for not participating in job-related courses (see Table 9.11) by both men and women and in all countries except Poland is lack of time. For Polish women the first reason not to participate is that a course is "too expensive". However, response categories such as "too busy" must be interpreted carefully, because people might opt for giving "socially accepted" answers.

Differences between men and women appear when one analyzes the second and third most frequently given reason for not participating. The category "too expensive" is the second reason generally mentioned by both men and women, although the percentages vary for both. In Canada, Poland and the United States the third reason for not participating is "family responsibilities", whereas for the Western European people this reason appears only in sixth (Switzerland) or seventh (Netherlands) place. However, in all the countries family responsibility is more important for women than men. In the Netherlands the fourth most important reason not to participate for women is "family responsibilities" whereas for men this only occupies ninth place. In the United States and Poland thhay rank third for women and seventh for men.

Table 9.11.   Most frequently mentioned reasons for not participating in job-related courses (percentages *)

	Canada	Switzerland (German)	Switzerland (French)	United States	Netherlands	Poland
Too busy						
Men	45.0	47.1	42.3	48.7	47.4	39.0[1]
Women	43.9	41.1	38.0	41.8	41.4	28.6[1]
Total	**44.5**	**44.2**	**40.2**	**45.0**	**44.6**	**34.3[1]**
Too busy at work						
Men	13.4	16.3	23.5[3]	19.8	15.6[2]	18.8
Women	10.8	12.6	10.0[3]	14.4	7.2[2]	11.6
Total	**12.1**	**14.7**	**16.8[3]**	**16.8**	**11.9[2]**	**15.5**
Course not offered						
Men	12.7[3]	12.0	8.8	3.8	6.2	14.7
Women	5.8[3]	16.9	11.8	5.3	7.6	14.5
Total	**9.3[3]**	**14.4**	**10.3**	**4.6**	**6.9**	**14.6**
Family responsibilities						
Men	13.5[3]	3.5[3]	3.2[3]	6.2[3]	3.1[2]	10.3[3]
Women	23.0[3]	12.2[3]	16.2[3]	28.7[3]	9.8[2]	26.8[3]
Total	**18.1[3]**	**10.9[3]**	**9.6[3]**	**18.4[3]**	**6.2[2]**	**17.9[3]**
Too expensive						
Men	24.9[3]	6.8[3]	18.1	32.3	16.1	27.6
Women	38.9[3]	21.2[3]	20.6	34.4	20.0	35.3
Total	**31.7[3]**	**13.2[3]**	**19.3**	**33.4**	**17.9**	**31.2**
Lack of employer support						
Men	5.2[3]	6.2	7.9	7.0	9.4[2]	10.4
Women	2.1[3]	6.2	7.8	5.5	3.4[2]	12.6
Total	**3.7[3]**	**6.2**	**7.8**	**6.2**	**6.6[2]**	**11.4**
Other reasons						
Men	16.0[3]	23.3[1]	14.9	9.2	11.1	21.6[2]
Women	9.5[3]	13.3[1]	14.7	8.1	13.9	9.2[2]
Total	**12.9[3]**	**12.5[1]**	**14.8**	**8.6**	**12.4**	**15.9[2]**

*   *Unflagged estimates not statistically significant.*

[1] $= p < .05.$
[2] $= p < .01.$
[3] $= p < .001.$

Reasons not to participate: Non-work related courses

The reasons for not participating in non-work related courses are generally the same as for the job-related courses reviewed in Table 9.11. As Table 9.12 shows, "too busy" is the most frequently mentioned reason also in the non-work context, for both men and women, although the proportion of men considering themselves too busy is higher than that of women in all countries. The second most important reason for all women, except for the German Swiss, is the cost of the course. Even for Canadian, Dutch and Polish men high costs are the second reason not to participate, although in these countries the proportion of women is higher than that of men in this respect.

In all of the countries surveyed, "family responsibilities" is the third most often cited reason for non-participation among women but not among men. "Being too busy at work" is the third or even the second reason for not participating for men. For them, "family responsibilities" are a less important factor in their decision forenrolment.

Table 9.12.   Most frequently mentioned reasons for not participating in non-work related courses (percentages *)

	Canada	Switzerland (German)	Switzerland (French)	United States	Netherlands	Poland
Too busy						
Men	67.2[2]	62.4[1]	64.6[3]	61.4	67.8	53.6
Women	60.3[2]	57.2[1]	47.9[3]	59.4	63.5	44.2
Total	62.9[2]	62.1[1]	55.2	60.1	65.4	48.6
Too busy at work						
Men	14.1	27.0	27.3[3]	24.4[3]	6.7	20.6
Women	16.7	20.4	14.1[3]	11.8[3]	7.3	12.3
Total	15.7	23.3	19.9[3]	16.2[3]	7.1	16.1
Family responsibilities						
Men	9.4[3]	5.2[3]	8.0[3]	7.5[3]	3.2[3]	11.6[1]
Women	18.1[3]	12.5[3]	18.3[3]	21.3[3]	12.3[3]	22.8[1]
Total	14.7[3]	12.9[3]	13.8[3]	16.4[3]	8.4[3]	17.8[1]
Too expensive						
Men	22.1	6.2	9.8[3]	22.5	15.2	40.4
Women	21.5	10.0	21.3[3]	27.1	17.4	36.6
Total	21.7	8.3	19.2[3]	25.4	16.5	38.3

Table 9.12.   Most frequently mentioned reasons for not participating in non-work related courses (percentages *) (Concluded)

	Canada	Switzerland (German)	Switzerland (French)	United States	Netherlands	Poland
Course offered at inconvenient time						
Men	5.4	12.0	6.2	6.3	2.1	5.4
Women	7.5	8.8	8.1	6.9	4.3	3.9
Total	**6.7**	**10.2**	**7.3**	**6.7**	**3.3**	**4.6**
Other reason						
Men	6.7	9.7	12.0	6.3	12.1	13.0
Women	6.0	10.7	12.8	3.2	10.7	14.1
Total	**6.3**	**10.3**	**12.4**	**4.3**	**11.3**	**13.6**

*   *Unflagged estimates not statistically significant.*

[1] $= p < .05.$
[2] $= p < .01.$
[3] $= p < .001.$

Also in the non-work context the differences between men and women in their reasons for non-participation offer indications of hidden discrimination, with women more often at the short end of the draw. However, the mechanisms of discrimination are more subtle than they are in the world of work, because they operate within the symbolic cultural world where the image of the "good woman" and "family responsibilities" are stereotyped. The archetype of the traditional mother continues to condition the life of many women who, despite enjoying economic independence, are still considerably conditioned by the traditional division of roles. This type of deterrent to participation is part of people's cultural background.

Having economic independence does not necessarily mean that women also have personal autonomy. The tendency toward dialogue, democracy and symmetric relations within the family does not reach every woman in the Western countries. There are a growing number of women who develop new and more autonomous social relations, but there are an equally large number of women who assume or tolerate more traditional roles. For instance, many professional women think that the income they generate is less important than the one generated by their husband. Their relationship with men continues to be defined by the traditional division of labour between the sexes. Even when the external conditions have changed, there are many socio-cultural contexts in which women keep living in a traditional way. It is precisely in these traditional ways of living and thinking that many cultural barriers to participation in adult education and training can be found. Many women are struggling with these contradictions, and this may explain why they tend in all countries to look for the kind of course that aims at enhancing self-confidence and autonomy, developing different patterns of social participation, and opening new ways of solving communication problems.

9.5   The Scope for Policy Intervention

The participation pattern between gender observed in Sweden may be an indication that alternative policies do make a difference in the learning opportunities of men and women. In Sweden in 1975, men were twice as likely as women to participate in employer-sponsored education or training, but by 1994 there as no longer a significant gender difference in this respect. As Rubenson (see Bélanger & Valdivielso 1997) points out in his chapter on Sweden: "Not surprisingly, the participation rate was somehow higher among women than among men, 55 versus 51 percent. The difference originates in a larger share of women participating in non-employer sponsored adult education while at the same time receiving employer sponsored education and training to the same extent as men. It is this that explains why the average length of study was longer for women than for men, 92 versus 72 hours".

The motivation to participate and the choice between work and non-work related courses are complex issues, and they cannot be properly studied in a limited statistical survey. Adult learning is a transformative process for the person concerned. The motivation to learn and the educational aspirations are changing not only along the lifespan but also during the learning encounter. One has some reasons for participation at the beginning of a course and develops other during the learning process.

In a qualitative research study conducted in the Canary Islands by Valdivielso and Rodriguez (1996), a group of women enroled in a basic education programme were asked about their reasons for doing so. Most of them answered that at the beginning of the course the reasons were to get the certificate or to help their children with school work, but that after some time the reasons had changed. They discovered later on, at the time of the group interview, that their reasons for participation had more to do with themselves than with their children. The educational process had given them opportunities to meet other women and to share many aspects of their life with them. Through this sharing they became aware that many of their problems, which at the beginning were seen as individual problems, were also present in the family and personal life of other women. This had helped them to better understand the social dimension of their problems— the "structural nature" of their difficulties to participate.

The same transformative process occurs in the development of the motivation to undertake job-related studies. The growing recognition of the artificiality of the divide between general and vocational education indicates how important it will be to study more in-depth the complex and dynamic motivational processes at work. The growing overlap between the formal and informal economy, the "new professionalism" and changing patterns of mobility give rise to the same question.

Workplaces are changing and becoming increasingly divided between knowledge-intensive production on the one hand and more repetitive and precarious work on the other. This requires a more highly qualified work/force, capable of taking decisions on a high level of skill, flexibility and autonomy, but it also requires an "employable" work/force ready to take jobs in the secondary labour-market. More studies are needed to assess whether this dualization of the labour-market is characterized by a gender bias, with implications for the patterns of participation in adult education. It can be hypothesized that this dualization is already present in the current provisions of adult learning. The main sources of supply tend to be directed to the core of the labour-market, with financial incentive, time sharing facilities and motivation support. Women, reflecting the gendered division of labour in Western societies, would tend to be employed in majority in the secondary labour-market where adult education programmes may be more centred on employability than skill development. Yet, at the same time, women tend, often at their own expense, to join programmes focusing on life skills, quality of life requirements, empowerment and communication. More studies are required to understand the difficulties encountered by women in their effort to adapt themselves to the changing requirements of labour-markets and their capacity to use non-work related education in their effort to integrate into the job market. Women, having fewer training opportunities, have fewer possibilities to find regular jobs. Having a less secure job status, they also have less chance to continue their education.

9.6   Conclusions

The national surveys explored in this chapter have shown that, even if the overall participation rate of men and women is about the same the patterns, types, and conditions of adult learning are far from being equal between the genders. Women have to overcome more difficulties and obstacles than men. The increasing proportion of job-related courses in total provision will tend to reinforce the profile of the majority participants: adults working in regular jobs, at a higher level of the occupational structure, having had a better and longer initial education, with higher incomes, and with more possibilities to organize their free time. The gender character of this profile is inescapable.

The barriers to participate are very different in nature. The circumstantial, institutional, dispositional, informational, and psycho-social barriers (Cross 1981; Wikelund, Reder, & Hart-Landsberg 1992; Merriam & Caffarela 1993) are clearly present in the countries surveyed. The circumstantial ones, like "lack of time", "too expensive" or "course not offered", seem to be more important than the other ones if studied using aggregate participation data only. Both men and women mention such circumstantial barriers as the most important ones, but the percentages vary between them.

The dynamism of social life makes it necessary for working hypotheses to be constantly reviewed. The changes taking place in society affect the contexts and conditions in which men and women live. For instance, the massive incorporation of women in the labour-market has had knock-on effects in the workplace and the family. Nowadays the social space of women is extended beyond the confines of the household, and their destinies are no longer defined by tradition alone. The emergent relations are more and more based on "dialoguing democracy" (Giddens 1992) and less on the sexual division of roles. The transformation of intimacy and the growing up of social reflexivity are producing a cultural and social transformation in which men and women are less defined by their sex and more by their life style.

Life has become a reflexive project and as Giddens says: "The reflexive project of the self generates programmes of actualization and mastery" (1991: 9). Many people who participate in organized learning activities register for courses where the main objective is learning how to construct this reflexive project of the self.

The gap between those who have access to information and education and those who do not is widening in industrialized countries. New technologies bring us closer to one another, but at the same time they produce social exclusion which brings us more and more apart. From the results of this survey one can infer that adult education and training is not contributing to the democratization of access to information and to the creation and use of knowledge.

But inequality goes beyond gender. It is clear that women have to overcome more difficulties when they seek to participate in adult education. However, being a woman is not a static concept. There are also differences among women. Those women who are working outside the household, who have a personal income, and who are at the highest level of formal educational attainment, participate more than those who do not hold a job or who have low education. This last group has more problems to participate.

In a society that is characterized by segmentation, by inclusions and exclusions, the response to the condition of women must be local as well as universal, individual as well as generic. The local ecosystem is at the same time intimately linked to the global ecosystem. Changes in one influence the other. This dialectic process explains the building of "learning societies". In the current ecosystem, however, the learning societies that are being built are full of contradictions, exclusions, and inequalities in access to and in the production of knowledge and information. The learning societies currently emerging are gendered both in the explicit and the silent educational demand and in the conditions that encourage or deter adults to continue learning.

References

Courtney, S. 1992. *Why Adults Learn: Towards a Theory of Participation in Adult Education.* London: Routledge.

Cross, K.P. 1981. *Adults as Learners.* San Francisco: Jossey-Bass.

European Commission. 1996. *Teaching and Learning. Towards the Learning Society.* Luxembourg: Office for Official Publications of the European Communities.

Giddens, A. 1991. *Modernity and Self-Identity: Self and Societies in Late Modern Age.* Cambridge: Polity Press

Giddens, A. 1992. *The Transformation of Intimacy: Sexuality, Love & Eroticism in Modern Societies.* Cambridge: Polity Press.

Gobierno de Canarias 1995. *Memoria Estadística de Educación de Adultos: Curso 1993/ 94.* Las Palmas de Gran Canaria: Dirección General de Promoción Educativa.

Merriam, S.B., and Caffarela, R.S. 1993. *An Update on Adult Learning Theories.* San Francisco: Jossey-Bass.

OECD. 1996. *Lifelong Learning for All: Report of the meeting of the Education Committee at ministerial level, 16-17 January 1996.* Paris: Organisation for Economic Co-operation and Development.

OECD and Statistics Canada. 1995. *Literacy, Economy and Society: Results of the First International Adult Literacy Survey.* Paris and Ottawa: Organisation for Economic Co-operation and Development and Statistic Canada.

Rubenson, K. 1995. *Adult Learning and Social Participation: The Paradoxical Status of Adult Education Research.* (Paper presented at ESREA 95).

Rubenson, K. 1997. "Sweden: The Impact of the Politics of Partcipation". In: P. Bélanger and S. Valdivielso (eds.). *The Emergence of Learning Societies: Who Participates in Adult Learning?.* Oxford: Pergamon Press.

Valdivielso, S., and Rodriguez, G. 1996. *La Participación de las Personas Adultas en Educación y Formación en Canarias.* Las Palmas de Gran Canaria: Consejería de Educación Cultura y Deportes del Gobierno de Canarias.

Van der Kamp, M. 1997. "The Netherlands: Impacts of a New Policy Environment". In: P. Bélanger and S. Valdivielso (eds.). *The Emergence of Learning Societies: Who Participates in Adult Learning?.* Oxford: Pergamon Press.

Wikelund, K.R., Reder, S., and Hart-Landsberg, S. 1992. *Expanding Theories of Adult Literacy Participation. A Literature Review.* (Technical Report TR92-1) Philadelphia/ PA: University of Pennsylvania, National Center on Adult Literacy.

Chapter 10

Adult Education Participation:
A Policy Overview

Abrar Hasan and Albert Tuijnman[1]

10.1 Introduction

The aim of this concluding chapter is to provide a policy overview of the field of adult learning. Given the wide diversity in the socioeconomic context and institutional set-up among countries, and among regions within countries, the overview can only be given in very general terms. The focus will be on the OECD countries—for which the term industrialized countries will be often used—although some references will also be made to the developing economies. Section 10.2 provides the policy context. The reasons why there is renewed emphasis on adult education are best examined in the context of the evolution of the concept of lifelong learning. The dimensions of the un-met learning demands of the adults population are treated in Section 10.3. Given the policy context and the task at hand, the considerations that go into developing policy responses are treated in Section 10.4. The special role of the knowledge-base in supporting policy development is taken up in Section 10.5. The final section of the chapter offers some concluding remarks.

---

[1]   *The views expressed here are those of the authors and do not necessarily reflect the views of the Organisation for Economic Co-operation and Development or of its Member countries.*

10.2 The Policy Context

Evolution of the Lifelong Learning Concept

The concept of lifelong learning, in modern times, first emerged in the late 1960s. Later, in the early 1970s, the term became internationally popular through the efforts of the OECD, UNESCO (1972) and the Council of Europe (1978). Mr. Olof Palme, then the Swedish Minister of Education, coined the exprssion "recurrent education" at a conference of European Ministers of Education in 1969. The concept was embraced warmly by the industrialized countries and the OECD, through its Centre for Educational Research and Innovation (CERI), produced a framework for policy development in *Recurrent Education: A Strategy for Lifelong Learning* (1973). In 1975, OECD Ministers of Education adopted a resolution endorsing recurrent education as a strategy for the long-term structural planning of education.

The basic principle underlying the notion of lifelong learning as it was understood then was that post-school education should be provided on a recurring basis. It aimed at redressing the balance between youth and adult education, in favour of the latter, making for a more equitable and more efficient distribution of educational opportunities across the population as a whole. Developments over the last two decades have brought new meaning to the concept of lifelong learning. These have been described in detail in reports from the OECD (1996a), UNESCO (1996a) and the European Commission (1995). The concept is no longer restricted simply to recurrent education, or to a second chance for those who missed out in the first instance. Rather, it is a genuine lifelong endeavor, from the cradle to the grave. The cardinal principle is that each individual, young and old, should be both *motivated* and *equipped* to engage in learning on a continuing basis throughout life, in formal and informal, institutionalized or other settings. This means that learning needs to be viewed in a systemic context, and in the perspective of lifespan development.

By including learning in informal and non-formal settings, the new concept of lifelong learning recognizes the increasing blurring of work and learning. Not only that much training takes place on the job, but there are many examples of employers setting up training schools and even universities. At the other end of the spectrum, schools are setting up their own businesses and providing opportunities for students to learn through hands-on experience. There is also the increasing need for frequent renewal of skills of the adult population. Viewed in this context, the concept of adult education becomes broader than literacy development or remedial education.

The new concept gives much greater emphasis to the *demand* for learning and the capacity and motivation of the learner to undertake self-directed learning. This has several implications. The search for improved motivation raises a number of questions: Are the teaching methods appropriate to learner needs; is learning best achieved when the curriculum focuses largely on theory or when theory and practical experience are optimally combined? One element of motivation comes from relevance: if transversal skills, such as communication, problem-solving, and team-working skills are in greater demand in the job setting, is the curriculum structured to provide them? The new concept also pays greater attention to the longer-term consequences of how learning is organized: Does a particular learning activity lead to future learning?

The New Impetus

The concept of lifelong learning, as presented above, is a very comprehensive one. Yet there are powerful new stimuli which underpin the new view, making it a viable concept for policy making. These come from both the economic and social domains and forces that cut across them.

Human skills and competencies have always been key to social and economic advancement. What is different now is that their importance is being more widely recognized. As explained in Chapter 1, the gathering momentum of globalization and technological change, the changing nature of work and job stability, and the aging of the population in the industrialized world have all contributed to this heightened realization that education and learning cannot be treated as a once-for-all experience. There is a need to learn and re-learn work and life-skills throughout the lifespan.

The economic impetus for lifelong learning in the industrialized world is coming from many changes at the workplace. The nature of skill demand is changing, along with a rise in threshold skills. This is going hand in hand with changes in management practices. The main management paradigm in vogue since World War II, variously described as Taylorism or Fordism, tended to downgrade the skills required from workers. In this paradigm, the large majority of relatively unskilled workers specializing in narrowly defined assignments was directed by a small group of skilled workers, generally charged with problem-solving and innovative thinking. There is a growing realization that this paradigm has become outdated as it does not utilize the potential human resource available to enterprises. The quality and commitment of workers are an essential component of a firm's competitive edge and are being recognized in the shaping of new management practices.

Firms' drive for greater flexibility has injected greater precariousness to jobs, and the use of non-standard forms is increasing. Reflecting more volatile product markets and short product cycles, there is a tendency towards shorter job tenures. Individuals are now experiencing more changes in jobs over the life-cycle than before. As a consequence of these developments, skills are changing more rapidly than in previous times. In order to retain jobs or find new ones workers have to update their skills on a continuing basis.

The unemployment situation provides a major impetus for adopting the new concept of lifelong learning. As shown in Figure 10.1, unemployment in most OECD countries has been on a rising trend since the mid-1970s. In view of the worsening unemployment situation in OECD countries a major study was commissioned in 1992, with the purpose of "identifying the causes of and remedies for persistently high levels of unemployment". The resulting *Jobs Study* (OECD 1994) produced a package of nine sets of recommendations designed to combat unemployment and to promote high-wage, high-productivity jobs. The package gave central importance to the adaptive and innovative capacity of the economy and the society. An adaptive and innovative economy requires a flexible and adaptive labour force, which in turn depends on how rapidly the skills of the workforce can be renewed and expended.

Figure 10.1. Unemployment rates in OECD countries

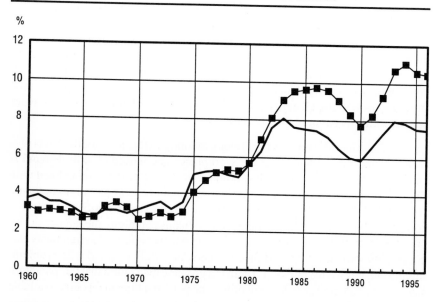

Source: OECD, ADB.

These developments in the labour-markets and the globalizing world economy provide a major impetus for the renewed emphasis on lifelong learning. However, economic pressures are not alone; there are equally compelling social forces. There is, on the one hand, an increasing diversity of demand for learning opportunities, especially at later stages in the life course, coming from both social and economic sources. on the other hand, the large structural changes engendered by globalization, technology and demographic change are threatening to create new forms of social polarization. In the burgeoning information society, there are risks of an emerging gap between the knowledge haves and knowledge have-nots; and this, in turn, can threaten the very basis of democracy. The risk of social polarization can be seen from the following six observations:

Research evidence that opportunities for training later in life depend heavily on the qualifications with which one enters the labour force;

- The learning opportunities open to the unemployed and the disadvantaged groups in the society are far limited in scope and quality than those available to the employed group;
- The training opportunities open to workers in small firms are significantly less than those open to workers with large firms;
- Training opportunities available diminish significantly after the age of 45;
- The earnings gaps between those who attain some post-secondary education and those who do not are large and widen over the lifetime; and
- The earnings gap itself has increased between the 70s and the 90s.

The general picture that emerges is that a range of forces are redefining the concept of lifelong learning and investing it with new urgency. It is widely accepted that education and training serve multiple purposes, ranging from personal development to social, cultural, and economic objectives. The new impetus for lifelong learning is that the economic, personal, and social imperatives are coming together to underline that the new concept is not a luxury but fast becoming a necessity. Future economic prosperity, social and political cohesion and the achievement of genuinely democratic societies with full participation, all depend on a well educated and trained population. Lifelong learning is now seen as an investment, not in the narrow economic sense, but more broadly—as an investment in the social, cultural and economic future of societies. These considerations led OECD Education Ministers to call for implementing strategies for "lifelong learning for all" (OECD 1996a *Communiqué*).

The Benefits of Investment in Learning

This broader concept of investment in learning takes account of the social benefits of learning activity, such as its contribution to personal development, better health, lower crime rates, better environmental outcomes, and so on. These and the contribution education makes to cultural enrichment and the democratic traditions of societies, may well be the more important contributions of learning than those economic benefits that are easier to quantify. Nonetheless, there are solid economic returns from investment in learning as well—for example those measured in terms of earnings and employment differentials.

Figure 10.2a.   Unemployment rate by level of educational attainment for persons 25 to 64 years of age, 1994

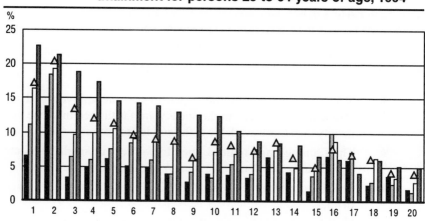

Countries are ranked in descending order of unemployment rate for below upper secondary attainment.

Figure 10.2b.   Distribution and rates of employment by level of educational attainment for persons 25 to 64 years of age, 1994

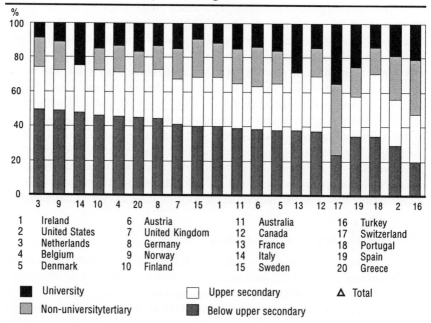

1	Ireland	6	Austria	11	Australia	16	Turkey
2	United States	7	United Kingdom	12	Canada	17	Switzerland
3	Netherlands	8	Germany	13	France	18	Portugal
4	Belgium	9	Norway	14	Italy	19	Spain
5	Denmark	10	Finland	15	Sweden	20	Greece

■ University   □ Upper secondary   △ Total

▨ Non-universitytertiary   ▨ Below upper secondary

Countries are ranked in descending order of the percentage of the unemployed with less than upper secondary attainment

Source: OECD (1996b).

As can be observed from Figure 10.2, the unemployment rates for persons with post-secondary qualifications are more favorable than for labour force participants lacking such qualifications. The unemployment rate for persons with high levels of tertiary education (ISCED level 6 or 7) is lower than for those with some tertiary education (ISCED level 5) and significantly lower than for those with only upper secondary education (ISCED levels 2 or 3). This result appears to hold generally across countries even though there are large differences in the distribution of educational attainments.

The data on employment growth show a significantly high rate of growth in employment of the white-collar workers. For each of the eight countries shown in Figure 10.3, employment growth over the 1980s was positive for white-collar workers, whether low or high-skilled, while the rates were generally negative for blue-collar workers.

Figure 10.3 Employment growth decomposition by skill

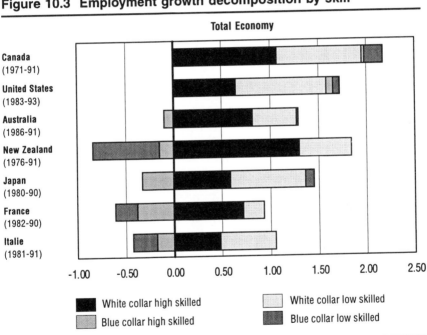

Source: OECD, STI/EAS Division, October 1995.

A comparison of the earnings experience of adults with and without post-secondary education, depicted in Figure 10.4, shows that even though the supply of university graduates is increasing, the demand continues to outpace the supply and produces significant earning differentials in favor of the university graduate. Better-educated gain in another way. As shown in Tables 10.1 and 10.2, university graduates also enjoy greater opportunities for formal training than others, both among the employed and the unemployed.

Figure 10.4. Mean annual earnings of persons 25 to 64 years of age by level of educational attainment and gender relative to mean annual earnings at the upper secondary level (1994)

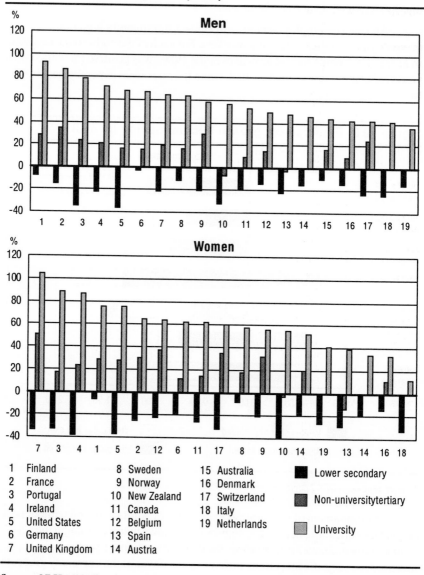

1	Finland	8	Sweden	15	Australia
2	France	9	Norway	16	Denmark
3	Portugal	10	New Zealand	17	Switzerland
4	Ireland	11	Canada	18	Italy
5	United States	12	Belgium	19	Netherlands
6	Germany	13	Spain		
7	United Kingdom	14	Austria		

Lower secondary

Non-universitytertiary

University

Source: OECD (1996b).

Table 10.1.   Participation in job-related continuing education and training as a percentage of the employed population aged 25 to 64

	Year	Gender	Primary education	Lower secondary	Upper secondary	Non-education	University-level education	Total
During the 12-month period preceding the survey								
Australia	1993	M+W	20	33	35	53	67	38
		Men	18	32	33	50	66	37
		Women	21	34	38	57	69	40
Canada	1993	M+W	6	12	25	35	43	28
		Men	6	13	22	36	40	27
		Women	5	11	28	34	47	30
Finland	1993	M+W	x	27	40	61	61	41
		Men	x	26	37	58	58	38
		Women	x	29	44	63	65	44
France	1994	M+W	8	28	42	72	57	40
		Men	7	26	40	76	46	38
		Women	8	30	46	69	75	43
Germany	1994	M+W	x	15	28	43	50	33
		Men	x	m	29	44	50	35
		Women	x	14	28	40	50	31
Switzerland	1993	M+W	m	16	39	51	53	38
		Men	m	(14)	41	52	52	42
		Women	m	17	37	45	56	34
United States	1995	M+W	7	13	24	36	49	34
		Men	8	11	21	34	45	31
		Women	6	15	27	38	54	36
During the 6-month period preceding the survey								
Sweden	1995	M+W	28	31	41	60	60	44
		Men	27	30	38	58	53	40
		Women	28	32	44	62	68	47
During the 4-week period preceding the survey								
Belgium	1994	M+W	1	1	2	4	6	3
		Men	1	1	3	5	6	3
		Women	0.5	1	2	3	6	2
Denmark	1994	M+W	x	7	14	21	24	15
		Men	x	5	11	19	21	13
		Women	x	8	17	22	29	18
Greece	1994	M+W	m	m	m	m	m	1
		Men	m	m	m	m	m	0.5
		Women	m	m	m	m	m	1
Ireland	1994	M+W	1	2	5	7	8	4
		Men	1	2	4	6	8	3
		Women	1	3	6	8	9	6
Italy	1994	M+W	m	1	2	a	3	1
		Men	0.3	1	2	a	2	1
		Women	m	1	2	a	3	2
Spain	1994	M+W	0.3	1	6	5	8	3
		Men	0.2	1	5	4	7	2
		Women	1	2	8	6	9	4
United Kingdom	1994	M+W	x	3	12	24	24	13
		Men	x	3	11	21	22	12
		Women	x	4	13	26	28	14

Source: OECD 1996.

Table 10.2. Participation in job-related continuing education and training as a percentage of the unemployed population aged 25 to 64

	Year	Primary education	Lower secondary	Upper secondary	Non-education	University-level education	Total
During the 12-month period preceding the survey							
Australia	1993	12	25	25	43	53	24
Canada	1993	6	6	15	24	30	16
France	1994	14	22	38	66	75	35
Germany	1994	8	10	19	24	21	16
Switzerland	1993	m	m	m	m	m	33
United States	1995	6	10	11	17	24	14
During the 4-week period preceding the survey							
Belgium	1994	m	m	m	m	m	5
Denmark	1994	m	7	12	10	18	11
Greece	1994	m	m	m	m	m	1
Ireland	1994	0.4	1	4	8	9	2
Italy	1993	m	m	m	m	m	1
Spain	1994	1	5	16	14	35	8
United Kingdom	1994	m	2	7	15	14	6

Source: OECD 1996.

The contribution education and training make to economic growth has been documented in many studies. Some 24 studies were surveyed in a recent OECD review and confirm the positive contribution (OECD 1994: Chapter 7). Studies also confirm the positive impact on productivity levels. These studies are, if anything, likely to understate the contribution as most use either simple measures of labour force skills and competencies and none has been able to take into account the many facets of skills in a comprehensive way. At the enterprise level, too, the skills and competence of workers make a valuable contribution to performance. Evidence on the pay-off to firms comes from comparative studies, which have compared firms making the same products with similar technology but with employees possessing different levels of skills. Several studies of manufacturing find that productivity differences between similar firms do not stem from production machinery but from poor maintenance, poor production control and poor diagnosis of faults, all of which have thier origins in technical skills at the level of foremen and operators. Studies of the service sector, such as the hotel industry, have often reported high productivity levels linked to the formal qualifications of the staff and opportunities for training. Often productivity differentials are attributed to the use of new technologies, but this too, depends critically on worker qualifications.

10.3 Dimensions of Unmet Needs: Patterns of Participation in Adult Learning

Impressive gains have been made in the industrialized countries in the provision of education and training over the preceding three decades. Most industrialized countries have achieved virtually universal secondary education. The drive now is for the "massification" of tertiary education, which comprises not only university education but other technical and general education at the post-secondary level.

Given this background, the data on patterns of participation in adult learning are sketchy. Information is especially lacking on the duration and quality of learning activity and on costs and outcomes. Adults engage in a variety of formal and non-formal learning, but the data relate mostly to the formal type, with little systematic information being available on the non-formal components. The patterns subrequent description of draws upon two sources of information, the labour force survey and the International Adult Literacy Survey (IALS). The IALS, described more fully in the acompanying volume of this publication (Bélanger & Valdivielso 1997), is the first ever comparative international survey of literacy of the adult population and provides, for the first time, direct measurement of outcomes or the skills and competencies of the adult population,

Data drawn from the labour force surveys of 15 countries are reported in Table 10.1 for the years 1993/95, for different reference periods (OECD 1996). The pattern varies considerably among countries, measured over a twelve-month reference period from data for seven OECD countries, between 34 to 40 per cent of the 25-64 year-old employed adults were reported to engage in job-related learning activities. The participation rate for Sweden is the highest (44 per cent), even though it is measured over a six-month period. The rate is naturally lower for a shorter period of reference: measured over a one-month period, the participation rate ranges from 1 per cent in Greece and Italy to 15 per cent in Denmark, among the seven countries for which such data are available. These data refer to all organized systematic education and training activities, whether financed by government, employers, or by the participants themselves. Learning activities at the primary, secondary, upper-secondary, non-university tertiary and university level are taken into account, but full-time studies at the tertiary level were not included. Compared to the employed, the participation rate among the unemployed is significantly lower, as can be seen by comparing the data from Tables 10.1 and 10.2.

The International Adult Literacy Survey sheds further light on the extent and patterns of participation in seven OECD countries (OECD & Statistics Canada 1995). Data reported in the previous chapters show that overall, the participation rate ranges from 34 per cent to 53 per cent for the 15-64 age group. Participation is generally lower for females than for males, and the rate drops significantly after 45 years of age. Participation is also significantly lower for those outside the labour force. For example, in the age group 36-45, the rate ranges from 43 to 63 per cent among the employed; 19 to 64 per cent among the unemployed, but only 10 to 26 per cent for those outside the labour force.

The IALS also provides information on several other features of adult learning. As reported in Chapter 6, the duration or intensity of training ranges from typically 500 hours on average for the 16-25 year group to less than 100 hours for the 56-65 age group. The pattern of financial support also differs among countries, but the general pattern is that the role of government is rather small, varying from 10 to 20 per cent. Financial support from employers is the most important source; it accounts for between 40 and 60 per cent of adult training in the countries investigated. Self-financing is the second most important factor: from one third to one half of the training activities are self-financed, the rate being higher for women than for men. A very large percentage of training, some 70 to 90 per cent for males, is undertaken for job-related reasons, with personal interest making up the rest. The provision of adult education and training comes from diverse sources. Employer-provided training is the most important source in all the countries. Commercial educational organizations are the second most important source; whilst colleges and universities rank third as the most important providers.

The main conclusion that emerges is that a majority of adults in the industrialized countries do not participate in lifelong learning. The situation is considerably worse for the under educated adults. As Tables 10.1 and 10.2 show, only around 10 per cent of the adults in the labour force with primary education participate in learning activities.

If the target of "lifelong learning" for all is defined as equipping individuals with at least secondary-level education, then some 76 million adults in the age group 25-64 years would need to be reached (OECD 1996: Chapter 8). If the IALS criteria of reaching at least literacy level 2 is chosen as the target, some 65 million people would need training in the age group 26-65 in the United States alone. A rough estimate of the direct cost of reaching the first target comes to between 1.3 to 4.4 per cent of GDP for the OECD countries. The nature and requirements of adult education in developing countries are of a quite different order. Even though concepts of functional literacy are now being invoked, the usual definition as, for example, in the case of India, is completion of three to four years of schooling. Even if calculated on this basis, the literacy rates in many developing countries are low. Bangladesh, where the rate is 49 per cent for males and 26 per cent for females (UNESCO 1996b), is a typical example. Thus, in developed and developing countries alike, reaching the different targets of lifelong learning for adults represents a large task.

10.4 Policy Issues

If lifelong learning does indeed capture societal expectations of citizens in these countries, clearly much remains to be done. The preceding section gives some very rough estimates of the financial costs of bringing the adults up to the secondary education level. But the policy issues go beyond the resource question. A useful approach is to consider the barriers to participation in adult learning activities.

Barriers to Participation

A number of major barriers to adult learning have been identified in the research literature and OECD's work on adult learning and recurrent education (OECD 1975; OECD 1977-81; Levin & Schütze 1983; Schütze & Istance 1987; Kawan 1993). The barriers framework developed by Cross (1982), depicted in a modified form in Figure 5.1 (Chapter 5) consists of three types of barriers: situational, institutional and dispositional. Situational barriers capture the influence of circumstances that include questions about the economy, culture, family structures, and technology. Behind the institutional barriers lie issues concerning the cost of education, programme availability, the availability of pathways, supply technology, marketing, etc. Finally, dispositional barriers cover dispositions, values and attitudes to education and learning. While these manifest themselves in the individual and are personal in nature, they do not lie outside the realm of policy intervention. These dispositions are shaped by life experiences, by the situational and institutional factors cited above, and, in their turn, shape the situational and institutional forces. It is important to remember that there is considerable interaction between the three types of barriers.

Further Considerations

Developing appropriate policy responses needs to address these barriers. Since adult learning involves many actors and stakeholders, a key to successful policies is that they are brought together. However, as Papadopoulos (1992) observes, progress in OECD countries has been limited because policy development has failed to achieve two types of integration which are essential for such a cooperative effort:

a. a vertical integration of adult education opportunities with initial schooling has been difficult to achieve. Resistance to this type of integration has arisen from fears that it would result in a radical transformation of existing education systems;

b. inadequate horizontal integration—There has been weak coordination of education and training policies with other policies, in particular employment, social and economic.

The observation about the inadequacies of horizontal integration is supported by a review of the policy setting in six industrialized countries (OECD 1992). For example, lack of policy coordination is a feature of the experience in the United States, where responsibility for adult education and literacy programmes is mostly with the state. Funding for many programmes comes from the federal government. At this level, responsibility is shared among at least three agencies—Education, Labour, and Health and Human Services—with some English language programmes run by the Justice department. Funding for the programmes is highly fragmented, under the Job Training Partnership (JTPA) programmes, adult basic education, and several other smaller programmes. In Canada, another federal state, lack of coordination among different levels of government and among various jurisdictions has resulted in very uneven provision. The federal role is limited to post-secondary education and federal support for adult literacy programmes is filtered through several different federal departments. The federal role is largely one of providing services and policy support that cannot be handled by the provinces. There is a high degree of local autonomy and provincial governments have been supportive of community-based groups.

In France, the literacy training system is quite separate from the rest of the education system. The Interministerial Committee set up in 1984 to combat "illiteracy" does not have its secretariat in the Ministry of National Education, but is located in the Ministry of Labour. Thus, the initiatives have remained fragmented. Potentially powerful vehicles for addressing the problem are already in place but remain underutilized. In the United Kingdom, voluntary organizations have played a particularly significant role. While literacy campaigns, with the support of media, were very successful in the initial stages, later developments showed that local-level action cannot be successful on a sustained basis without the provision of sufficient funding or infrastructure from the national level. In Germany, there is no national funding of the literacy programmes, and the budgets of the provider institutes are met by the communities they serve. This results in inequities of access and the commitment to training is uneven. Rural populations are generally underserved. Bridging of programmes in institutes with training in other types of institutions, including the private sector, remain major challenges in Germany.

Government, at all levels, needs to develop new partnerships with the private sector, the social partners and community organizations to overcome barriers to the expansion of adult education and training to meet the increasing diversity of demand and new modes of teaching and learning. Governments are in a better position to set the policy framework for achieving greater horizontal coordination. They can adopt a strategic role to set goals and targets and to direct policy towards gaps in provision.

A major issue concerns the relationship between adult education and secondary and post-secondary institutions. While it is agreed that these institutions should be involved in the delivery of programmes, questions about the capacity of the regular education systems to accommodate adults continue to be asked in many countries. In regard to schools, experience in some countries, for example Sweden and Hungary, shows that folk high schools rather than regular schools have adapted better to the needs of the adults. A key consideration remains as to how to take into consideration what has been learnt outside the formal system in designing delivery programmes through the formal system. In addition, if governments adopt a strategic steering role and schools and other education institutions are given new responsibilities, their capacity to exercise them must be developed through improved support structures, training and evaluation.

In regard to workplace training, the data presented above show its growing importance. This has raised two sets of questions. First, there is the problem of inequity of access—employer-sponsored opportunities are generally available to better-qualified workers and those with large firms. There is a need to explore alternative types of incentives to encourage firms to provide more quality training to meet the growing and diverse social needs of the workplace. Second, there are questions about the quality of the training provided. Some studies suggest that often the employer-sponsored training tends to be narrowly focused and repetitive and does not effectively serve the promotion of self-directed, "investigative" learning. This emphasizes the growing role of the social partners. The Swedish experience in this regard provides a good example (OECD 1992).

To take account of the contextual barriers "programmes will be most effective when they 'situate' instruction within the activities, lives, values and cultures of their individual learners" (see above, Chapter 5). There is a general consensus among experts that education should be based on the lived experiences and needs of learners, and that there needs to be some overlap in the content of vocational education, adult basic education, and literacy programmes, so that basic skills training can be applicable both to daily life circumstances as well as to the demands of the work place. On an institutional level, there are many inherent problems for the under educated—scheduling, access issues, and availability of information are prime examples. Many under educated adults cannot responsibly attend adult education programmes, and still care for their children, hold jobs, deal with health or income problems and cope with other situational barriers. On a personal level, research has shown that some non-participants have had negative experience with schooling. For these adults, it is not the availability of opportunity but the nature of the provision to suit their particular needs. Quigley and Arrowsmith (See above, Chapter 5) make a persuasive case that research so far has focused unduly on the participant population, and that policy-making can benefit from examining more closely the situation of the non-participants.

A general conclusion reached in OECD research (1992) favors a multiplicity of delivery modes that include support for mainstream institutions as well as work-based and community-based groups. Given the new pressures for lifelong learning, there is need for more basic training in the work place, more integration of work-related and non-work-related content, more support for participating organizational models in both work and training, and closer ties to the community organizations and local interest groups.

10.5 The Role of Monitoring and Evaluation

To develop and implement policy for lifelong learning, policy-makers will need to have access to an adequate knowledge base. Information is needed not only for assessing the dimension of the problem at hand but also for developing a framework for evaluating alternative approaches, both substantive and administrative, including financing. Since 1988, the OECD, with crucial support from many of its member countries, has been in the vanguard of a large-scale international effort aimed at developing internationally comparable indicators of education systems (INES). The INES project was launched primarily because decision-makers in many countries felt the need to get together to discuss the instruments that would help them to better assess and evaluate the quality, efficiency and effectiveness of their education and training systems and monitor their evolution and progress towards specific goals against the backdrop of data that are external to the functioning of any one system.

The programme of work devoted to the development of international education indicators can be seen as an extension of the research programme on social indicators that was pursued during the 1960s mainly, but not exclusively in the United States. There were clear demonstrations at that time that such indicators could be used for tracking the magnitude and direction of changes in specific economic activities at the national level. Social scientists were keen to extend these economic indices, so as to cover also broader social welfare considerations within society such as improvement in qualitative aspects of life, industrial democracy, the development of culture, and equity in race and gender relations.

The new interest in adult education indicators is the result of several factors. First, globalization and the opening up of national borders has led to an increased need for knowledge about the education and training systems of neighbouring countries and trade partners. The signing of the Maastricht Treaty which established the European Union, the ratification of the North America Free Trade Agreement (NAFTA), the growth of the Asia-Pacific Economic Co-operation forum, and the emergence of the Common Market of the South (Mercosur) in Latin America are examples of the gradual economic integration processes which have consequences for trade, industrial production, and the competitiveness of nations. Second, new priorities for adult education policy have emerged. New goals have been adopted, such as making upper secondary education a common experience for all young adults, and realizing an expansion of enrolment in tertiary education and adult education.

The OECD-led education indicators movement has until recently, concentrated its efforts mostly on the development and refinement of measures of the inputs, processes and outcomes of the formal school system. That a limited orientation was advocated initially is understandable, given that the better-known domains needed to be explored first, that results needed to be produced quickly, and also because the majority of the policy-makers and researchers involved were interested mainly in the welfare of the regular school system. But at a time when a solid international consensus as emerged on the importance of developing a culture of lifelong learning for all, the dearth of reliable and comparable statistical information about adult education and training is felt greatly.

A monitoring system that includes evaluation and performance assessment of programmes is important both for accountability and reform. In the absence of proper evaluation there is a temptation to continue with existing programmes even though their shortcomings are known. The acceptance of new approaches is much enhanced if demonstration results are available on their performance. Although policy in recent years has favored support for a multiplicity of delivery modes, few evaluation studies are available on the effectiveness of alternative modes.

10.6 Conclusions

This chapter has argued that policy development for adult education is best viewed in the context of the concept of lifelong learning. Although the new impetus for this concept comes from economic pressures there are equally compelling social factors. Education and training serve multiple objectives—social, cultural, economic and personal. The call by the OECD Ministers of Education for "lifelong learning for all" (OECD 1996) meets to these multiple demands. Lifelong learning is no longer a luxury that some enjoy, but has become a necessity for all. This concept means that all individuals are equipped and motivated to engage in learning and re-learning throughout life. Within this policy framework, adult education becomes a broader concept that is not limited to literacy improvement programmes or basic adult education.

Although some progress has been made in the preceding two decades, since the term "lifelong learning" became popular in the industrialized countries, much remains to be done. A major gap in the provision of lifelong learning concerns the adults. If the lifelong learning target is defined as reaching at least secondary-level education for all, some 76 million adults in the OECD countries need to be reached. Adult learning targets are defined more modestly in developing countries, but still represent a huge task. The question is not only one of resources but also concerns appropriate policies and practices.

Participation in adult education is hampered by many barriers, situational, institutional and dispositional. To handle the situational barriers, a focus on linking the learning activity to the functional aspects of daily life would be desirable. More research is needed on pedagogy that is especially suited for adults and on the effectiveness of various mixtures of theoretical and experiential. Institutional barriers can be lowered through greater attention in programming the provision to the special scheduling needs of adults, their family circumstances, and to making information more widely available to them. In regard to dispositional barriers it is important to study more closely the impediments faced by the non-participants, rather than devise programmes for them on the basis of the experience of the participants.

The delivering adult education programmes requires collaboration among a range of actors and stakeholders. Policies for adult education need vertical integration of adult learning with other forms of formal learning. For a variety of reasons, this has been difficult to achieve. Equally, governments have failed in delivering a coordinated set of horizontally linked education, labour, social, and economic policies. New partnerships among the diverse group of actors are essential, and governments need to provide a framework of well coordinated policies. As more and more adult learning takes place at the workplace, the roles of the social partners become more prominent. The role of government is to ensure that incentives are in place and that a framework is available for setting standards and assessing and recognizing the outcomes. Governments also need to provide the necessary information and data bases not only for their own policy development purposes but also to individuals for making informed decisions.

References

Bélanger, P., and Valdivielso, S. (eds.). 1997. *The Emergence of Learning Societies: Who Participates in Adult Learning?* Oxford: Pergamon Press.

Commission of the European Communities. 1995. *White Paper on Education and Training: Teaching and Learning - Towards the Learning Society.* Luxembourg: Office of Official Publications of the European Communities.

Council of Europe. 1978. *Permanent Education: Final Report.* Strasbourg: Council of Europe.

Cross, K.P. 1982. *Adults as Learners.* San Francisco: Jossey-Bass.

Kawanobe, S., Yamada, T., Tanaka, M., Kajita, M., Yamamoto, Y., Ichikawa, S., Kimura, H., & Inoue, S. 1993. *A Study on Lifelong Education in Selected Industrialised Countries.* Tokyo: National Institute for Educational Research.

Levin, H.M., & Schütze, H.G. (eds..) 1983. *Financing Recurrent Education: Strategies for Increasing Employment, Job Opportunities, and Productivity.* London: Sage Publications.

OECD. 1973. *Recurrent Education. A Strategy for Lifelong Learning.* Paris: Organisation for Economic Co-operation and Development.

OECD. 1975. *Recurrent Education. Trends and Issues.* Paris: Organisation for Economic Co-operation and Development.

OECD. 1977-81. *Learning Opportunities for Adults* (Vols. 1-5). Paris: Organisation for Economic Co-operation and Development.

OECD. 1992. *Adult Literacy and Economic Performance.* Paris: Organisation for Economic Co-operation and Development.

OECD. 1994. *The OECD Jobs Study* (Vols. I-II). Paris: Organisation for Economic Co-operation and Development.

OECD. 1995. *Education at a Glance: OECD Indicators.* (3rd ed.) Paris: Centre for Educational Research and Innovation.

OECD and Statistics Canada. 1995. *Literacy, Economy and Society.* Paris and Ottawa: Organisation for Economic Co-operation and Development and Statistics Canada.

OECD. 1996a. *Lifelong Learning for All: Meeting of the Education Committee at Ministerial Level, 16-17 January 1996.* Paris: Organisation for Economic Co-operation and Development.

OECD. 1996b. *Education at a Glance: OECD Indicators.* (4th ed.) Paris: Centre for Educational Research and Innovation.

Papadopoulos, G. 1994. *Education 1960-1990: The OECD Perspective.* Paris.

Schütze, H.G., & Istance, D. 1987. *Recurrent Education Revisited.* Stockholm: Almqvist and Wiksell.

Faure, E., Herrera, F., Kaddoura, A.R., Lopes, H., Petrovsky, A.V., Rahnema, M., & Ward, F.C. 1972. *Learning To Be: The World of Education Today and Tomorrow.* Paris: UNESCO Press.

UNESCO. 1996a. *Report of the Commission.* Paris: International Commission on Education for the Twenty-first Century, UNESCO.

UNESCO. 1996b. *Education for All: Achieving the Goal.* (Statistical Document for the Mid-Decade Meeting of the International Consultative Forum on Education for All, 16-19 June 1996, Amman, Jordan).

Appendix A

International Adult Literacy Survey: Data-Collection Procedures

Introduction

The Adult Education Participation Survey (AEPS) was designed as an integral part of the first International Adult Literacy Survey (IALS)[1]. The survey was a collaborative effort by national governments, statistical agencies, research institutions and international organizations.

The development and management of the survey was coordinated by Statistics Canada, the statistical arm of the Canadian government, in collaboration with national research teams from the participating countries where large representative samples of adults aged 16-65 were interviewed.

Purpose of the Survey

Conceived as an adult literacy survey aimed at studying the literacy skills of people from different countries, the second purpose was to describe and analyze the patterns of adult education and training participation (see Appendix B for the instrument used) and collect background information from the respondents, so that an attempt could be made to explore possible explanations for the observed variation in participation patterns.

---

[1]   *Jointly published by OECD and Statistics Canada under the title* Literacy, Economy and Society: Results of the First International Adult Literacy Survey, *Paris and Ottawa 1995.*

How the Survey Was Conducted

Besides the literacy part which took one hour on average, about half an hour of each interview was devoted to obtaining adult education data as well as background and demographic information from the respondents. These data provide a means for exploring how adult education participation is related to social, educational, economic, and other variables, and whether these relationships are similar across cultures.

Target Population and Survey Coverage

Each country was obliged to draw a probability sample from which results representative of the civilian, non-institutionalized population aged 16 to 65 could be derived. Countries were free to sample older adults too, and several did so. Table 1 displays the survey coverage and the exclusions for each country.

Table 1.   Survey coverage and exclusions from a sample frame

Country	Coverage	Exclusions
Canada	98%	Residents of institutions, persons living on Indian reserves, members of the Armed Forces, residents of the Yukon and Northwest Territories, Francophone residents in the province of Ontario who lived in geographic regions where 20 persons were Francophone
Netherlands	99%	Residents of institutions
Poland	99%	Persons residing in Poland for less than three months
Sweden	98%	Persons living in institutions (including those doing their military service), persons living abroad during the survey period
Switzerland	89%	Persons in Italian and Rhaeto-Romanish regions, persons in institutions, persons without telephones
United States	97%	Members of the Armed Forces on active duty, those who reside outside the US, those with no fixed household address

Table 2 shows that the survey was carried out in one national language in four countries. In Canada, respondents were given a choice of English or French; in Switzerland, samples drawn from French-speaking and German-speaking cantons were required to respond in those respective languages (Italian and Rhaeto-Romanic-speaking regions were excluded; these languages are to be assessed in a future survey round). When respondents could not speak the designated language, attempts were made to complete the background questionnaire to allow for an estimation of their literacy level to reduce the possibility of distorted results.

Table 2.   In-scope population, language of test, and sample yields

Country	In-scope population aged 16-65	Language of test	Sample yield
Canada	13,676,612 4,773,648	English French	3,130 1,370
Netherlands	10,460,359	Dutch	2,837
Poland	24,475,649	Polish	3,000
Sweden	5,361,942	Swedish	2,645
Switzerland	1,008,275 3,144,912	French German	1,435 1,393
United States	161,121,972	English	3,053

All sampling plans were reviewed by a sampling referee, in order to ensure that they met the specified design criteria. However, no uniform sampling methodology was imposed because of the differences in data sources, survey practices and resources available in the countries. Table 3 indicates that all countries used probability sampling methods for some of the stages of selection. However, Switzerland selected one household member using an alphabetic sort. The Swiss demographic statistics line up with estimates provided by independent data sources.

Table 3.   Sampling methods used by the countries

Country	1st stage of sampling	2nd stage of sampling	3rd stage of sampling
Canada	Labour force survey probability	LFS households probability	1 person/hhld probability
Netherlands	Postal codes probability	Addresses probability	1 person/hhld probability
Poland	Cities/counties probability	Individuals probability	
Sweden	Municipalities probability	Individuals probability	
Switzerland	Telephone number probability	1 person/hhld non-probability	
United States	Current Population Survey probability	CPU PSU's probability	Individuals probability

Data Collection

Each country was provided with a standard set of data collection and administration manuals and the associated questionnaire protocols. While countries were free to adapt these models to their own requirements, they were also asked to respect a number of key features. First, they were obliged to conduct the interview as an unaided personal interview in the household. Second, respondents were not permitted to use aids such as calculators. A detailed non-response coding structure was specified for use. Countries were instructed to obtain a background questionnaire at all costs.

Most countries adhered closely to the guidelines provided for the data collection. However, some countries did deviate from the instructions in certain instances. Sweden offered incentives to encourage individuals to participate. However, in experimental studies conducted in the United States (Jones, in: Kirsch & Murray 1997; Mohadjer et al. 1997) it is found that minor incentives such as those offered in this case have little impact on survey responses and estimated literacy proficiency.

Table 4 presents summary information about the data collection procedures used by the countries.

Table 4.   Data collection summary by country

Country	Number of interviewers engaged	Average number of response interviews per interviewer	Introductory letter sent by data collection agency
Canada	250	23	Yes
Netherlands	150	21	Yes
Poland	200	15	Yes
Sweden	100	30	Yes
Switzerland	300	10	Yes
United States	149	21	Yes

Survey Response

Originally, the design specifications included a requirement to select a sample large enough to yield 3000 responses. This requirement proved to be unrealistic, however, because of the financial constraints faced by several of the countries. A respondent was defined as a person who has fully or partially completed the background questionnaire. This background information was used for the imputation of literacy scores in cases where incomplete assessment data had been obtained.

Table 5 shows the ages sampled, the number of respondents for each country, and the achieved response rates. In terms of response burden, the full protocol imposed high demands on respondents. The average respondent took 30 minutes to answer the background questions and an additional 60 minutes to complete the IALS test.

Table 5.   Ages sampled and number of survey respondents

Country	Ages	Response rate per cent	Respondents n=
Canada	16 and older	69	5,660
Netherlands	16 - 74	45	3,090
Poland[1]	16 - 65	75	3,090
Sweden	16 and older	60	3,090
Switzerland	16 and older	55	3,000
United States	16 - 65	60	3,053

1.   *Poland's response rate only refers to the first stage of sampling selection.*

Weighting Procedures

Countries used different methods for the weighting of their samples. For the countries with known probabilities of selection, base weights were applied using the probability of selection. Data were also weighted by adjusting the rough estimates produced by the sample to match known population counts from sources external to the survey. Table 6 shows that all countries post-stratified their data to match known population counts and adjust for non-response.

Table 6.   Post-stratification variables applied in the survey

Country	Benchmark variables
Canada	Province, economic region, census metro-politan area, age, sex, in-school youth, out-of-school youth, unemployment insurance recipients, social assistance recipients
Netherlands	Region, age, sex, education
Poland	Region, urban-rural, age
Sweden	Region, education, age, sex
Switzerland	Number of household members aged 16 to 65, total number of persons in the house-hold, level of education, size of community, age, sex
United States	Education

Data-Quality Review

The IALS project has been subjected to an extensive review of data quality by independent experts. The findings reached by these reviewers as well as the detailed analyses subsequently undertaken are presented in Kirsch and Murray (1997). The main shortcomings of the IALS have been the differences in test administration between countries and the low response rates. But experts from Statistics Canada and the Educational Testing Service judge the results to be highly plausible and not to be impaired by serious bias. Valid conclusions can therefore be drawn on the basis of the IALS data analyses presented in this publication.

Appendix B

Adult Education Participation Survey[1]

1. The following questions will deal with any education or training which you may have taken in the past 12 months.

    During the past 12 months, that is, since August 1993, did you receive any training or education including courses, workshops, on-the-job training, apprenticeship training, arts, crafts, recreation courses or any other training or education?

2. In total, how many courses did you take in the past 12 months?

3. What were the names (titles) of these courses or the program* associated with these courses?[2]

*   Note: A program is a collection of courses which leads to a specific degree, diploma or certificate.

4. Now I'd like to ask you about ...(name of course or program name).

Was this training or education financially supported by

    a)   yourself or your family?

    b)   an employer?

    c)   the government?

    d)   a union or professional organization?

    e)   anyone else?

    f)   no fees

    g)   don't know

[1]   *Reproduction of Section F of the International Adult Literacy Survey questionnaire (English version) as designed by the Special Surveys Division of Statistics Canada in 1994.*

[2]   *Question no. 3 allowed for up to three mentions which were thereafter treated separately (from questions no. 4 to 14). Programmes/courses to be mentioned were the (three) most recently completed by the respondent.*

5.   Were you taking this training or education towards

a university degree/diploma/certificate?
a college diploma/certificate?
a trade-vocational diploma/certificate?
an apprenticeship certificate?
an elementary or secondary school diploma?
professional or career upgrading?
other
(mark one only)

6.   Was this training or education given by

a)   a university or higher education establishment?
b)   a further education college?
c)   a commercial organization (for example, a private training provider)?
d)   a producer or supplier of equipment?
e)   a non-profit organization such as an employer association, voluntary organization or a trade union?
f)   an employer or a parent company?
g)   other

7.   Where did you take this training or education?

a)   Elementary or High School
b)   College Campus
c)   University Campus
d)   Business or Commercial School
e)   Work
f)   Training centre
g)   Conference centre or hotel
h)   Home
I)   Community centre or sports facility
j)   Elsewhere
       (mark one only)

8.   For how many weeks did this training or education last?

9.   On average, how many days per week was it?

10.   On average, how many hours per day was it?

11. What was the main reason you took this training or education? Was it for

career/job-related purposes?
personal interest?
other?

12. To what extent are you using the skills or knowledge acquired in this training or education at work?

To a great extent

Somewhat

Very little

Not at all

Not applicable

13. Who suggested you take this training or education?

a) You did
b) Your friends or family
c) Your employer
d) Other employees
e) Part of a Collective Agreement
f) Your Union or trade association
g) Legal or professional requirement
h) Social Services or Employment Centre
I) Other
j) Don't know

14. Was this training or education provided through

a) classroom instruction, seminars or workshop?
b) educational software?
c) radio or TV broadcasting?
d) audio/video cassettes, tapes or disks?
e) reading materials?
f) on-the-job training?
g) other methods?

15.   Since August 1993, was there any training or education that you
       wanted [3] to take for career- or job-related reasons but did not?

16.   What were the reasons you did not take this training or education?

       Too busy/lack of time
       Too busy at work
       Course not offered
       Family responsibilities
       Too expensive/no money
       Lack of qualifications
       Lack of employer support
       Course offered at inconvenient time
       Language reasons
       Health reasons
       Other

17.   Since August 1993, was there any other training that you ***wanted*** [4]
       to take but did not, such as hobby, recreational or interest courses?

18.   What were the reasons you did not take this training or education?

       Too busy/lack of time
       Too busy at work
       Course not offered
       Family responsibilities
       Too expensive/no money
       Lack of qualifications
       Lack of employer support
       Course offered at inconvenient time
       Language reasons
       Health reasons
       Other

---

[3]   *Underlined in original text.*
[4]   *Underlined in original text.*

Notes on Contributors

Stephen Arrowsmith is a Project Manager with the Special Surveys Division of Statistics Canada. Managing the National Adult Education and Training Survey programme since 1989, he was responsible for coordinating the major redesign of the survey methodology and instruments prior to the 1992 national survey.

Paul Bélanger is Director of the UNESCO Institute for Education, Hamburg, Germany and currently responsible for the preparation of UNESCO's Fifth International Conference on Adult education of which he will be the General Secretary. He has been the author of many studies on adult education in Canada and Africa and most recently has been the editor of *Lifelong Education* (with E. Gelpi, Dordrecht 1995). He is chairman of the editorial board of the International Review of Education.

Pierre Doray is Associate Professor at the University of Québec at Montréal, Canada, and distinguished researcher with the Centre interuniversitaire de recherche sur la science et la technologie (CIRST). He is a specialist for vocational education as part of initial education as well as of adult education. His publications include studies on the relation of economy and education and on the educational consequences of technological change in the workplace.

Abrar Hasan is the Head of the Education and Training Division of the Directorate for Education, Employment, Labour and Social Affairs of the OECD. Prior to this he served as the Head of the Central Analysis Division and was responsible for OECD's annual publication, Employment Outlook. He has published widely in the fields of education and training, labour markets, technology and work organisation, and energy economics.

Willem Houtkoop is Programme Manager of the Max Goote Centre for vocational education and training at the University of Amsterdam. He was the National Study Manager for the Dutch part of the IALS and has published extensively in the fields of adult and continuing education, vocational training and literacy. He is currently working on a dissertation in the field of adult literacy.

Max van der Kamp is Professor in Adult Education at the University of Groningen in the Netherlands. He was scientific supervisor of the Dutch part of the International Adult Literacy Survey. He wrote several books on adult education and was co-editor of *Learning Across the Lifespan: Theories, Research, Policies* (together with A.C. Tuijnman, Oxford 1992). He is currently supervising adult education projects in South Africa and Mozambique. Edwin Leuven is a staff member in the Education and Training Division of the OECD. His professional affiliation is with the Department of Economics, University of Amsterdam. His interests are in the economic dimensions of education and training.

T. Scott Murray is currently Director of the Special Surveys Division of Statistics Canada, which specializes in large-scale population surveys designed to address emerging policy issues. He was the international Study Director for the International Adult Literacy Survey.

David C. Neice is Senior Strategic Research Analyst for the Department of Canadian Heritage, and was previously the Director of the Social Trends Analysis Group of the Department of the Secretaryof State. During 1995 he was seconded to Statistics Canada as Communications Manager for the launch of the International AdultLiteracy Survey (IALS). He has written on literacy and adult education for the O.E.C.D.and other organizations. Currently, he is working on federal policy questions concerning "access to the information highway", including the adult skills required for participation in a knowledge-based economy.

Hessel Oosterbeek is Assistent Professor in economics at the University of Amsterdam, staff member of the Max Goote Centre for vocational education and training, and fellow of the Tinbergen Institute. His main professional interests are in the fields of education economics and labour economics. He has published articles in several economic journals and is Associate Editor of the Economics of Education Review. B. Allan Quigley is Associate Professor and Director of Adult Education at Penn State University in Pennsylvania, United States. As of August, 1997, he will be Associate Professor of Adult Education at St. Francis Xavier University in Nova Scotia, Canada. He has published several research studies on the non-participation of undereducated adults and the barriers and deterrents to participation.

Kjell Rubenson is Professor at the Department of Educational Studies and Director for Policy Studies in Education at the University of British Columbia, Vancouver, Canada. Before joining UBC he held a Chair in Adult Education at the University of Linköping, Sweden where he still is an adjunct professor. He has published extensively in the area of participation in adult education. His most recent publications in this area are *The Role of Popular Adult Education: Reflections in Connection to an Analysis of Surveys on Living Conditions, 1975 to 1993 and An analysis of Statistics Canada's 1994 Adult Education and Training Survey.*

Jo Scheeren is a researcher with the Department of Adult Education, University of Groningen. His main interest is in the field of labour market analysis and education. He has worked on several research projects involving adult education, with a focus on older adults. At present he is writing a dissertation on literacy and older adults.

Albert Tuijnman is Principal Administrator in the Education and Training Division of the Directorate for Education, Employment, Labour and Social Affairs of the OECD, where he was responsible for the preparation of the Background Report for the 1996 Education Ministerial, Lifelong Learning for All. Prior to this he worked in the Centre for Educational Research and Innovation on successive editions of Education at a Glance: OECD Indicators. He has published extensively in the fields of comparative and adult education. Most recently he edited the revised edition of the International Encyclopedia of Adult Education and Training (Oxford 1996).

Sofa Valdivielso Gomez has been working since 1992 as a Research Consultant for the UNESCO Institute for Education. After directing various research projects on functional literacy, basic and adult education on behalf of the Ministry of Education in the Canary Islands/Spain, she has now specialized in literacy and basic education of adults.

Gongli Xu is a doctoral student in adult education at the University of British Columbia, Vancouver, working on a dissertation on long term effects of adult education. He is co-author of the report An analysis of Statistics Canada's 1994 Adult Education and Training Survey (with Kjell Rubenson).

Author Index